P9-DNL-145

HONOR BOUND

Mark,
Thank you for your continued leadership and love of our Country!

HONOR BOUND

Live your courage.

An American Story of Dreams and Service

With much Respect,

Amy McGrath

with Chris Peterson

Amy McGrath 2021

ALFRED A. KNOPF · NEW YORK · 2021

THIS IS A BORZOI BOOK
PUBLISHED BY ALFRED A. KNOPF

Copyright © 2021 by Amy McGrath

All rights reserved. Published in the United States by Alfred A. Knopf,
a division of Penguin Random House LLC, New York, and distributed in Canada
by Penguin Random House Canada Limited, Toronto.

www.aaknopf.com

Knopf, Borzoi Books, and the colophon
are registered trademarks of Penguin Random House LLC.

Library of Congress Cataloging-in-Publication Data
Names: McGrath, Amy, [date] author.
Title: Honor Bound: an American story of dreams and service /
Amy McGrath ; with Chris Peterson.
Description: First edition. | New York: Alfred A. Knopf, 2021. |
"This is a Borzoi Book published by Alfred A. Knopf."
Identifiers: LCCN 2020036303 (print) | LCCN 2020036304 (ebook) |
ISBN 9780525659105 (hardcover) | ISBN 9780525659112 (ebook)
Subjects: LCSH: McGrath, Amy, [date] | United States. Marine
Corps—Women—Biography. | United States. Marine
Corps—Officers—Biography. | Women marines—Biography. | Air pilots,
Military—Biography. | Fighter pilots—United States—Biography. | Women
political candidates—Kentucky—Biography. | Edgewood (Kenton County, Ky.)—Biography.
Classification: LCC VE25.M38 A3 2021 (print) | LCC VE25.M38 (ebook) |
DDC 359.9/6092 [B]—dc23
LC record available at https://lccn.loc.gov/2020036303
LC ebook record available at https://lccn.loc.gov/2020036304

Jacket photograph by Mark Nickolas
Jacket design by Jenny Carrow

Manufactured in the United States of America
First Edition

To whom much is given, much is expected.

(LUKE 12:48)

To my mom and dad. My parents raised me to experience the world, to not be afraid, to love life, to care for others, and to follow my dreams. It is my hope that I can teach my own children to soar with purpose in their lives.

And to CAPT Asbury Coward IV, USN, 1942–2021. He was my champion, my leadership role model, my friend.

HONOR BOUND

INTRODUCTION

TWENTY-FOUR YEARS as a Marine officer and F/A-18 aviator taught me how powerful the idea of home can be. That lesson was etched on my heart during my first combat deployment. In the spring of 2002, my squadron was sent to Ganci Air Base, a gritty green-and-beige collection of tents in Kyrgyzstan, on what had once been a Soviet long-range-bomber base. Comfort isn't a consideration on bases built to support combat operations. Sleeping twelve to a tent in a busy air base where missions are flown twenty-four hours a day means hectic schedules and little alone time. The exception is an overnight shift as operations duty officer, or ODO.

Fighter attack jets have to be in the air around the clock to support ground operations at a moment's notice. F/A-18s are incredibly complex and powerful machines, and so much can go wrong when one is in the air. It's essential that an aircrew member—an F/A-18 pilot or weapons systems officer—be listening at all times on the ground radios so that there is an expert to respond and assist any pilot experiencing a potentially catastrophic situation in flight. It's hard to keep your eyes open during the overnight shift. Sleep being a precious commodity in combat, ODO duty isn't popular. Regardless, I eagerly signed up for the first Sunday night in May. The shift corresponded to Saturday afternoon in America, where the Kentucky Derby would be in full swing. I'm a proud Kentucky native, with a love for the Commonwealth that runs bone deep and mirrors my love for America. The ready room tent had one of the few televisions on base. As ODO, I would have that TV to myself, and I desperately wanted to watch the derby.

It was a way to connect to family and home, to what I knew to be true. My family would be throwing our traditional Kentucky Derby party. My dad would greet people at the door and have drinks in their hands before they could even finish saying hello. My parents' modest living room would be packed with people creating a soundtrack of laughter. I could see my dad telling a joke or funny story as our neighbors waited for the punch line. I could smell the mint in the juleps. They would all watch the race on TV at the same time I did. It felt like a tangible link to that place, to my roots, and to all the people I cared about.

I turned on the thirty-inch Samsung, and the happiness flooded over me. It was a minor miracle that the American Forces Network was broadcasting the derby. The network isn't predictable in what it chooses to broadcast, so it was a bit of Marine luck to find the race on the schedule. The radios were quiet. The Kyrgyz mountains were still draped with snow down to the foothills, and the tent was chilly. It didn't matter. In Louisville, at Churchill Downs, the weather was sunny and warm. Decked-out women in flamboyant hats waited in the grandstands for the race to begin. Men in blue-striped seersucker or white linen suits stood behind them, looking like country gentlemen from a century ago. Everyone had a drink in hand, and it was obvious they were having tons of fun. I reveled in the spectacle.

Right before the race itself began, everyone stood to put their hand over their heart for the playing of the national anthem. If you're serving in uniform, "The Star-Spangled Banner" means something profound. It touches on why you're serving. The next song, though, struck an even deeper chord. Churchill Downs began playing "My Old Kentucky Home." What seemed to be the entire well-dressed crowd, in the bleachers, throughout the paddock, and even in the box suites at Churchill Downs, began singing the words.

My whole life, from as far back as I could remember, my parents had always thrown a fantastic party for the Kentucky Derby. A native son, my father loved having people over and celebrating what he saw as a special and unique feature of the Commonwealth. The tradition meant a lot to him. Because of that, it meant a lot to all his kids. Dad loved his family, God, the church, teaching, America, and Kentucky (not necessarily in that order). I learned to love all those things as well.

Watching the wonderful, colorful, derby happening sixty-eight hundred miles away, I ached for Kentucky. All the people in my parents' living room would be joyful and singing together, laughing when they forgot the words, and clapping at the end. Alone, bundled in my steel-toed boots, a flight suit, and my leather jacket, inside a cold canvas tent plunked down on a gravel plain next to a busy military airstrip, I got up out of my folding chair and stood while they played "My Old Kentucky Home," just as I had been taught. I cried and thought, "Wow, I'm glad there are no other Marines in this tent." I wouldn't have wanted to try to explain my tears to a fellow Marine.

I cried because I love Kentucky as fiercely as I love America. Like America itself, Kentucky is more than a place. It is home. I'm forever connected to the state and to the people who have always made it such a wonderful place for me to live.

I dried my tears and sat back down. I watched every minute of that derby, which was cold well water for a great thirst. I can't say I remember which horse won. I just knew it was the closest I would be to home for a long time.

When we say that we're missing home, we're not just missing a place we call Kentucky, or South Dakota, or Ohio, or Virginia, or even America. Those are all just lines on a map and soil on the ground. Our love of place isn't about a place at all. It's about people and the ideals those people share and hold dear. It's about what holds us together as one country. Home is, to me, my family's cathedral, attended by the faithful on any given Sunday. It is a Marine Corps unit and the camaraderie we all felt in being part of an elite group in the greatest military in the world. It is the modest, three-bedroom ranch house I grew up in, one of many on a pretty suburban street in Edgewood, Kentucky. It is my parents, who believed in being good citizens and that service and sacrifice were essential threads in the American fabric.

That undistinguished house on a plain suburban street in middle-class America was pure happiness for me growing up. A single address on Brookwood Drive represented the heart and soul of America for me.

My Kentucky, like my America, is about the people who have inspired me day in and day out, people who taught me about the most important ideas in the world: faith, patriotism, service, and sacrifice. Those people understand the importance of dignity, decency, honor, and compassion. Those are so much more than words to the Kentuckians I know and respect, and they aren't just words to most Americans. They are lights along the road that winds through American democracy, from 1776 to today. They are also responsibilities, obligations of how we must act as citizens. They represent the best that America—be it Kentucky, or California, or Texas—can be. People hold those words in their hearts. For so many of us, they are principles that serve as the North Star for the country itself. Like air, those ideals are most noticeable in their absence.

We seem to be straying from those guiding lights, from the true meaning and value of what it is to be American. America is at its best when everybody shares opportunity, as I was able to after federal law was changed to allow women to fly combat aircraft. This country embodies the idea that you run or fall according to your own skill, ability, and drive. The problem is, you can't get far if you never have the chance to run in the first place.

When I was ten years old, I met a Romanian refugee named Viorel. He was staying with my parents' friends Carlotta and Lloyd. They were hosting Viorel, who had fled the hardship and repression of his communist homeland, until he could find a job and an apartment and sort out his path to immigration. He was a tall, sturdy man in his forties, with a horseshoe of hair around the sides of his head and bald crown. His English was thickly accented, but he made it clear that he was incredibly happy to be in America.

"Romania," he said, shaking his head. "It is so . . . tough. To eat, to buy food. We have bad leaders, cruel leaders. There is no hope in Romania."

He got teary as he talked about his new home, America. It seemed over the top, the way he described a country we all knew so well, that everyone at the table laughed. But he raised his bushy eyebrows and insisted, "No, no, no . . . this place is wonderful. It has . . . everything!" Listening to him speak, I saw Kentucky and America in a new light. The idea of freedom was made tangible for me, and I connected it to all the people serving in the military to preserve that freedom.

America has always shone when we shared this type of deep, honest patriotism. Not a fist-pumping gesture, but a pride of country honoring the original American ideals. There is so much emphasis these days on that word "patriotism," but it seems as though the people who use the word the most understand it the least.

Patriotism is the unwavering love of the place we call home, and true patriots honor the finest principles of that place. Real, heartfelt patriotism is why I joined the military and spent twenty-four years serving this country. In America, patriotism has always been about service, about skin in the game. It is, to me and the people I know, a verb. It's why I was sitting there in a tent, one of a few hundred in a loud, smelly tent city at a combat air base in Kyrgyzstan. It's why my father taught high school students for forty years and why my mother dedicated herself to her patients as a pediatrician and a psychiatrist without ever once complaining about the demands on her time. It's why we never missed a Fourth of July parade in Edgewood. We were a patriotic family. That meant understanding, from a young age, that you serve, you sacrifice, and you give for the greater good. Our view of patriotism wasn't limited to love and sacrifice for America. It included service to community, to church, even to family. That's the Kentucky I love and the America I know.

The aftermath of the 2016 presidential election brought all that into sharp focus for me. Before that election, I prided myself on not being partisan. I didn't grow up beholden to a given political party or its dogma. I was never indoctrinated into a particular strain of political ideology. I grew up learning in conservative organizations like Catholic schools, and my adult life has been spent within the conservative institution of the Marine Corps. I don't reject the conservative principles I've learned. But my parents, teachers, and life experience led me to think independently, to question and adopt positions guided by essential American principles. I've always been more concerned about what is right, decent, and fair than whether a given idea was labeled "conservative" or "liberal."

I have wondered many times in the last few years just who we want to be as a nation. It's always wise to look at the best examples of the past when you're charting a path into the future. What I see in America's finest moments is that the country had leaders and citizens who were not afraid of change. They opened doors and focused on equality and opportunity for all. As citizens at our best, we have always valued hard work, the power of wise public investment, and the importance of putting country before party. Paying your dues has historically been part of the fabric of the American ethic, as have tolerance, decency, and fairness.

In a way, this book is a look back at how I was gifted those values. How I learned and internalized them. They are a part of me, and I think the best part of me. I am not alone. There are vast numbers of Americans like me. Some people call these traits "middle-class values," but they don't belong to a class. They are simply American values, the ones I learned growing up: hard work, honesty, sacrifice for the greater good.

My story is a study in those values, a tapestry of how good Americans have taught me right from wrong, care and tolerance rather than hate and ignorance. It is also a tale of imperfect and heartbreaking things about our country. All along the way, my path has been studded with object lessons that have never been more relevant than they are at this moment in history.

Mine is a suburban, middle-class story. It explains why I place so much importance on my family, where I get my faith, and the support I got in going through the challenges in my life.

The values I hold dear have always been powerful influences in my life. By describing how that came to be, the events and ideas that molded me, I'm hoping they can be part of a greater solution. I see them as what could be landmarks on a road back to the wonderful America I cherish, a country with an infinite ability to grow and change. America can be what it has so often been—a wonderful example for the world of how to face adversity with strength, dignity, and honor and, through it all, still be capable of compassion.

Faith, honor, and service. These are America's values. They are my values and the bedrock of my story.

1

EVEN AS A YOUNG GIRL, I knew that my mother's beeper signaled something incredibly important. She wore the beeper when it was her turn to be one of the pediatricians on call for the Cincinnati Children's Hospital. My sister, brother, and I might be watching *The Muppet Show* while my mom made her wonderful spaghetti sauce, the enticing smell filling the house. She liked to sing as she cooked, adding a cheery background to dinnertime. Suddenly the shrill alarm of the beeper would shatter the pleasant calm.

Mom would turn the beeper off and call the hospital using the wall phone in the kitchen. She'd stretch the spiraled phone cord to move as far from us as possible and hear the person on the other end clearly. Even so, Dad would say, "Turn it down. Mom's got a beep. She's on the phone!" We went quiet in an instant. We knew it was serious business.

She would hang up and, many times, head out to the hospital.

In my young mind I envisioned her rushing to the bedside of a sick child suffering a dire medical emergency. Dad would take over cooking, and we would go back to watching TV. Still, it would linger, the same thought every time: "Wow, my mom is important. She's going to go save a life right now." It was my earliest brush with how service to others translated to action. My mother was a healer, had chosen to be a doctor. People—children—counted on her. She took that obligation to heart.

She was my strongest influence and most powerful role model. Mom, the oldest of eight kids, had been struck with polio when she was ten years old. She survived, but the disease left her with a leg that was largely useless. She drag-limped it as she walked. Regardless, she refused to let it stop her or even slow her down. She exemplified the determination of pure will. At a point in history when few women even went to college, my mom went to medical school and became a pediatrician.

I'm sure there were days when she would have loved to let that call go, to ignore the beeper. Times when she was tired from a long day of seeing patients, checking homework, and reining in three kids. There must have been evenings when all she wanted was to sit down on the sofa, take a breath, and stare out the window. That is surely true, but I never once heard my mom complain. Not about the beeper, her work, or her leg. She had important things to do, and those things required sacrifices. She had made the choice to serve, and as far as she was concerned, there was no other option. You put your head down, and you got on with it.

That dedication was coupled with a keen mind. She has always been one of the smartest, most thoughtful people I've ever known. She taught her children to constantly question the world around them. We were raised to always be respectful but never take anything at face value. She showed me that the only true limitations are the ones we impose on ourselves. Safe to say I would never have so tenaciously pursued my dream of being a fighter pilot had she not been such an example of possibility realized.

Her immense inner strength, quick mind, faith, and love of family were deep values she shared with my father. They were both compassionate, strong people of durable religious belief, faithful but forever intellectually curious.

My mom was short and huggable, with a beautiful smile. Dad was a sturdy man whom people knew they could lean on for support. He, too, had immense inner strength matched by a physical heartiness. He was built thick and strong, with a laborer's beefy hands. He had brown curly, almost frizzy hair and an unruly beard and mustache that framed a quick and infectious smile. He loved a good practical joke. He once parked our station wagon down the street while we were asleep and replaced it in the garage with a look-alike toy car. He told my five-year-old brother, Matt, that the car had shrunk and tried to contain his laughter as Matt's eyes grew wide. It was his lighter side, and his eyes often danced behind the Coke-bottle lenses of his glasses as he looked for an opportunity to have some fun at our expense.

He loved people and enjoyed life. He was also one of the most gregarious people you might ever meet. Visitors to our home would barely get their coats off before they had a beer in their hand and my father was coaxing a story out of them.

That didn't mean he lacked a serious side. Like my mom, he was a person of service and faith. He was particularly passionate about knowledge—increasing his own and helping others learn. He taught English for forty years at Roger Bacon High School in Cincinnati, just over the border. He carefully balanced the striking contradictions in his life, the rigorous pursuit of empirical wisdom and the leap of faith involved in his Catholic beliefs. He had once been a seminarian and an aspiring priest. Though he'd given up that path, it didn't temper the flame of religious devotion that burned inside him. He embraced it with a New Testament joy and compassion. I never heard him proselytize, and he rarely talked about Catholic doctrine at all. He simply lived his faith. He studied his Bible and went to church—with the family in tow—every Sunday without fail and on holy days throughout the year.

It was no coincidence that the people who most showered me with love were also faithful churchgoers and devout believers. They embraced their religion in a deeply thoughtful way. It grounded me in my own. The role models for faith didn't stop at my mother and father. My parents were friends with a couple named Ron and Kathy Eckerle. My mom mentioned to Ron that she was looking at day-care options. Ron told her, "Well, my mom is looking for work and she loves kids. She's a housekeeper as well."

That simple interaction was how I came to know one of the most influential people in my early life. As young as my brother, sister, and I were, we couldn't pronounce "Eckerle," so she became and always would be "Mrs. Eck." She was my nanny when I was three and four and picked me up after classes once I started attending the local Montessori school. She showed me boundless patience and affection.

My early role models all gave me the space and guidance to learn, think, and come to grips with my own beliefs. I was never going to be a worshipper who blindly followed church doctrine or literal interpretations of the Bible. The support I had helped me question everything without ever losing my faith. Something is there, I'm sure of it. Sometimes the light burns bright, and sometimes it barely flickers. Mrs. Eck gave me one more example of living to the brightness.

It was my father, though, who most nurtured my spiritual beliefs. He created a living, breathing Catholicism that made faith seem accessible and relevant. Some of my fondest memories are of sitting in the front pew at St. Mary's Cathedral in Covington, watching

Dad read a passage from the scripture. He served as a reader, a layperson who read scriptures to the congregation prior to the sermon proper. He projected his deep, strong voice, reaching those at the very back of that cavernous cathedral.

We lead best when we lead by example, and my father showed me how faith translates into action. Every Good Friday, I would join him in quietly "climbing the steps at Mount Adams," an honored tradition local to the Cincinnati area. We would stop at each step to silently recite a Hail Mary or Our Father. It would take an honest hour to reach the top step and then enter the church for more prayers. There was a joy in my father as we made that pilgrimage every year. It was solemn but uplifting. That, and so many occasions like it, taught me that faith could be a verb.

Both my parents instructed me, clearly, that I shouldn't think of Catholicism as the "right way" or the "only way," but that it was "our way." They were accepting of other religions as different but equal, not lesser. It would open me to the world, and one of my best friends at Mercy Montessori was Jewish. Her family invited me to their Hanukkah ceremony, and I was excited to go. It was fascinating to me to watch a family just as devout as mine pray in Hebrew. That early framework would stick with me and open me to other cultures when I encountered them overseas as a Marine.

Of course, for a young, energetic girl, life is not all prayers and devotion. From a young age I loved to move. I relished the feel of my body responding to my commands. I wanted to climb trees and run like the wind. I was also competitive, and I welcomed the physical challenge of sports, especially against tough opponents. Seeing my mother struggle with her disability made me forever appreciate the fact that I had two good legs, and two good arms, that I could do without thinking things she could never hope to do. I was lucky to have good health and was going to use my body to its full advantage.

That made me an unapologetic tomboy. Fortunately, I lived in a town and grew up with parents who didn't judge or force me to be something I wasn't. I'm sure that Edgewood, Kentucky, had its share of small minds; every place does. But the people who mattered most to me were fine with me being exactly who I was— a budding athlete, an independent-minded competitor who gave no quarter on any field. My older sister, Janie, had a mean backstroke in the pool, wrote beautiful poetry and engaging, entertaining stories, and loved playing with Barbies. That wasn't for me. Those activities didn't speak to me the way they enchanted her. I enjoyed the swing of a bat, kicking a goal, or sledding at breakneck speeds down the steep hill of our long backyard. That's how I became my brother Matt's smaller shadow and his athletic protégée.

It never failed that Matt would be one of the captains for our school's lunchtime football game. He and the other captain would face the rest of us, lined up along the brick wall of the building next to the practice field, hoping to be picked early rather than late (and certainly anything but last). When it was time for him to make his first pick, he would make a show of putting his finger on his chin and running his eyes along the line of possible candidates. We both knew it was a ruse. He would always pick me first, because we practiced together nearly every day.

"I'll take Amy."

The other captain would look shocked. "Okay, your loss."

Little did he know. Matt was always the quarterback, and I was forever the wide receiver. He would drop back on the first play of the game, looking downfield. Nobody would cover me, assuming this spindly girl couldn't possibly reel in a pass. Then Matt would launch a perfect spiral that I would catch with confidence, not even breaking stride as I ran unopposed into the end zone. By the end of the game I would be dragging double coverage, but the damage had been done. We won a lot. I played football, baseball, basketball, and soccer. "Playing with the boys" would set me up for success in the face of greater challenges later—most pointedly the military.

Even though it was a prosperous, intimate suburb, Edgewood had an old-fashioned, small-town feel. People there embraced traditional values. We waved our flags proudly. Edgewood, too, helped shape me. I learned that neighbors were people you helped when they needed it. The greater good mattered. Certainly, the intimacy of a small community can breed its fair share of gossip, but that closeness also fosters cohesion, a coming together. From the time I was old enough to run outside and play in our front yard, I knew all the neighbors up and down our block. Elderly Dr. Maloney lived across the street, and my parents would send Matt and me to check up on him from time to time. We would deliver meals or just sit and talk with him. The Schepers lived next door and were some of the nicest people you could ever hope to meet. Once, the old woman who lived a few doors down walked over in the snow wearing only her nightgown. She knew Mom was a doctor. She had experienced some disorientation and actually fell at our doorstep. Mom immediately assessed the situation, called 911, and wrapped a blanket around her. She talked quietly to calm the flustered woman and us kids. Dad went to her house to get her family. This was what you did for neighbors.

Edgewood was a solid, middle-class place. Most people, if they weren't retired, commuted to Cincinnati for their jobs or worked in the local hospital. There were small towns in Kentucky worse off, but drive from one to the other, and values weren't any different.

The core values in my town ran deep and true. The seven thousand souls of 1980s Edgewood, Kentucky, tolerated differences and celebrated common bonds. Most were followers of one religion or another. All believed in fairness and decency. Edgewood citizens knew the Constitution and Bill of Rights and deeply valued both. It was all a part of their patriotism.

The town exhibited that love of country every year, in its own wonderfully quirky Fourth of July parade. It was like a million others held in small towns across the country, hokey and heartfelt. The parade was a chaotic collection of funky old cars dressed in comical banners advertising local businesses or politicians, school bands and Boy Scout troops marching in formation, and the uniquely American spirit pervading the day's events. I marched in the parade at six and proudly waved my miniature flag so that everyone lining the parade route would get a good look.

Although the town was rich with patriotic enthusiasm, it was my dad's thoughtful love of America that really taught me what citizenship was all about. It was intertwined with an innate fascination with learning and discovery. He would pick us three kids up from school each day and drive us to the library in Covington. There, we would do our homework or explore while he graded papers. It seemed the most natural, welcoming place. He taught us that the library was a civic institution to be valued, used, and supported.

Beyond books, Dad made history real for us. Matt and I would be enjoying a catch out back on a lazy summer morning when the back door would fly open and Dad would yell, "Pack a lunch. We're going on a trip." Off we went on a modest voyage of discovery, prying into yet another historic corner of America. We'd pile into the station wagon, the trusty workhorse with its faux-wood panels and much-used roof-mounted luggage rack, and head to whatever new location had captured my father's imagination. It might be south-central Ohio, where we'd spend half a day touring the Great Serpent Mound, a grass-covered rolling burial site built by prehistoric Native Americans a thousand years before. Maybe it wasn't Machu Picchu, but it was enough history for an interesting day trip. Dad's radar was always up for any vestige of history, any new discovery that would expand his knowledge. We'd be driving through some town on our way to canoe the Little Miami River when he would whip the station wagon over to the curb.

"Look, a historical marker. Everyone out." Something had happened on that site, and Dad wasn't going to drive another ten feet without finding out what exactly it was. All of us would reluctantly pile out of the station wagon, read the marker for ourselves, and discuss it for the next twenty miles. Sometimes a minor Civil War battle had been fought there, or a political figure had been born in the town. My dad taught me that history was everywhere and the echoes of the past were worth listening to and learning from.

These were the lessons that formed my worldview. The borders of that perspective exploded in the summer of 1985, when I was ten. My family drove off for a five-week journey of exploration to the West Coast and back. All five of us planned the trip for months based on a wonderful concept: each person got to pick three destinations.

We studied the map, read guides to each state, and endlessly discussed the possibilities. Three favorites hardly seemed enough. My choices were based on my passions of the moment. Reading about California, my mother said, "You know, the best chocolate in the country is made by Ghirardelli in San Francisco." The best chocolate in the country? How could I, a young and budding chocolate aficionado, not choose Ghirardelli?

My second choice was driven by love. I had been drawn to puppies and kittens as far back as I could remember. I loved watching wild animal documentaries on TV and was dying to see more exotic species in person. I thought I might want to be a veterinarian. So, it was no surprise to my family when I chose the San Diego Zoo—the largest zoo in the country at that time—as my second destination. I chose my third, the High Rockies, because it just sounded wild and untamed.

The trip took us through fourteen states on our way out west and back. We saw amazing sights: Wall Drug Store and the Corn Palace in South Dakota; the Badlands National Park; Fort Laramie in Wyoming; Mount Rushmore; and so many more. My father picked a stunningly scenic ride on the Durango & Silverton Narrow Gauge Railroad in Colorado, skirting a mountainside so steep you had to wonder how the tracks stayed in place. My brother's pick was Alcatraz, a different experience altogether, and part of our long stay in the San Francisco Bay Area.

San Francisco had already impressed me with its postcard hills, unique architecture, and a drive down Lombard Street—"the crookedest street in the world"—when we headed off on our tour of Alcatraz. We returned four hours later to discover someone had broken into the station wagon. Crime was exceedingly rare in Edgewood, and the break-in seemed almost personal. The thief had rifled through all of our personal possessions, taking anything of monetary value (including my trusty Walkman radio). I was heartbroken. This too was a lesson. The diversity of America included the people. All types called this country home. That included the finest people on earth as far as I was concerned. Now I understood that any group had some bad as well. There were bound to be those in it only for themselves, working against the best interests of the group. I thought about that a lot on the way home. The entire trip was full of real-world lessons.

Perhaps the most powerful, though, was just how vast and varied America truly is. Before our vacation, I had the limited perspective any child has. Kentucky was Edgewood to me. So was America. Then we drove six thousand miles, and I saw the reality, the awe-inspiring wonder of a magnificent country. I was amazed at the incredible gaps between populated areas. We often traveled five or six hours never once seeing a building or any sign of civilization. The only sign that there were other people anywhere were the FM stations we'd pick up, only to drop an hour or two later.

Thanks to my parents, I became used to learning organically. Education was a part of life and curiosity-driven exploration. Like my brother and sister before me, I attended Mercy Montessori grade school. The classroom experience was unique for every student, and each was allowed to learn at his or her own pace. The school fostered self-discovery and was engaging from the first class in the morning until Dad or Mrs. Eck picked me up in the afternoon. There were no report cards, but there were endless opportunities to learn, test your own boundaries, and grow. I loved it.

It was no small shock to graduate and move on to a Catholic middle school. Matt and Jane had been so far ahead of the kids in middle school that they had opted to skip those two years and go right into high school. I was offered the same opportunity, but that would have meant putting myself at a huge disadvantage competing in sports at the high school level. I would have been up against kids six years my senior. Given how much I loved sports, it just made sense to do my two years in middle school. It turned out to be a disappointing time. The teachers were nice but the classes weren't challenging, and the structure of the school day was far more rigid and less adaptable than what I had known in grade school.

My education outside school, however, continued as it always had. My parents provided endless shining examples and teachable moments about what was most valuable in life. When I was twelve, my mother received the Marvin Rammelsberg Distinguished Service Award from the Greater Cincinnati Association for Counseling and Development. The presentation ceremony was held on a gorgeous late spring day, the rows of redbud trees in stunning full bloom at the Peterloon Estate in Cincinnati. I stood at the back of the handsome main room in Peterloon's stately Georgian brick building, angling for a better view of the stage as my mom received her award. I was watching her give her short acceptance speech, when a woman approached me. She was about thirty, pretty, with a wide smile and long, light brown hair.

"You're Dr. McGrath's daughter, aren't you?"

"Yes," I said.

"You should know how special your mother is. She's an amazing person, and you're lucky to be her daughter." She hesitated for a moment, a little choked up. "Your mother saved my life. And I'm not alone; she's helped a lot of other people. She is an incredible doctor. I just wanted you to know that."

"Thank you," I said, a little stunned.

The woman walked away, and for about the millionth time I felt a deep pride in my mother, in what she did and who she was. I ached to be useful in that way, to help people, and do something important in the world. Soon enough, I would figure out exactly what that was.

2

Wᴏ's ᴛᴏ sᴀʏ what role divine providence might play in any
life? I don't think of my fate in those terms, but the truth is
that the direction of my life was forever altered by a simple, seventh-
grade history class assignment. I had found middle school unin-
spiring until I decided to focus on military airpower for my term
project. I thought World War II aircraft would make an interesting
subject to research and write about and for the teacher to read.

I found a model of a P-47 Thunderbolt turboprop fighter in a
local shop. The plane was a fighter-bomber, one of the sleekest of its
era. It was a key weapon for the U.S. Army Air Corps in the skies
over Europe. I built the model and began researching the European
military missions for which the plane was used. I soon had a sense
of the pure excitement, the thrill of flying this powerful, nimble
aircraft in combat.

I wanted to learn more about the P-47. I discovered a television documentary on military aviation. The footage was awe inspiring, tracing the use of airpower in the military all the way back to World War I and then up to the present day. The show ran grainy footage of F-14 Tomcats landing on carriers, which seemed about the most exciting thing I could imagine doing. Near the end of the riveting hour-long film, a navy pilot talked at length about training for naval aviators. He said only the best of the best could fly jets onto aircraft carriers. Just about anyone could get a pilot's license, but if you wanted to fly the fastest, most advanced, and most awesome military aircraft in the world, you had to be something special. It was the perfect intersection of my love of a challenge and my drive to do something patriotic, to contribute to a greater good. Truth be told, it also spurred my deep competitive streak. Right at that moment, at the end of a weeknight one-hour documentary, I decided that I would become a naval aviator and fly fighter jets.

I threw myself into the history project, because now it was personal. I checked out every book I could find in the library and watched every program on TV that even briefly mentioned fighter aircraft. How did somebody become a fighter pilot? How long did it take? What was the training like? There were so many questions and details to learn.

I memorized the names and weaponry of every fighter attack aircraft the United States had in its inventory. Unfortunately, all that research turned up less exciting news. Although the navy allowed women to fly, they were prohibited from carrier landings and couldn't fly combat missions. By law.

I was shocked. How could that be? I was competing with and beating boys my age in every sport I played. I was as dedicated and patriotic as anyone in Edgewood, and I simply wasn't going to buy that there was a physical challenge I couldn't handle. But the law was going to stop me from reaching my newfound passion? My new goal in life? The idea of flying one of those planes at the speed of sound and beyond, defending America while I did it, spoke to me in a way no other possible future ever had. The only thing that came close was the possibility of playing second base for the Cincinnati Reds, and that really did seem like a bridge too far.

I wasn't going to accept that a law stood in the way of my dream. I switched gears. I did different research and went down the rabbit hole of federal legislation—how laws were enacted, reformed, and, most important, repealed.

It wasn't the first time I had felt marginalized because of my gender. I had chafed at many of the Catholic Church's teachings and practices regarding women. It is an archly conservative, patriarchal institution. It made no sense to me that women could not be priests. I couldn't even be an altar boy as my brother had been. The church was different, though. At fourteen, I understood that the Catholic Church was not a democracy. The layperson could not effect profound change within the church. The best you could do was question the tenets of your faith, seek answers, and hold your own counsel.

But the law? Heck yeah, the law could change. That there was even a law that limited women's role in the military pissed me off. At fourteen, I vented mightily in my journal:

I read something that made me so angry. The stupid, prejudice, ignorant rule about women in combat. Which does not let women fly fighters or go on a ship at sea except for a stupid refueling ship. I am so angry about that. It wasn't because we weren't smart enough. It was because of the physical differences. That's what the books and congress said. It doesn't take much muscle to use a computer on a destroyer, to find enemy subs on a radar or sonar, to watch and call for next flights on an aircraft carrier, or to be a pilot. There are stress levels under high-G circumstances, but even the scientific tests prove there is no difference on how the two sexes cope under those kinds of situations. Ever since I was very young, I played football, and baseball, collected baseball cards, watched WrestleMania, watched every football game I could and just about any other thing stupid people would call "boy things." At Mercy the motto was "you can be what you want to be!" I always thought that was true. Out of all the things I wanted to be, I picked the one thing I couldn't—not because I wasn't smart enough—not because I wasn't physically capable but because I was a girl, a female, but now all of a sudden a second-class citizen. It hurts. Sometimes it tears me apart so much I cry. It makes me wonder, why care? I pray it will change soon. I still have some hope and I still have a dream!

PS: dear Lord, please make some of this unfair prejudice go away.

Frustrated though I might have been, I wasn't raised to fold in the face of adversity. Maybe I couldn't change a law all by myself, but I knew people who could. I sat down and wrote a letter to my district's representative, Congressman Jim Bunning. Then I wrote two more to Senators Mitch McConnell and Wendell Ford. Congressman Bunning was the only one who bothered responding. He made no bones about the fact that he wasn't going to work to change the law, because he thought it was just fine as it was. That got my hackles up even more.

I headed to the Covington Library and researched the name and contact information for every single member of the House and Senate Armed Services Committees. I sat down with my stack of gleaming, bright white paper and my favorite pen. I started writing more letters. I told them all who I was and what I wanted to do. I asked them to repeal the law barring women from flying combat missions.

Most didn't reply. I wasn't their constituent and couldn't vote, so why bother? Several did write me back, and the responses could be divided into one of two camps. The first group basically said that women shouldn't be in combat. The second group wrote letters that boiled down to this: The U.S. military exists to fight and win the nation's wars. We should have the best people in combat and leadership positions, and Amy McGrath should be allowed to compete to fly in combat just like anyone else. The split was largely down partisan lines, with Republicans opposed to changing the law and most Democrats in favor of changing it. For the first time, I understood how political party affiliation affected, or even determined, a politician's stance on an issue. Yet another lesson.

Ever the optimist, I was determined that I would achieve my dream. The law might say I couldn't, but I decided that once I was older (at least old enough to vote), I would make it happen. I'd continue to write to any politician I could and to be a one-person lobby to change that unjust law. In the meantime, I needed to work hard and act as if I already had the green light.

The more I researched women naval aviators, the more it became clear that my path to being a fighter pilot ran through the U.S. Naval Academy (USNA). In seventh grade, I came across a brochure about the naval academy. I brought it home from school and read it again and again. It was worrisome. The back of the brochure described the percentage of people who actually get in among those who apply. It was less than 10 percent. I wasn't sure that I could academically and athletically be among the top 10 percent of students in the country. It seemed like an incredibly high bar.

I showed my mother the brochure and pointed out the entrance statistic. I knew she would be honest with me, because she always was. She and my father had been noncommittal about my fighter pilot ambitions, because they had seen me be just as passionate about becoming a veterinarian. As they saw my anger at the law and my devotion to the topic, they began to realize that this was a real aspiration for me.

"Mom, it's really hard to get in." I didn't have to say anything more, because what I was thinking was written on my face: "I don't know if I can make it."

She took the brochure and quietly read it over for a moment, then two, then three. She read it over carefully and refolded it. She handed it back to me, looking me right in the eyes.

"Amy, you can do this."

She said it as if she were saying, "You can do a four-mile run," or, "You can catch a hard line drive." She believed it. It was the best boost of confidence I could possibly have asked for. I would come back to that moment many times over the course of the next six years. I'd think back to that quiet exchange in our wood-paneled kitchen even after I got into the academy, when Plebe Summer became a grueling nightmare, or when the workload from a class was threatening to overwhelm me. "Amy, you can do this." That from the person I admired most in all the world.

Unfortunately, not everyone was so supportive. One of my idols growing up was Bobby, the son of my mom's friend Carlotta. Bobby was a Marine artillery officer. He was home on leave when I went with my parents to visit Carlotta and her husband, Lloyd. I excitedly told Bobby of my plans.

He was trained to think like a Marine. Marines deal with what's in front of them without blinking. It doesn't matter if the reality is grim; you deal with it. So, I'm sure that he was only being honest, being a Marine, when he told me, "Look, Amy, hang it up. First, they are never going to allow women to do these jobs. And second, your eyes are too bad for you to be a pilot."

He was doing what he thought was right. Better to give it to me straight so that I could change course early and make other plans. I think he really didn't want to see me work so hard to get into the naval academy or dream of a military career just to have my dreams crushed down the line. Women were second-class citizens in his military. It was the reality of the time. The only path he saw for a woman in the military was the medical corps or logistics. Things far from combat and far from being a warrior. And he was right, I did have bad vision. I had inherited my father's eyes.

All that didn't matter one bit to me. As we drove home from Carlotta and Lloyd's that night, and I sat in the backseat of the station wagon, his words bothered me to my core. Not because what he was saying was a cold, wet dash of reality. It was because I believed I could do what I set out to do. My mother believed too.

How could Bobby not see? I knew perfectly well that he cared about me and had my best interests at heart, but how could he not know that I wouldn't give up? I understood that getting there was going to mean brutally hard work, overcoming huge obstacles, competing and excelling at sports like never before, acing academics even in my worst subjects. Lining up A after A, semester after semester. Even as young as I was, I had no illusions that it might be easy. Now I clearly understood that it would also mean changing a lot of people's minds. It would mean proving Bobby and scores of other men wrong. Long before we pulled in to our driveway that night, that was exactly what I vowed to do.

3

THE MAIN BUILDING of Notre Dame Academy in Park Hills, Kentucky, was a serious, rectangular, businesslike brick structure. The way I saw it, that building was like a dull-brown cardboard box concealing the Hope Diamond. The incredible stuff happened as soon as students walked through the unremarkable double glass doors.

I could not get to the first day of high school quick enough. The summer after my graduation from middle school, I thought about Notre Dame every day. It was where the march to my master plan would begin in earnest. Notre Dame was an all-girls Catholic school with off-the-charts academics and competitive athletic programs. I was no stranger to the school. My sister had gone there before me, and I had seen what an incredible education she had received. I'd shouted myself hoarse at Notre Dame basketball and soccer games. I could so easily envision myself wearing the Notre Dame blue-and-gold colors in that gym or on those fields. More than anything, though, the school represented that final stepping-stone, my launchpad into the U.S. Naval Academy in Annapolis, Maryland.

Everyone around me now realized that flying fighter jets was not some passing fancy. I was doggedly determined, and my parents and siblings did what good families do: they stood behind me and supported me. I was laser focused on the goal even in the summer before my freshman year. I ran Edgewood's three-mile Fourth of July race as what I saw as preparation for my airborne future. It inspired another journal entry:

Back in November, when I decided to do this race, I believed it was my personal ticket to USNA. I thought if I could accomplish this, I could accomplish anything. I reached that goal today. A first long goal for me. That's what makes this a very special day for me. I don't have the full confidence yet, but now I know what it's like to reach a goal you've worked so hard to accomplish. I'm going to be accepted into USNA. I don't care if I have to do the race again a thousand times. I guess if I had to pick one word to describe the day I couldn't, because the feelings in the beginning and the end of the day were so different. Determination . . . confidence. Scared . . . proud.

My next personal challenge was making the Notre Dame soccer team. Tryouts were held the week before school started and were a highly competitive five-day ordeal. After the last day, the coach taped a piece of paper to the front door of the school listing the kids who had made the team. Seeing my name on that list was an incredible boost to start the school year. Not only did it mean I had a place on the field, but my teammates became my first friends in the new school.

Walking up to the school's entrance on that first day, I felt as though I were finally attacking the big goal on the horizon. I thought, "Let the games begin. I'm ready, let's do this."

I liked Notre Dame. Even though it was an all-girls school, there was a distinctive lack of cattiness and drama. The teaching staff, too, was easy to get along with. Half my teachers were nuns. They put the lie to the stereotype of stern, frocked taskmasters wielding wooden rulers as knuckle-rapping weapons. The nuns at Notre Dame were dedicated, thoughtful, and talented teachers revered by students. I respected them. They were yet another vivid example of faith translated to action. They took their vow of service seriously and were invested in their students.

They were just what I needed. Good teachers were crucial if I was going to get the stellar grades I'd need for admission to the naval academy. Beyond the marks I earned, my four years at Notre Dame would also be a time of immense personal growth. Those years would also be a period of radical change for America, especially for the U.S. military. My high school experience would be inextricably intertwined with a real-time evolution of military culture. Game-changing military events were happening around the globe and at home. They would all, to one degree or another, strengthen my case for flying in combat.

In December of my freshman year, the United States invaded Panama. The CIA had propped up Panama's dictator, General Manuel Noriega, for decades. But the mid-1980s saw a backlash from the Iran-contra affair that revealed, in part, that Noriega was intimately involved in the drug trade. The Bush administration distanced itself from Noriega. The dictator then adopted a Soviet-friendly policy that openly rejected thirty years of U.S.-Panamanian partner relations.

Tensions were high, because the United States maintained a significant and unwelcome military presence in Panama to protect our interests in the Panama Canal. Things boiled over when four U.S. military officers left the Fort Clayton military base to go to dinner in downtown Panama City. At a checkpoint, their car was surrounded by hostile soldiers and Noriega supporters armed with guns and other weapons. The pack was on the verge of violence. The U.S. military officers were trying to prevent conflict by driving away when they came under fire. A Marine lieutenant was killed, and a Marine captain was shot in the foot. In response, President Bush ordered the military invasion of Panama the following day. The Pentagon called the invasion Operation Just Cause.

It was a display of overwhelming force, involving American ground and air troops. Although military operations continued for weeks, the actual battle was decided in days. The invasion received a lot of media coverage and I followed it, even though I didn't really have a firm grasp of the politics or history behind our involvement in Panama. I was particularly interested in the role women pilots played in the war. Female army pilots flew Black Hawk helicopters to transport troops and supplies and took fire from the ground. The same happened to women air force pilots flying cargo and refueling missions. It became apparent that women were enduring combat even if they were never officially designated as combat troops.

The conflict ultimately didn't move the needle on allowing women in combat, but I saw it as a small skirmish in the greater struggle for gender equality in the military. I wasn't so naive, even at fourteen, to expect everything to change overnight. After all, I had written a book's worth of letters to members of Congress and newspaper editors, to no apparent effect. I took the long view. I was enjoying school so much that it would have been hard to get me down regardless.

My freshman year passed in a flash. I was so focused on schoolwork and sports that I didn't have a social life. That first semester blended into the winter break, which seemed to melt into May and softball practice before I realized it. The summer break was no less hectic. It would set the tone for all my high school summers. I competed on a summer swim team as I had since I was five, volunteered, and tried to do everything I could to become a more attractive candidate for the naval academy.

Sophomore year started on the heels of a dramatic military action that made the Panama invasion look modest by comparison. Just as I was preparing for my first day at school, the U.S. military launched a defense of Kuwait against an Iraqi invasion. It would become the first Gulf War. Although the initial "Shock and Awe" campaign was extremely successful in repelling Iraqi troops, the conflict lasted through February 1991. The troop buildup in Kuwait and Iraq would ultimately include more than thirty-seven thousand female troops, including women aviators who piloted supply helicopters and reconnaissance planes. Although those women often flew over combat and even took fire, they were flying craft with no weaponry to fire back. The irrational nature of the military's policy regarding women in combat was thrown into a bright spotlight when the army major Rhonda Cornum was captured as a prisoner of war near the end of the conflict.

Major Cornum was a flight surgeon attached to the 229th Attack Helicopter Regiment. She was part of a Black Hawk crew on a search-and-rescue mission looking for a downed F-14 pilot. Her Black Hawk was shot down. Not only did Major Cornum suffer massive injuries—including two broken arms and a gunshot wound to the back—but she was quickly taken into custody and tortured. Her torture included sexual assault. This was exactly the scenario military and political leaders had used as reasoning to deny women combat roles. And yet the majority of POWs were men, and they were often sexually abused because the Iraqis felt it was a way to humiliate Westerners. Just the same, Cornum's experience shocked the sensibilities of much of the public. The wounds and abuse she suffered as a POW repulsed a lot of Americans.

My parents were fearless in facing the hard issues, such as what had happened to Major Cornum. It had to hit home a little harder for them, given that I was single-mindedly focused on a military career, one that could quite easily put me in a similar situation. Despite that reality, my mom took a rational approach to a topic that was creating so much discussion in homes across America.

After we watched an evening news report about Major Cornum's homecoming, I said, "She went through hell."

My mother said, "War is terrible for everyone."

"A lot of people are saying it's worse because she's a woman."

"Honey, let me tell you something. Being a prisoner of war is horrifying whether you're a man or a woman. The things they do to prisoners are awful, no matter what."

That was the point that Major Cornum herself would make in interviews after her release at the end of hostilities on March 5, 1991. With her ramrod-straight posture, no-nonsense demeanor, and quiet authority, she was perhaps the perfect spokesperson for the cause I so embraced. An obviously forthright, well-spoken, and extremely strong military leader, Major Cornum played down the sexual abuse element of her experience. Again and again, she emphasized that torture was torture. Male POWs had also been tortured by the Iraqis, some in horrible, even disfiguring ways. She made a compelling case that a soldier was a soldier. Regardless of gender, a captured soldier had to follow the training: the warrior endured, resisted, got through it, and moved on. She was the perfect example that women were just as tough as men in high-stress battlefield conditions. Her eloquence and personal fortitude revealed the hypocrisy of a military policy that was antiquated and quite obviously made no sense. Much as I would have wished she never had to experience what she went through, I was thrilled by how poignantly she made the point.

The reality of the military's gender policy was sinking in for the public, thanks to CNN and other cable channels that covered the war extensively. Viewers saw footage of women in action in Iraq. They saw the interviews with Major Cornum. It felt as if the tide could be turning. Women in the military were becoming more vocal proponents of change, because without the ability to go into combat—or more accurately, get credit for their combat experience under fire—they couldn't be promoted above a certain rank.

Just the same, I supported President Bush's decision to go to war in the Gulf. So did almost everybody I knew in Edgewood and at Notre Dame Academy. America had come through the Cold War and we had won, emerging as the sole, valid superpower in the world. What Iraq was attempting to do violated international norms, and Kuwait was a valuable U.S. partner in the region. I felt it was a rightful use of American military power. Certainly, occasional guests on CNN would promote the position that the war was all about oil and U.S. corporate interests in the region, but I didn't agree with that. My parents, as thoughtful as anyone I had ever known, weren't sure.

One night at the dinner table I asked my mom, "Do you believe the war is justified?"

"I don't think you and I have all the information. I certainly hope that our leadership isn't getting us into a war just for oil."

I wanted to believe the best of American leadership. "But Iraq invaded Kuwait. Shouldn't that be enough? They can't get away with that. Don't you think we need to liberate the people of Kuwait?"

Matt, who always played the skeptic in any dinner table conversation, said, "Are we really liberating the people of Kuwait, or are we just liberating the oil? If this were about liberating people, why aren't we doing the same thing in other parts of the world?"

My mom nodded, conceding the logic of Matt's point. "Well, there are a lot of nations behind this effort. All wars are terrible, and I just hope this thing ends as quickly as possible."

These were the kinds of thought-provoking conversations that were fostered under my parents' roof. I learned from a young age that it was okay to challenge ideas and positions, as long as you did it thoughtfully, with reason and facts. That principle would serve me well in high school and beyond.

By junior year, I was on fire. I started out anticipating big things on the soccer field and focused on maintaining a 4.0 grade point average. I was determined to do everything I possibly could to ensure I'd be accepted into the naval academy. If I failed, it wasn't going to be for lack of trying.

About a month after school started, yet another incident occurred that would drastically impact military culture and gender. It became known as the Tailhook scandal, and it rocked the navy to its core. That event had implications across the armed services.

The Tailhook Association Symposium was a yearly, three-day gathering of naval aviators, officers, and commissioned aircraft carrier crew. It was put on by the Tailhook Association, a nongovernmental, fraternal organization dedicated to supporting "aircraft carrier sea-based aircraft" and associated aircrew members. The symposium was started as an educational conference. But by 1991, it had become a yearly social gathering where male naval officers and personnel gathered for a rowdy, macho drinking party.

The symposium was held in Las Vegas. In 1991, things got out of hand. Shortly after the symposium wrapped up, the media reported on what was revealed to be a frat party gone off the rails. There were more than four thousand active and retired military personnel at the symposium, and more than a hundred were accused of sexually assaulting eighty-three women and seven men. The allegations were incredibly gross. There were photos of naval aviators wearing T-shirts with "Women Are Property" written on the front. Some women had to run a gauntlet of drunken men groping them just to get to their rooms.

The investigations in the aftermath of the scandal led to the widespread conclusion that the navy—and military at large—needed to do much more to integrate women into command positions and foster respect for female service members. Dozens of officers would be demoted or even forced to retire. Tailhook ruined careers, changed lives, and made the strongest case yet for gender equality in the services.

Tailhook hit me hard. I saw it as a foreseeable result of the combat exclusion law that prevented women from holding combat roles. No woman wants to see other women sexually assaulted, but part of me thought, "Well, now the whole world sees. I like the swaggering, confident culture of the naval aviator, but I want to be part of it, and I don't want it to be sexist. The only way to change the sexist part is to open up those positions to women so that men don't see women as inferior. The only way the sexual assault stuff and demeaning crap will stop is if women are doing the exact same jobs as these guys and doing their duty well."

I was energized and having a much better year than the navy. I was killing it in the classroom and putting together a rock-solid athletic career. I felt invincible, as if nothing could stand in my way. Little did I know that I was about to get a harsh wake-up call.

Near the end of my junior-year basketball season, I was putting up the best numbers of my athletic career. I played forward and was known for aggressively fighting for rebounds under the basket. We were playing a tournament game and had a reasonable shot at winning the whole thing. The crowd in the bleachers was roaring when I jumped for a rebound amid a tangle of players. In the jumble of arms and legs going for the ball, I came down awkwardly, right on the point of my knee. The pain was instantaneous and excruciating. My coach and teammates carried me off the court, and my parents drove me home. My mom's expression made it clear how serious the injury was. She managed to get me into an orthopedic surgeon first thing the next morning.

One X-ray and a twenty-minute wait later, the doctor showed up with the black film in his hand and a frown on his face. He stuck the film in the wall-mounted light box and shook his head at what he saw. My mom stared at the film, saying nothing but obviously concerned. It looked like ink blots to me, but my heart sank as the doctor turned to me.

"I'm sorry to say this, but you've injured your knee in a way we only see in old ladies who fall down stairs. The kneecap is cracked clean in half."

"What?" I was shocked. I knew it hurt worse than any injury I had ever suffered, but that sounded really serious—like, athletic-career-ending serious. "What do I do about it?"

"Normally, we'd operate. But the fracture's limited enough that I can fit you with a removable cast, what we call an immobilizer. We'll try to let it heal on its own rather than jump into surgery. But I'm going to warn you: this is going to be a very long rehab period. This will take some time to heal. If it doesn't, surgery will be the only option."

Just like that, my basketball season was over. And the doctor wasn't exaggerating. I lost my softball season as well. That stung bad, because softball was my best sport. The one saving grace for me, the thought I held close, was that I still had a full year to recover and get ready for the naval academy. I had forgotten that God has His own plans for us.

Blocked from sports or even getting around much, I aced my homework and watched CNN with my mom and dad every night. The presidential race was under way. Bill Clinton was the Democratic candidate; George Bush was fighting for a second term. I liked and respected President Bush. He had been a naval aviator and was a war hero. I thought he made sound decisions and was an honorable man. As for Bill Clinton, I knew he had been the governor of Arkansas and that a lot of sordid stuff was coming out about him. A woman named Gennifer Flowers alleged that she and the married

Clinton had engaged in a decade-long sexual affair. The Clinton campaign did all it could to discredit her. It was ugly stuff. Clinton was undeniably smart and talented at communicating complicated policy positions in a simple, understandable way. But a lot of people in both parties felt that he was less than honorable or trustworthy.

I was conflicted. You didn't have to be a political insider to know that a Clinton administration was likely to overturn the combat exclusion rule, at least for combat aviators if not for all troops. I knew perfectly well that if President Bush won a second term, he would almost certainly not overturn the rule. It would remain in effect for his four years, which would line up almost exactly with my time in the naval academy. I was thankful I wasn't old enough to vote.

I continued to follow the campaign closely as the school year wore on. I rehabbed and looked for opportunities to boost my chances of getting into the naval academy. I was shocked when a golden opportunity presented itself.

I had a good friend who was a hardworking, smart student. Laura was near the top of our class academically. We had all taken the PSATs in preparation for the actual SATs, and Laura had done exceptionally well. I did far less well. Everyone in the whole school, including Laura, knew that my goal was the naval academy because I had never hidden my mission. One day in spring, Laura found me eating lunch in the cafeteria and sat down across from me.

"Hey, Amy, remember the PSATs?"

"Yep."

"Well, the naval academy checks out those scores. I guess they send out invitations for their Summer Seminar to certain kids that do well." She pulled a few stapled, official-looking documents out of her backpack. "Anyways, they sent me an application, but I'm not really thinking about the military. Do you want it?"

I felt like Charlie getting the golden ticket to Mr. Wonka's factory.

"Really? Yeah, I'd love to use it. Thanks, Laura."

I filled in the blank application that night. There was nothing about it particular to Laura, so I didn't think there was anything wrong with submitting it myself. I wrote in all my information including my PSAT scores. The next morning, I put it in the mail and thought, "Well, I gave it a shot."

It paid off. A week later, I came home from school to find a letter on the kitchen table addressed to me. The crisp white envelope had the USNA logo in the upper left corner. Inside was an invitation to the Summer Seminar's mid-June class. I could hardly believe it. My knee was at 90 percent and getting better every day, and now I was going to see the naval academy up close. It would be a preview of what it was like to be a midshipman. I felt as if a dream were coming true. Although I did a lot during the summer after my junior year—summer swim team, volunteering at a nursing home—the most exciting event by far was the Summer Seminar.

My dad was always up for an interesting road trip, so he offered to drive me to Annapolis in the dark red Chevy sedan he affectionately named the Cardinal (the replacement for our old, well-traveled Ford Country Squire station wagon). He decided to spend the week exploring Maryland and pick me up at the end of the seminar. We got there a day ahead of when I needed to check into the dorm. We took a walk around the school. I was bowled over.

Annapolis is a majestic, impressive place. It is steeped in history and myth. You can feel the presence of all the midshipmen who have toiled on the fields and gone to war right after graduating. My dad and I stood shoulder to shoulder, looking out at the Chesapeake Bay, the tang of salty, brackish air all around us.

"It's really something, isn't it?" he said.

"It's amazing." I didn't have any other words to describe it.

I thought about all those who had come before me. Admirals who had engaged in fiery naval battles. Naval aviators who had flown in dogfights in World War II, or piloted hundreds of missions in Vietnam. People like John McCain who had gone from combat attack pilot, to prisoner of war, to serving as a leader of the country in Congress. I was standing on a vantage point where midshipmen had looked out at the water for more than a hundred years. It was surreal, and wonderful, and overwhelming. I badly wanted to be part of this line, part of something so great and honorable. I looked up, to the cloud-dappled Maryland sky, and thanked God that I was there.

The actual seminar was a jam-packed preview of what life at the academy was like for a midshipman. It's meant as an opportunity for kids from around the country to see what the day-to-day routine at a military college is really about. It's also a chance for the academy's leaders to see what individual students are made of.

The seminar spans five days. It's a nonstop schedule of moving from all-out physical training, to classes in engineering, to team building and squad special events like competitions. You're busy from the time you wake up to lights-out and bedtime. I loved every minute of it. The physical sections of the seminar were as tough as any sport I'd ever done, and I was glad my knee was almost fully healed.

To be so close to my dream, to be experiencing what it would be like as a midshipman on the path to flight training, was exhilarating and motivating. I respond well to pressure like that. I hit the ball out of the park; I returned home as one of the highest-ranked students in my class. That would serve me well because it went into my permanent file and would be considered in my application.

The experience lit an even bigger fire under me as I started my senior year. I was more pumped than ever. Although I never doubted what my goal was, the Summer Seminar made it clearer than ever that the academy and a military career were exactly right for me. All I had to do was finish high school strong, get accepted, and get on with it.

Leadership experience is one of the key measures the naval academy uses in considering potential enrollments, so I was excited to be made a co-captain of the Notre Dame women's soccer team. I loved the camaraderie in soccer; we were a tight-knit group, supporting one another as teammates should. I was home one October afternoon rushing through my homework in preparation for a soccer game that night when the phone rang. I heard my mom answer it. Then she called me into the kitchen. Her eyes sparkling, she handed me the receiver.

"Amy, this is Captain Sandy Coward, director of candidate guidance at the United States Naval Academy."

I thought my heart was going to beat right out of my chest.

"Good evening, sir."

"I wanted to be the first to congratulate you on being accepted to the United States Naval Academy for the class of 1997."

"Oh . . . thank you, thank you so much." Then something struck me. "Captain Coward, are you sure? I haven't gotten the notification of nomination from my congressman."

As part of the application process, all candidates have to be nominated by their congressperson.

"That's not an issue. The superintendent can select ten candidates on his own, and those candidates don't have to go through the nomination process. He selected you and we want you here next year."

I could not remember ever being happier. "Thank you, sir. I can't wait."

I was still on cloud nine when I joined my teammates for the game against St. Henry. I couldn't wait to tell them the news, and they were all thrilled for me. We had become such a close group that we were more like sisters than teammates. Every one of them hugged me. The game itself was just one more part of a magical day. It went into overtime, and I scored the winning goal.

The next morning, I sat in homeroom, my head still buzzing. We listened to the day's PA announcements, which normally mentioned any senior who had been accepted into a college.

The voice on the PA said, "And congratulations to Amy McGrath, who has just been accepted into the United States Naval Academy." Everyone in my homeroom began cheering and clapping, and I could hear that other homerooms were applauding too. I had always let people know about my ambition to get into the academy. From the moment I walked through the doors on the first day of my freshman year, anyone who knew me at Notre Dame knew my singular focus. Pretty much the whole student body knew what my goal was. Now I had achieved it.

It took all the strength I had to keep from crying at the amazing outpouring of support from all these incredible people. This was my community and the heart of my America as I understood it at that moment. It was one small Catholic school in one tiny corner of Kentucky, but it was, for me, America idealized.

Being accepted to the naval academy took a weight off my shoulders, but I was still driven. My competitiveness was nowhere near quenched. The soccer team played well, and we made it into the final game of the state tournament—the first women's state soccer tournament in Kentucky's history. It was a chance to win big and end my high school soccer career on an epic note. We had a chance to tie the game with a corner kick. There were just two minutes left in regulation play, and Coach Wolf brought me up from my defender position. I had a talent for heading in goals off corner kicks. I'd done it all season long. This time, though, I was a beat too slow. I missed the ball by an inch, and we lost the game.

I was devastated. I felt I had let the team down in a truly ugly way. Our failures are often the most poignant teachers. Coming to grips with that game, I turned to what my parents had taught me. My mom and dad never focused on what they didn't have. They were thankful for their blessings. The more I thought about it, the more perspective I gained. My faith, God's plan for me, that was all much larger than one soccer game. I trusted Him and could be nothing but thankful that I was assured a spot in the naval academy and surrounded by supportive people. It seemed silly to waste time pining for what might have been or hanging my head in shame. I would learn from it and move on.

It helped that my high school soccer career was overshadowed by a world-shaking presidential election that November. Bill Clinton was elected president, and the largest group of women ever to be voted into Congress swept in behind him. Seismic cultural and political shifts toward equality were under way. I knew now that it was only a matter of time before the combat exclusion rule was overturned. Everything seemed to be lining up for the future I had dreamed of for so long.

If only it had been that easy.

In March, my basketball curse struck again. I went up for a rebound in the last game of the season, only to come down tangled with another player. My lower leg was pinned in the wrong direction. I felt something pop, but the pain wasn't excruciating. Then, as I stood up, my lower leg snapped back into place and the pain spiked, making my eyes water. It wasn't as painful as my first knee injury but would turn out to be worse. My teammates helped me off the court, and the trainer checked me out. I could tell by his face as he frowned down at my knee that I was headed to the orthopedic surgeon again. I saw the doctor the next day, and he ordered an MRI for the following week. I held my breath. A week later, the surgeon gave me the bad news.

"I'm sorry, but you've torn your anterior cruciate ligament."

The blood pounded in my head. I had been around enough athletes, and followed pro sports closely enough, that I understood exactly what those words meant. In 1993, an ACL injury was a major setback, one that could end a pro athlete's career. My mother squeezed my shoulder. The surgeon gave me a second to process and then continued. "We're going to take a ligament from elsewhere in the body, and we're going to screw it into place above and below the joint."

I did the mental math. It was March. I had to be ready to go for the intense physical demands of Plebe Summer at the end of June. "How long will the rehab take?"

He looked at my mom and then at me. "Typically, six to nine months. But if you work hard, you might be able to accelerate it. Better you do it right, though. Are you in a hurry?"

"I need to be ready for Plebe Summer at the naval academy, starting at the end of June. It's mostly physical training."

"Look, I'm not sure that's realistic, Amy. It's a significant operation. There's going to be a lot of pain in your recovery. Even after you heal, the knee will be stable, but the leg will be weak for some time."

He could tell by my face that I was devastated. Maybe he was throwing me a bone, but I took what he said next as gospel, as purely hopeful.

"I can't guarantee anything; everybody's different. But if you work really hard in rehab, there's an outside chance you could be good enough to go. I'm not saying you'd be at one hundred percent, but the knee would probably hold up."

I smiled. I'd take it. Any chance was a big improvement over no chance at all. I had a new goal: I was going to have to cut the rehab time about in half.

I had to let the academy know what had happened, but making that call was almost as bad as talking to the surgeon. I dialed Captain Coward's number and waited. As soon as he picked up, I told him about the injury and my rehab outlook.

"I'm sorry, Amy. That's a tough break. It means that you're no longer physically qualified for entrance. You can reapply for the next year, but you probably won't make it this year. I just think it's unlikely that you'll be able to recover in time for Plebe Summer."

I was seventeen. A year seemed like an eternity. I had already waited so long and fought so hard for my spot. I understood what he was saying, but it was frustrating and unfair. There had to be a way to make it work.

"Well, how about if I just go to prep school for a year?"

"I hear you, but you don't want to waste your time in prep school. Get a year of college under your belt."

I had been accepted at Jacksonville University in Florida, through the navy ROTC. The location would keep me close to a naval base at least, and I could get some of the basic requirements out of the way toward graduation from the naval academy.

"Okay, that'll be my fallback. But I still think I can make Plebe Summer."

There was a moment of hesitation on the other end of the line. Captain Coward knew the odds, and he didn't want to give me false hope. "Okay, Amy. Keep me in the loop and let me know how rehab goes."

Ironically, three weeks after my injury, Secretary of Defense Les Aspin lifted the combat exclusion policy preventing women aviators from flying combat missions. I was so close to what I had wanted for so long, and now fate was trying to pull it away.

The surgery scared me. I had nightmares of being saddled for life with a leg that didn't work right. What if something went wrong? It wouldn't be just a year lost; it could kill any chance that I would ever get into the military, much less inside the tiny, physically demanding space of a fighter jet cockpit. In the end, though, there was no option. My mother held my hand, literally and figuratively, through the whole process. I went in for the surgery in early April, and she was there sitting by my bed when I woke up. My knee was horribly swollen and discolored. I avoided looking at it. I needed to stay positive. As the drugs wore off and I became completely aware, I realized that it wasn't the pain I had to worry about. It was the panic. The knee looked awful, but the bigger problem was that I could not lift it.

Major surgery traumatizes nerves, and those nerves take time to heal. The pain I could manage. The hard part was going to be staying upbeat, staying focused mentally, and keeping the panic from overwhelming me every time I tried to move my leg.

Both the surgeon and my mom reassured me that the nerve connection would regenerate. At seventeen, though, crises can take on an unreasonable size and shape that overwhelms all rational thought. A little voice somewhere in the back of my head kept saying, "How do they know?" and "What if it doesn't ever work again?" I spiraled into a dark place heading into my first rehab sessions. I wore a massive, clunky knee brace and had to rely entirely on crutches. The first step in rehab was the thoroughly unrewarding work of making the mind-leg connection. Day by day, I lay on the workout mat and just focused on controlling the leg. Each day I could feel the clock ticking, time running out as my naval career slipped away. I wanted to do something so simple, something even children can do without thinking about. I had never wanted to run so badly.

There is a special kind of fear that arises when your mind is rudely disconnected from a part of your body. Walking is so automatic. We don't even realize that our brain is constantly sending electrical signals to our muscles. It's a seamless connection that we never have to worry about. We perform this task of standing on two skinny sticks, balancing and motoring around as if it were nothing. We move deftly to avoid obstacles, control a vast number of muscles, and coordinate a series of extremely complex joints. Even highly sophisticated robots struggle to mimic walking. We take it for granted. I took it for granted. Until, suddenly, my leg would not obey me. In fact, it ignored me.

I kept thinking, "What if I can never control my leg muscles again?" It seemed like the end of the world. At one point, angry, afraid, and overwhelmed, I hobbled into the living room. My mother was reading on the couch. I lay down on the floor and began to cry. I wanted my mom to make everything better. I wanted her to see that I was trying so hard but that it wasn't working. I wanted her to fix me.

She marked her place and put the book down on the arm of the sofa. Leaving her cane leaning there, she limped over and sat down on our beat-up old beige ottoman. She sat silently and watched me. She listened as I literally yelled, and complained, and cried. Calm as anything, she reached down and put her hand a couple of inches above my leg.

"Come on, Amy, touch my hand. You can do it."

In my frustration I yelled at her, "No I can't. I'm trying, but it's not working."

Again, a little more firmly, she said, "C'mon, Amy, I know you can do it."

I made a feeble attempt to move the leg and nothing happened.

I got even angrier and yelled again, "See! It won't move. You don't understand. It won't move."

That struck a nerve with my mom. Didn't understand? This woman had physically struggled through her life every day since she was ten years old. She could not go out for a jog. A long, leisurely walk in the evening wasn't even a possibility. Every day must have taken a herculean effort just to get where she was going, yet I had never once heard her use her leg as an excuse.

I could hear the change, the raw emotion that colored her determined yet calm voice, as she said, "Amy, you can do this. Lift your leg and touch my hand. Right now."

She wasn't messing around. She had put special emphasis on the words "you" and "can." I could see the pain in her eyes, the angst of worrying for your child, but also the heartache of realizing that I would eventually get better but that she would never be able to lift her leg as she was asking me to do. She understood me, and she understood anatomy, and she knew it would be only a matter of time before I was walking, running, and doing all the things I loved to do. She knew what it was to actually never again be able to will your leg to do the simplest thing. In an instant, I saw all that. I understood it. How small I felt.

I was crying as I squeezed my eyes shut and willed my leg up with all my might. I needed to lift it for both of us. I concentrated harder than I ever had, my eyes closed tight, thinking about that one very simple thing. "Raise your leg." Then I felt my mom's hand. I felt it with my leg. My eyes popped open, and she was smiling at me as I held my leg three inches off the rug. We were both crying now, but smiling too. I made a silent vow never to feel sorry for myself again.

May that year was the longest month I would ever endure. Good days were followed by small setbacks. After I was able to control the damaged knee's movements, I had to move on to more complicated exercises. By the end of April, I had mastered walking again and could walk increasing distances every day. But walking wasn't running. And it sure as heck wasn't the obstacle course at Annapolis.

Attending the end-of-season basketball banquet to applaud my teammates, I was reminded that we don't get where we're going alone. Americans value independence and personal achievement, but I was constantly being supported by an incredible network well beyond my family. As I sat off to the side, watching everyone walk around freely on two good legs, Coach Westerman came over to say hi. He could tell I was wrestling with anxiety about the injury. He looked me straight in the eyes and said, "Amy, you need to always remember you aren't done. You're going to do great things. Character, Amy. You have it, and that will get you there. Trust me." The intensity of how he said it, how he looked me in the eyes, moved me. It gave me strength.

The people in my life helped me focus on the positives. I was managing the pain. I stumbled once in a while as I tried to refine my coordination, but I was making progress. You hold on to hallmark moments, like when I handed my crutches to the physical therapist who said, "I'm not giving these back." There was the moment when I actually jogged about twenty yards on the track at the boys' school across the street. By the third week in May, I was jogging short distances. At first, a quarter mile was enough to prove to me how weak my leg still was. I held a lot of fear about reinjuring the knee. Each day, though, brought a little bit more distance, a little bit more leg strength and trust in my own body. I had three weeks to make Plebe Summer.

Finally, with two weeks to go, I called Captain Coward as I did every week, to let him know my progress. As usual, I was careful with my words. "I ran three miles, sir. There was hardly any pain." "Ran," not "jogged." It had hurt more than I let on, but pain wasn't going to kill me. Captain Coward was on my side. He would become my mentor for the course of my career, and he was my champion during the admissions process. He saw my drive and wanted me to succeed.

"That's good news, Amy. I took your case to what we call the demolition derby, where we review every candidate who's been injured since acceptance. Here's the deal. You'll need to show up two days before induction. We'll have the navy doctor check you out. If you get the green light from him, your case will go directly to the commandant and it will be his decision. So, you can come, but I want to be clear that there's no guarantee you'll be inducted."

That's all I needed. Just a shot. It was better than nothing, and it was all I was going to get. "Yes, sir. I'll be there."

Three days before my induction on July 1, 1993, my mom, dad, and I drove to Annapolis in the Cardinal. Captain Coward had graciously offered to put us up in his home, and we spent time with him and his wonderful and welcoming wife, Croom. I tried to relax. I didn't have much success.

The next morning, my dad drove me to Hospital Point on the academy's "Yard," or campus. I was examined by a navy orthopedic surgeon. He reviewed all my charts from the doctors back home, performed a battery of movement tests, and made me do duck walks and squat thrusts. Finally, he sent me for X-rays. It was a long day, but the hour after hour of waiting that night seemed truly endless. Finally, Captain Coward came home and sat me down to deliver the navy's verdict.

"Here's the deal. The commandant has decided you can be inducted, but you'll have to wear a knee brace for Plebe Summer. It's going to be a bear, but that's the price of admission. You'll have to pass all the evolutions except for the obstacle course. We'll hold off until September on that one, and you'll have to pass that as soon as the brace comes off."

"Oh my God, thank you, sir. I won't let you down."

He smiled and said, "I know you won't."

Twelve hours later, I was standing in line on the sidewalk outside the USNA admissions office, one of a thousand kids with my paperwork in hand and my mom and dad standing next to me. All the candidates were hustled through the process with military efficiency. Our paperwork was checked, we were fitted for uniforms, hurried to the barber to have our hair cut, rushed to supply to get our bedding, and then ordered to Bancroft Hall. Bancroft was the dorm building, and we had to learn how to move properly through the hall and make a bed to pass muster. There wasn't time to think through any of it. Upperclassmen were everywhere, yelling at us, telling us where to go, what to do. Pity the poor plebe who failed to listen.

Finally, dressed in our "white works," the first uniform we ever got in the military, we lined up to enter Tecumseh Court, the area in front of Bancroft Hall. We were ordered to stand and raise our right hands as the commandant of midshipmen read the oath in which we all swore to defend the Constitution of the United States against all enemies, foreign and domestic. Then we screamed, "I do," in unison. Just then, four EA-6B Prowlers roared overhead in a flyby that rattled the entire regiment and all the spectators. It was incredibly loud and purely awesome. In that moment, I said a silent prayer, thanking God for this opportunity and asking Him to guide me to my ultimate goal.

I was officially a U.S. Naval Academy midshipman.

I was the lowest rank of naval officer you could be. I was a plebe, not even a human worthy of consideration by any upperclassman. I was given the alpha code 974098, and I was nothing more than that number as far as the navy was concerned. I was going to be wearing an uncomfortable, clunky knee brace and facing an excruciating amount of work under some of the most rigorous and onerous regulations of any college student anywhere. I was about to endure endless abuse each and every day for the better part of a year.

I was the happiest I had ever been.

4

THE U.S. NAVAL ACADEMY can take your breath away. An intimidating sense of legendary history saturates the campus, and every midshipman realizes that he—or she—is incredibly lucky to be attending one of the finest universities in the country, a school unlike any other.

Unfortunately, it's easy to lose sight of that majestic allure when you're humping a stiff, four-strap, ten-pound knee brace across the hard-packed dirt of a parade field. Plebe Summer is incredibly challenging in the best of times, but even more so dragging a restrictive medical appliance along for the ride. The pace of the seven weeks is relentless. A few classes break up the schedule, but the majority of each day is spent doing physical things. You hustle from one place to the next, forever behind, with red-faced upperclassmen screaming at you, "Hurry up, plebe." Strapping in and out of an awkward knee brace only complicated my commute. The brace was always in the way, and after the first week of my sweating on an hourly basis, it got a bit ripe.

You can get lost in momentary discomfort and make the mistake of thinking that the punishing schedule and constant abuse are arbitrary. That's not the case. Plebe Summer is a midshipman's initiation into the military way of thinking. There is a time-tested method to the madness and profound reasons for what goes on in training. Plebe Summer drives home the reality of responsibility in the military. The yelling, the performing under pressure, being driven to your extremes, are all part of the ultimate goal: preparing midshipmen for combat. Forget a single piece of crucial information or move a shade too slowly in battle and someone can die. Looking at it that way, I realized that the abuse was a means to an important end.

Plebe Summer was physically the hardest thing I had ever done to that point in my life, but it led to a big reward. I knew that by making it through, I'd be preparing for even greater challenges to come. It was a journey of discovery, of learning that I could actually perform on far less sleep than I might have thought I could. I learned that with the proper inspiration, I could run six miles at the same pace I ran one. I got to the core of who I was and what I was capable of.

The summer serves as the academy's boot camp. It broke us down and stripped us of any sense of individuality. We were a team now, each of us just one among many. I would be relying on others and had to be reliable in return. Everything was about the corps, country, brigade, platoon, and unit. It started with memorizing the name of every classmate in my platoon, including knowing where they were from. My passion for team sports and my devotion to faith gave me a leg up. I was used to being just one of a flock among the pews. I knew what it was like to be a neighbor among patriotic citizens in a tight-knit small suburb. I already had a strong sense of community, a seasoned team mentality.

Being a link in a chain doesn't mean you don't get singled out. The upperclassmen who served as Plebe Summer trainers took a special interest in me. They didn't hide their irritation that I was being allowed to go through the summer with a brace and avoid the Hospital Point obstacle course evolution. It ticked them off, and they weren't shy about expressing their annoyance.

They rode me every day of the week. I did push-ups for being seconds late, for moving a step behind the class, for just about everything. I looked at it as good training for soccer season. Fortunately, the schedule left no time to dwell on how you were treated. Each day was full on morning to night, except for Sunday. Sundays before noon were dedicated to worship. Upperclassmen were not allowed to harass plebes during that time.

Just as I would many times during my military career, I turned to my faith as a way to connect with home and to my most meaningful values. Each week I would raise my voice as one among a chorus, singing hymns that were so familiar. I could almost hear my mother and father singing next to me. Those few hours in the academy's chapel each week were a precious renewal, rejuvenating moments that allowed me to just exhale and see the bigger picture. If you are one of the faithful, it colors all aspects of your life just as patriotism does. It puts everything you do in a more profound context.

There was also a less lofty reason for relishing Sunday mornings. After service, parishioners would gather for a coffee social. It was the only opportunity in the entire week to relax and just talk with other people, without an upperclassman yelling at me. Better yet, there was a spread of donuts, fruits, bagels, and more. For that one morning, I could eat my fill at a leisurely pace.

By the time my mom and dad arrived for parents' weekend at the end of the summer, I was a different person. I had lost almost fifteen pounds and gained the discipline of a true midshipman. I had actually begun a journey that, for so long, had been only an aspiration. Now I was hungrier than ever to see the inside of an F/A-18. Mom and Dad could see the fire in me, the desire that comes from getting closer and closer to a long-held goal.

My first academic year at the naval academy was in some ways an extension of Plebe Summer. Although I now had a full class load, as a "fourth class" midshipman I was still at the bottom of the pecking order. Upperclassmen treated me like a verbal punching bag. First thing every morning I jumped out of my rack, got dressed, and hustled to a different upperclassman's room to recite the "rates," that day's memorization task.

Memorizing the general orders of sentry or the names and classes of different naval warships can seem like an arbitrary rote exercise until you consider that in combat you don't get a chance to review your manual of emergency procedures or rules of engagement. The details have to be so ingrained in your memory that they are second nature. Memorizing the day's meal plan or the chain of command all the way to the president was just practice for quickly internalizing more important information.

All the traditions and rites serve the naval academy's overarching mission: creating and developing strong, capable, and responsible military leaders. They weren't training me to be a peacetime leader. They were molding me to be someone who could lead other warriors into the worst combat conditions imaginable. It's a tall order, but the academy has been doing it successfully for more than a century. Every once in a while I'd stop after a rotation on the drill field, looking out at the picturesque Chesapeake. I would reflect once again on all the midshipmen who came before me. Young graduates who went on to become admirals leading submarine and carrier strike groups. Naval and Marine Corps aviators who led squadrons into battle in the Pacific or flew bombing runs over Vietnam. I saw myself as part of a continuity of leadership that stretched back over a hundred years. That line of naval academy luminaries was a constant inspiration, from Chester Nimitz and Jimmy Carter, to John McCain, James Stockdale, and Alan Shepard. As a midshipman, I was standing on the shoulders of giants.

But day-to-day reality as a plebe is less grandiose than all that. The constant abuse can turn into nightmarishly bad days. It's easy to get ground down. You look for any break you can find, and my sanctuary became the soccer field.

I had been recruited for the USNA women's basketball team, but the academy had just elevated women's soccer from club sport to a varsity program. That meant we were now in the NCAA Division I. The former World Cup and soon-to-be Olympic women's soccer star Carin Jennings-Gabarra was hired as the naval academy's new head soccer coach. I had followed her career and respected her tremendously. She was tough and honest and a high-caliber competitor. I really wanted to play for her and prove myself. I strapped on my knee brace and walked on to try out for the squad. Making that team was a proud moment; all these strong women working together to build something new . . . and beat Army.

Army—the academy's most bitter rival—had a long head start on Annapolis. They had been fielding a varsity women's soccer team for many years and had been able to recruit behind that.

Naval academy players were dedicated to the military first and foremost. They were attending the academy to serve their country. Soccer teammates of mine would go on to become navy doctors and pilots commanding aviation squadrons. My teammate and friend Kerry Kuykendall would eventually become one of the navy's first female F-14 pilots. Ali Thompson would fly a helo as the Marine Corps' first female CH-53 pilot and first helicopter squadron commanding officer. Kate Standifer would rise to the rank of navy captain and command a C-130 squadron. Christine Weeks would become a navy brain surgeon. Anne Kipp Klokow would go from being a Marine combat pilot to an ER doctor. Nicole Aunapu Mann, a fellow Marine F/A-18 pilot, would become an astronaut. These were tough people and fierce competitors.

The soccer field was where we gathered in communion. We spent mornings running sprints together. We did drills all afternoon. We quickly bonded. Beyond the field of play, we shared our knowledge, insight, experience, and determination. We supported each other, and the team itself became like a unit—similar to a platoon. Anywhere in Bancroft Hall or on the Yard, at any moment, I was subject to abuse and punishment by upperclassmen. On the soccer field, though, we were all the same. Not plebes and upperclassmen—just teammates. We were a solidified small sorority in the midst of this huge naval academy fraternity. Off the field, my first-class (senior) teammates made sure I wasn't singled out or picked on as a plebe. Years later, I would return the favor as a first class, doing the same for the plebes on the squad. We pulled for one another, and that bled into our life elsewhere. Even in classes and physical training, you knew your soccer teammates had your back.

The soccer field and the academy at large offered constant lessons in leadership. There were examples of different leadership styles everywhere you looked. As a plebe, I got to see most of those in action and figure out which would work best for me. Would I be the hard-ass who relentlessly rode those beneath me, never giving them a moment's praise? Would I be the laid-back "buddy" leader, well liked but perhaps less well respected? No. My answer was to be the hard-but-fair leader. I saw that put to the test in an upperclassman who felt if you failed a rate assignment (knowledge we were required to learn and memorize), you did push-ups . . . and she'd do them right along with you because your failure echoed her failure as a leader.

The leaders I took as examples were quietly competent and even talented but never arrogant. The perfect example was my platoon commander when I was a third class (sophomore), Erik Kristensen. He was reserved, not a big one for yelling. But he knew his stuff and expected you to do the same. It was a quiet excellence, and it was the way I wanted to lead. Erik would go on to command Operation Red Wings as a Navy SEAL in Afghanistan and make the ultimate sacrifice when his helo was taken down with an RPG. Leaders like those could be hard on anyone below them, but only to help someone grow and improve. They were always teachers, honest and genuinely caring. My favorite leaders could also be fierce in competition and brutal to anyone who would attempt to hurt or denigrate a teammate. That made sense to me because what was war, what was combat, but competition? The most extreme form of competition.

The officers I admired most at the academy were almost all Marines. That drove my decision to abandon the idea of becoming a naval aviator and focus on Marine selection. The Marine Corps is elite, and the sheer challenge of becoming a Marine officer was alluring to me. The Marines were also the only service at the time that flew a two-seat version of the F/A-18. I had no illusions about my poor vision. I knew that I could not qualify as a pilot. If I wanted to fly in an F/A-18 right away—my dream since middle school—I could only do that in the backseat, and that meant with the Marine Corps.

Much as I reveled in life at the academy, it was essential to get off campus for a few hours each week. That's why midshipmen have local sponsors—people nearby who act as a family away from family. Mine were Bette and Joe DiNunno and Sandy and Croom Coward.

The DiNunnos were a wonderful, loving older couple, and Bette was a spectacular Italian cook. Home-cooked meals are a rarity for a midshipman, and eating Bette's lasagna as I listened to Joe's Cold War stories provided some of the most memorable moments during my plebe year. He had been a nuclear engineer working in the highest echelons of the Department of Energy. Raised in a poor Pennsylvania farm family, he got his degree using the GI Bill after World War II. He was a living example of what made America so incredible. He devoted his life to public service, using his expertise to ensure nuclear power was safe. He was one of the purely wisest men I had ever met, and I felt as if he were my own personal Yoda.

In terms of pure leadership, though, there were few examples quite as poignant for me as Captain Sandy Coward. Captain Coward had fought hard as the director of candidate guidance to help me get into the academy, and he would be an immensely valuable mentor to me. Early in that first year, though, I dealt with a surprising revelation from him, one that gave me a deeper insight into how true leaders think and act.

We had finished dinner one Saturday night, and Croom was cleaning up in the kitchen. Captain Coward had enjoyed a few drinks and was in an expansive mood. As we talked, I asked him what he thought about the navy opening up combat jets and aircraft carriers to women. I was certain that he would offer full-throated support of the policy change. After all, he had been a tireless champion for me as I struggled with my knee injury and rehab. He knew well what my goal had always been, and he was a combat pilot himself. He had an intimate knowledge of how deep the desire to fly runs in a military aviator. I quickly learned I had made a flawed assumption. He looked me right in the eye as he said, "I think it's a terrible idea. It's flat-out crazy. It's insane."

I was stunned. This was my sponsor, someone who had given me invaluable guidance and support. It was no overstatement to say I idolized him; he had been a navy attack pilot, had flown countless missions over Vietnam, and had been an attack squadron commander, a carrier air group commander, and a commanding officer of test pilot school. Here he was telling me that he didn't think I should be in combat? That I shouldn't achieve my dream simply because I lacked a Y chromosome?

He took a sip of his scotch and continued, "But if we in the navy are going to do this, then we've got to have the best women in the country. Otherwise, the whole thing fails miserably and people get hurt or worse. That, Amy, is why I recruited you."

It was the complexity that faces military leaders, in a nutshell. You don't give up your right to independent thought simply because you are a link in a rigid chain of command. In fact, critical thinking is an essential skill for a true military leader. But regardless of what your personal views or opinions might be, you ultimately follow lawful orders. As a leader, you must execute direct commands from above, and you must always seek to do what's best for the military and, by extension, the country. Captain Coward could have easily fought a counter-battle to keep women out of the academy. He could have undermined applications, or just not helped someone like me. That would have been dishonorable, and he was quite the opposite: one of the most honorable people I would ever know. We disagreed, which bummed me out. Still, I left their house that night respecting Captain Coward even more than I already had. I was determined to make sure the navy and the Marine Corps wouldn't fail in integrating women into combat roles.

Making room for different perspectives and personalities is a huge part of military experience. The naval academy—like every military institution in the United States—is a melting pot. I lived that reality in my own dorm room, with my plebe-year roommate, Rachel.

Rachel was a native of Queens, New York. She was Puerto Rican and Dominican and could not have been more culturally different from a wide-eyed Kentucky girl. We both held some stereotypes that we might not have admitted to each other. My first impression of Rachel was that she was a typical brash New Yorker, tough and blunt, bordering on rude. A fast talker who wore her emotions on her sleeve. I think Rachel probably expected me to be a bit of a backwoods Kentucky bumpkin with no sophistication or filters. We were, of course, both wrong.

We were people, just kids who had set themselves a gigantic challenge. On a campus where women made up less than 10 percent of the population, we were both in the minority, skin color be damned. What we were was Americans. We shared much more than whatever it was that made us different. We had very similar goals and aspirations. We were going to be proud members of the military. Perhaps on the streets of our respective cities, we would seem different from each other. But what would identify us most dramatically in the future was a shared uniform. Even beyond ideals, it was a matter of practicality. We needed to help and support each other. We became fast friends, the Kentuckian and the New Yorker.

We needed everyone we could get in our corners, because the first year at the naval academy is the toughest. You're setting the pace for all four years, and you're learning how high the bar is set. I was happy to see May come so that I could participate in the "plebes no more" ceremony (climbing the greased granite of the twenty-one-foot Herndon Monument) and drop that word "plebe" permanently. I earned my first stripe and jumped into a fully booked summer.

Midshipmen at the naval academy normally get a month off over the summer. The rest of the time, you're still on the clock for the military. For many in my class, including me, that meant Midshipman Leadership Training (MLT). MLT was a mandatory course at the time, rigorous training that further reinforced leadership skills, initiative, and responsibilities. I would go straight from MLT to serving as a squad leader for Summer Seminar. Although it had really been only a couple of years, it seemed like a long time ago that I had gone through the seminar myself. Guiding high school kids through that week gave me the chance to hone my leadership skills as well as evaluate the talent that would come after me in the academy.

I got only a couple of weeks of leave to visit home before I had to return early for soccer practice. Charging into my second year, I found my pace academically and began working on the academy's Foreign Affairs Conference. The conference is a yearly event held in the spring, but the planning and work begin from the start of the school year. I started in my sophomore year as a worker bee alongside more than a hundred midshipmen who handled the vast number of details that go into putting on the conference.

As full as my schedule was for my second academic year, it couldn't hold a candle to the summer that followed. I started with a trip to Basic Airborne Course in Fort Benning, Georgia. There are some purely fun opportunities as a midshipman, and learning how to jump out of planes is one of them. It's an exhilarating exercise. I came away with my parachute qualification, took a breath, and headed off to England in an exchange program with the Royal Navy and the Royal Marines. I have always been an international relations nerd, so it was incredibly interesting to see how a different military operated. I discovered that regardless of small differences in procedures or chain of command, the ethos driving military members is exactly the same. We share a dedication to honor, sacrifice, and patriotism. Core values remain core values regardless of the flag you salute.

I finished that summer on board the navy oiler USS *Seattle,* a supply ship on a cruise in the Mediterranean. We had ports of call in Greece and Italy, which meant visiting places I'd never been before. Even more important, though, was a two-hour stint aboard the aircraft carrier USS *Theodore Roosevelt.* Carriers had not yet integrated women, so I couldn't stay overnight. But even the short amount of time I spent there was a thrill. We arrived by helicopter amid frenetic activity on the flight deck. Carrier flight decks are busy, dangerous places, and everyone working there has to be incredibly precise in their jobs. There is literally no room for error. It was a shot of pure adrenaline to watch everything happening all around me. Although I didn't get to relish the sight—and sound—of a fighter jet landing or taking off, I did get to watch the flight deck crew launch an E-2 Hawkeye into the air. The compact turboprop plane carries a distinctive flat, round satellite antenna on top of the fuselage; watching it gather speed as it rushed down catapult 2 toward the bow of the carrier was a sight to behold.

We toured the cramped confines of the ship, including a typical rack where aviators attempted to get some sleep amid the mind-boggling noise and motion of the ship. I ate lunch in one of the mess halls and met the ship's captain. By the time I strapped into the helo for the flight back to the oiler, I couldn't wait to get myself into an F/A-18 and touch down on that flight deck. I started the school year with renewed passion and fire.

Junior year—second class—at the naval academy is a threshold. It's where midshipmen shoulder increasing amounts of responsibilities and start defining themselves as leaders. The people who aren't going to make it—those who drop out or wash out for one reason or another—are gone by junior year. The core of what will become the next wave of U.S. Navy and Marine Corps officers and leaders are all around you, in classes, in ceremonies, and on the soccer field. The reality of a military career and a military life sets in. I assumed a more prominent role in coordinating the Foreign Affairs Conference as an operations officer, responsible for making the three-day conference run as smoothly as possible. The keynote speaker that year was George H. W. Bush. As part of the command team, I got to meet the former president and even shared a short conversation with him. We talked about baseball, of all things, discussing his time as a first baseman for Yale and my devotion to the Reds. It was a hallmark moment for me because I admired President Bush; he had been a naval aviator, gone to war, and reached the pinnacle of public life. He was a tall, imposing figure with ramrod-straight posture and the bearing and gravitas I associated with the office of president. But he was also human, approachable, and kind, with a quick smile.

These types of magical experiences made me feel even more fortunate to be a midshipman at the naval academy. As hard as academy life might get, it was always rewarding and interesting. Even the tough days were made easier by the fact that I was living to my deepest beliefs, a personal engagement with patriotism, and the reality that I was part of something larger and important. Of course, some challenges were bound to be bigger than others. One of the hardest for me was Leatherneck training in the summer after my junior year.

The four-week training session is held at the Marine Corps base in Quantico, Virginia. We tackled many of the same field exercises we had in Midshipman Leadership Training, but the bar was set much higher. The performance evaluation was unstinting. I could feel the weight of judgment in every single task, every day. You're measured by crucial questions: Can you lead a squad with zero errors? Can you jump in as the person in charge and lead without hesitation? Can you command respect? Are you completely squared away, and can you help others be squared away as well? You had to have answered those questions for yourself if you were going to convince the Marine officer evaluating you that you could do the Marine Corps proud. I did well in the training and came out high in my class. That was essential if I was going to secure a Marine Corps billet.

I leveraged my evolving leadership skills as the regimental adjutant on the Plebe Summer staff, in charge of training the incoming plebes in the class of 2000. That role exposed me to the circular, "next man up" nature of the military. We were always striving to be the best leaders possible; part of that process was helping forge the leaders who would come after us.

For all that I had discovered about leadership and what type of leader I could be, my senior year would teach me one of the most important and bitter lessons about leadership: sometimes you fail.

In fact, the best leaders are adept at effectively dealing with and moving beyond failure.

I had become an elder on the soccer team. I was determined in my final soccer season that we would beat Army. We had lost to our fiercest rival all three of the previous years. The losses were a hard pill to swallow, especially given my finely honed sense of competition. Each year we had gotten closer to beating Army, and I was positive that my first-class year would be the delicious moment when we could celebrate that victory.

We were all amped on the bus to West Point in upstate New York. We checked into our hotel and tried to get a good night's sleep. The next day, we played our hearts out, and we had Army on the ropes. We went into double overtime tied. Then they scored the winning goal. It was the biggest disappointment in my time at the naval academy. It left a bitter taste in my mouth because it was so reminiscent of losing in the Kentucky state finals. We finished so late that it only made sense to stay another night at the hotel before heading home the next morning. About an hour after I settled in, there was a knock on the door. I answered it to find a teammate standing in the hall.

"I want to show you something."

"What is it?"

"You'll see."

She led the way to another teammate's room. We walked into the middle of a sorrow party that was just about to kick off. There were bottles of booze and a lot of beer on ice. They were quite obviously waiting for me.

This was an acid test. Drinking on a team trip was strictly against the rules, and I knew it. Everyone was waiting for me to go along before they jumped in. I was the upperclassman in the room, the responsible one. The right thing to do was crystal clear: I should have shut it down and made them pour out all the alcohol. Unfortunately, I was immensely frustrated and sad. Stinging so much from a defeat that could have easily gone the other way, I thought, "Screw it, we need to blow off steam and bond over this defeat." I grabbed a beer and twisted off the top. I raised it in a toast: "Beat Army!"

We didn't go wild. It was more like a wake than a college party. We drank enough to put on a buzz and ended up watching *Happy Gilmore*. I got to bed before midnight. It might all have been a regrettable slip of discipline if not for a simple misunderstanding. We had a civilian trainer who knew about the drinking. He wasn't military, so he didn't really care and wasn't going to go out of his way to give us up. The next morning, we all checked out of the hotel and got onto the bus, glad to put West Point behind us.

Our officer in charge, a submariner, sat down next to the trainer. A group of our soccer players had been stranded in a broken elevator at the hotel for an hour after we had first checked in. Referencing that episode, the officer in charge said to the trainer, "I don't know how I'm going to explain what happened at the hotel."

The trainer was surprised. "You mean the drinking?"

Now it was the officer in charge's turn to be surprised. "What drinking?"

The cat was out of the bag, and I knew it when the officer in charge called me up from the back of the bus. As soon as I sat down, he said, "Tell me about the drinking."

I was quite aware of the academy's honor concept: midshipmen do not lie, cheat, or steal. I knew I would never do the dishonorable thing. Bad conduct was one thing, but being dishonorable was much, much worse. I said, "That's what we did, sir. We had a few beers."

"All right. I'm glad you were honest with me."

That was far from the end of it. He reported us all as soon as we got back to the academy. We were duly informed that we were going to be adjudicated—disciplined and put on restriction. Two weeks later we had our adjudication. In a stroke of bad timing, the commandant had just made it his goal to crack down on midshipmen athletes' drinking. He had given a speech on it the week prior to our adjudication. At the hearing, I tried to take as much responsibility as I could. I stood in front of the deputy commandant presiding over the adjudication and said, "The rest of the team would not have done this had I not told them they could. It was my fault, and my responsibility to stop them." The statement made little impact; the judgment was swift and severe.

Each plebe (freshman) got a week's restriction; sophomores received two weeks' restriction. The juniors were tagged with a month. I got three months' restriction and a loss of all privileges until graduation. I would basically become a fourth-class midshipman until I graduated.

I lost all leave. While the juniors and the seniors lost Thanksgiving and Christmas, I lost Thanksgiving, Christmas, and spring break. I was dropped a hundred positions in class rank, from 50th to 150th. I wasn't surprised, because it was the right call and that's the way military discipline works. In an institution like the navy, the higher your rank, the more responsibility you carry.

The first order of business was to find out if I had screwed myself out of a Marine service assignment. I desperately wanted to be a Marine, more than ever before, and it was going to be bitter medicine if it turned out I had killed my chances. Even before my adjudication, I headed to the senior Marine's office. As I stood at attention in front of Colonel Michael Glynn, he let me unload my whole spiel. I told him everything, every detail and all my regrets.

"Sir, I screwed up. I don't care how long I'm going to be on restriction, or any other demerits. I just want to be a Marine. I'll do anything to make this right. As long as I haven't lost the chance to be a Marine."

He leaned back in his leather office chair and said, "Midshipman McGrath, you think that a drinking infraction is going to make the Marine Corps aviation community not want you?"

"Uh, I was concerned about that, sir."

A small smile tugged at his lips. As I would come to find out, Marine aviators are a hard-drinking group, tough in work and tough in recreation. "I think you're going to be okay, McGrath. Now get out of my office."

The relief was intense but not complete. I saw the drinking incident from two perspectives. We really needed to heal, commiserate, and bond as a team to deal with the biggest defeat most of us were going to be handed as athletes. And we had. We had supported one another and licked our wounds as a team. But I had knowingly broken the rules. I was fine with paying the price, but the worst part of that whole episode, the part I truly hated and regretted, was that the freshmen and sophomores would have a black mark on their reputations for the rest of their time at Annapolis. Me? I was on my way out. I was pretty much assured that I would become a Marine and still had a great shot at getting the billet I coveted.

I had allowed those fourth- and third-class midshipmen to get in trouble when they still had their entire academy careers in front of them. In a normal college environment, a little drinking might not seem like a big deal. But violating the rules so blatantly at the academy was a big infraction, one that could actually impact my teammates' training assignments and possibly their commissioned service assignments. It bothered me deeply, because they were all exceptional individuals. They were anything but partiers and dirtbags, which is exactly what they came out looking like. Fortunately, my final year at the academy would end on a much higher note.

The service assignment selection is one of the most exciting moments for a midshipman. Seniors file their preferences for service and assignment prior to the start of their senior year. The authorities then sift through academic achievements, qualifications, and general fitness to award billets—what you will become in your military career. You could only list assignments for which you had qualified. You filed your choices in order of preference. Mine were, starting from the top, Marine Aviation, Marine Ground, Navy Aviation, and Navy Surface Warfare. I would find out what my billet was along with the other seniors in 2nd Company. We were assembled in the wardroom by the company officer, and each of us was handed a folded piece of paper with our name on it as we walked in. The company officer said sternly, "Don't unfold your paper until my signal, after everyone has theirs." At the signal, everybody unfolded the paper. Mine said, "Marine Aviation." It was the happiest I had ever been at the academy. I was that much closer to the cockpit of an F/A-18.

Even though I had sabotaged any leave I might have had for the rest of my senior year, there was a consolation: more time to work on the Foreign Affairs Conference. I was the director of the conference, the top post. That meant I had more than a hundred midshipmen working under me and I was busier than ever. The keynote speaker was one of my personal heroes, Secretary of State Madeleine Albright. On the night of the conference I sat next to her at dinner. I was so awestruck that it was hard to pull up even one of the hundreds of questions I had always wanted to ask her. She was every bit as amazing as I had imagined. A strong, well-spoken, intelligent, and accomplished woman. She had seen and played a role in just about every corner of the world. She was also another example of what America is truly about. She emigrated from communist Czechoslovakia to become an American and went on to become an incredibly dedicated public servant.

The conference signaled that my time at Annapolis was drawing to a close. Almost before I realized it, I was sitting for finals. Then, in May, came the final hurrah—commissioning week. That point in a midshipman's final year is a pure celebration, five days of formal parties, a Blue Angels air show, and other cool events.

On Commissioning Day, my class filed into the Navy–Marine Corps Memorial Stadium for the graduation ceremony. Friends and family were there, and the lower classes in the brigades filled the stands out. We marched in proudly wearing our dress whites, aligned in perfect formation. I sat and watched the speakers give their speeches, and I thought back to all I had been through at the academy. So much had been packed into four years; it seemed like just yesterday I left my father and carried my bag into Bancroft Hall for the first time, as a green Summer Seminar resident. The beautiful morning wore on, and I reflected some more. Finally, we filed up to the stage in line to receive our diplomas.

When it was our company's turn, I stood in line until they called my name. I walked forward and shook the superintendent's hand, then the commandant's hand, and finally Vice President Al Gore's hand. He congratulated me as a staff member handed me my diploma. I was officially a graduate of the U.S. Naval Academy.

After the diplomas were all handed out, the lower-class midshipmen in the stands followed timeworn tradition and shouted, "For those about to leave us . . . hip, hip, hooray." All of us graduates replied, "For those we're about to leave . . . hip, hip, hooray," at which we tossed our covers—our hats—into the air. We wouldn't need them anymore because we'd be wearing officers' covers from that point forward. We were dismissed, and I joined my fellow Marine Corps officers in the locker room to change out of the dress whites into the corps' dress blue over whites. I was excited to pin on the gold bars of a Marine second lieutenant.

We headed back out to stand at attention in front of the Marine Corps Commandant and raised our right hands. Once more, I took the oath of office, swearing to protect the country and Constitution from enemies foreign and domestic. I was now officially a Marine Corps officer.

I took photos with my family and reveled in a day meant to be pure celebration. It was also a time for processing what I would take away. I had learned that the military rewards hard work. The academy had provided the tools I'd need to accomplish my goal, and all I had to do was use them with discipline and dedication. I had learned that you don't finish a hike in one step. You go step by step, and you break down achievements in the same way. Everything led to something beyond. I had gained confidence every time I conquered a new challenge, especially if it was something I might once have thought I couldn't possibly do. The best way to grow, to gain confidence in the military or anywhere else, is to challenge yourself.

More than anything, though, I once again felt the weight of opportunity. I had been given a chance that women before me had never been offered. Doors had opened, and I would be a fool not to do the hard work it would take to walk through. It was the familiar pressure of responsibility. I was responsible to the women who had fought so hard just to afford me such a profound opportunity. I was responsible to the mentors like Sandy Coward and Colonel Glynn who had put their faith, time, and effort into me. I was responsible to future women Marines, for whom I could provide an example.

Now I belonged to Uncle Sam, and I was incredibly proud of that. My country, America, had given me a handshake, a contract offering boundless opportunity to reach my dreams. All it asked in return was that I honor those fundamental concepts: service, duty, patriotism, and faith. I was bound and determined to uphold my end of that bargain.

5

THE MARINE CORPS MOTTO IS "Semper Fidelis," which translates to "Always Faithful." It means faithful to unit, corps, God, and country. There's nothing in there about the individual, because the individual takes second to all those things. That is the heart and soul of what's taught at the Marine Corps Basic School. Known by the acronym TBS, it's a brutal six-month slog through rain, heat, dust, mud, woods, every kind of discomfort, and your own personal physical limits. It's the crucible from which Marine Corps leaders are forged. It's where I learned how Semper Fidelis translates to action.

My days at TBS typically started at 0530. Marine Corps Base Quantico is sprawling and massive; sometimes we'd even get airlifted by helicopter to an exercise area. The evolutions and qualifications are unforgiving. Every bit of knowledge builds on what went before. The overarching mission is to teach officers how to lead Marines in ground combat, from land navigation to calling in air support. It's essential to have all the known variables down pat, because there is so much you can't know in battle. War is messy and chaotic. You may not know where gunfire is coming from, where the enemy is located, or if your map is accurate. Fields of combat are question marks. We call it the fog of war.

That unpredictability is why a Marine aviator finds herself at TBS. Maybe I would never see warfare except from the sky. It didn't matter. I needed to know the fundamentals of leading a rifle company not only so I understood what I was doing in the cockpit in relation to what was happening on the ground but so I could jump in should I ever find myself as the only officer available during a battle. It's a "utility hitter" philosophy, and any Marine officer needs to always be ready to step up. Ground warfare isn't academic. It can't be effectively taught in a classroom. To fully understand it, you have to live it. The Marine Corps can't drop you in the middle of a battle, so TBS is the next best thing.

The school tests your leadership, but I faced other challenges as well. Women were not integrated into every TBS class, and the idea that women officers should go through the exact same course was still debated. There were skeptics even among my peers. I was dead set on proving them wrong.

That meant establishing myself as a strong leader. I didn't have to wait long for the opportunity. Each company at TBS has to complete numerous forced marches. The hikes get longer as time goes on. Each platoon must carry several machine guns during long marches. The weapons are known by the acronym SAW (squad automatic weapon). It's a powerful weapon meant to supplement the M16s each Marine carries. In addition, each squad carries a larger heavy machine gun called the M240G. It's a grim reaper of the battlefield, perfect for engaging large numbers of enemy combatants in a heated firefight. The gun is heavy, but it's a shared burden; everyone takes a turn carrying parts of it.

Every two weeks, a different second lieutenant (the lowest-ranking officer) is rotated in as student platoon commander. It's harder to command a platoon of your peers than it is to be in charge of Marines of a lower rank. There's much more latitude for peers to criticize or mess with your leadership. When my turn came, I got to deal with a complainer.

He had a medium build and was just a little taller than I was, so he was hardly imposing. I wouldn't have cared if he had been. He had established himself as the malcontent, always griping about something. TBS is physically demanding and almost constantly uncomfortable. Humping fifty pounds of gear for twelve miles in all kinds of weather tests who you are at your core. As hard as that is, it's much harder hiking and executing maneuvers around someone who won't stop whining. When it came my turn to command the platoon, the complainer was assigned the SAW. It was the second time in a row he had carried it during field exercises, which wasn't all that unusual, even though we generally tried to rotate the duty. It set him off. After four miles of soaking in my own sweat and swallowing road dust to the sound of his bitching, I'd heard enough.

We had stopped for a quick hydration break when he started in again, spouting off to nobody in particular and to everybody. "This ain't right. I already carried this thing once. It's ridiculous." I squared off in front of him and said, "Give me your weapon."

"What?"

"Give me your weapon. I'll carry it and you'll carry mine."

He looked shocked. I could feel the eyes of the rest of the company on us both.

"No, no. It's okay, I got it." He suddenly realized how this was going to make him look, not only being stripped of his weapon, but having his load carried by a woman.

"Nope. I've heard enough from you. Give me your weapon. That's an order."

He reluctantly handed me the SAW, and I gave him my M16.

"There, now maybe you can do us all a favor and shut the hell up."

Word quickly got around that McGrath was not going to take any crap.

Those were the decisions you made in the field. They could be small, simple things in the heat of the moment, but they defined the type of leader you were. My philosophy was to lead by example, to solve problems with the unit in mind. I had come across guys who looked to personally excel. It was about *their* career, *their* excellence, *their* class rank. They were focused on making themselves look good and striving to be the best at everything. That's not the point of Marine Corps leadership. No, quite simply, it's about the unit. As soon as I got myself squared away, I wanted to look to my left and then to my right. Who needed help? How could I make the unit better? I saw it as part of a bigger picture. The idea extended far beyond the Marines. You could substitute "family," "community," "congregation," and "country" for "unit." That realization clarified leadership for me. I learned to ask myself, "What can I do for the greater good?"

The reality, though, is that TBS isn't all inspiration and success. It's long and arduous training, and admittedly I had my failures. Those are perhaps the best lessons of all. My Achilles' heel turned out to be a particular evolution called night land navigation. It's one of the more challenging skills to tackle. Night navigation is done with a compass with small fluorescent dots for indicators. You can't use a flashlight, because it could give away your position to an enemy. Setting the compass correctly to start with is essential. My mistake was turning the dial ninety degrees off true north.

That meant I wasted nearly two hours of the three-hour, timed evolution pushing through dark underbrush and unfamiliar wood terrain, headed in the wrong direction. I didn't realize my mistake until I stepped out of the woods onto the side of a paved road and saw a sign that read "FBI Academy Quantico VA."

"Damn it," I thought. I was on exactly the opposite side of the base from where I was supposed to be. The qualification entailed navigating to four boxes in sequence. The location of each put you in proper reference to the location of the next one. There was no way, in an hour, that I was going to find my way back and get to all four boxes.

I didn't see the point of fruitlessly heading back into the pitch-black woods, tripping into ditches, getting smacked by tree branches, running into spiderwebs, and encountering various other wildlife. So I began the long walk back, following the blacktop road to the exercise's starting point. I found my platoon commander, a Marine captain, and handed him my blank night navigation card that should have been marked with the contents of the four boxes.

"What the hell, Lieutenant McGrath?"

"I screwed up, sir. I set my compass wrong and didn't realize until I came out at the entrance to the FBI academy."

"So, get out there. Retrace your route and fix it."

"Sir, there's no way I make all four boxes in the time left."

He was angry, but saw the logic to what I was saying. "You failed this evolution, Lieutenant McGrath. You're going to have to do remediation, you know that, right?"

"Yes, sir."

I had already figured that much out. It meant I was going to stack extra night sessions onto days that began at 0530. It wasn't going to be fun, but I'd have to do it to pass the night land navigation test and graduate from TBS. Failing is frustrating. I hate it. It's easy to look at a failure as purely negative. I've come to see its value. Everyone falls down sooner or later. The getting back up is an unparalleled learning experience. I spent a lot of time and effort in remediation. I not only became proficient in night land navigation; I became really good at it. That particular skill would serve me well in the future.

I'm leery of Marines who have never failed. The longer you go without messing up, the more traumatic it is when it actually happens. For my money, give me a wingman who has failed a couple of times. I want to know that he's capable of correcting course and fixing a problem. I passed the night land navigation test on my second try. It's okay to miss the mark, but never make the same mistake twice. That was the moral of the story for me.

The rest of my time at TBS went more smoothly. After almost six months of hard evaluations, exercises, and training, it was time for the biggest challenge. One of the last things Marines do at TBS is a grueling twenty-mile endurance hike. It's nearly ten hours of misery, which begins in the middle of the night. You follow a featureless, dusty trail where boredom competes with pure exhaustion to destroy you.

It's a bear and a half under any circumstances. But the kicker is that each platoon is required to cart along a PRC-25 radio, a twenty-five-pound piece of Vietnam-era combat equipment. The PRC-25 is no longer used; satellite phone technology has replaced it. Didn't matter. We still had to carry it. Typically, the biggest guys in the platoon—the ones who looked as if they played offensive line in high school football—volunteer to carry the radio for a part of the hike. It's just basic math; twenty-five extra pounds is far less of a burden for a six-foot-two, 225-pound kid from Katy, Texas, than it is for a smaller Marine from, say, Edgewood, Kentucky.

By mile seventeen, though, we had plumb run out of beefy guys. That damn dinosaur of a radio sat there in the trail dust mocking us as we took a five-minute breather. We got ready to move out for the final push, but nobody was volunteering to carry the radio. Who could blame them? Seventeen miles in, our feet were blistered, we had sweated through our utility camouflage uniforms many times over, and each pack felt as if it had doubled in weight. The trail is about as boring as a trail could be, and it seemed as though it would go on forever. The last thing any of us wanted to do was drag some extra weight.

I thought to myself, "Well, this is gonna suck, but why not? I'm tough enough for this." I walked over, picked up the radio, and wrestled it into my pack. I didn't say anything. I looked toward the horizon and started walking. I carried it the rest of the way.

That's how you make your reputation as a leader. It's about not giving orders but setting an example. Those types of lessons are hard won. The good news is they're transferable. In the years to come, I'd think back many times to my experiences in TBS. I'd ponder the country's leaders. I'd come to believe that we needed more accountable servant-leaders in politics and the corporate world. America, it seemed to me, would be a lot better off if more of our elected officials had to carry their own twenty-five-pound radios.

As much as TBS had taught me, I was mighty happy to sit in the auditorium at Quantico for the brief, low-key graduation ceremony. I quickly packed my things and headed home to Kentucky for a short break. It was just enough time to catch my breath before I headed to the more exciting adventure of flight school. After two weeks, I hugged my parents goodbye, got into my Jeep, and realized that the next time I pulled up to that ranch house on Brookwood Drive, I'd be wearing my wings of gold.

Naval aviation flight training was a radical shift for me. It had a completely different pace and feel from either TBS or the academy. To start with, the school is a military melting pot. My class included Marine, navy, air force, and coast guard aviators, as well as pilots in training from abroad. There were students from Saudi Arabia, Germany, Italy, and other countries. That made the integration of women into the classrooms at Pensacola a more natural transition than it had been in the drill fields of the naval academy or the backwoods of TBS. Just the same, flight school was not entirely without its own gender controversy.

The school had a daunting obstacle course, known simply as the O Course. It was made famous by the movie *An Officer and a Gentleman,* in which Richard Gere ran the course and helped a female naval officer over the most fearsome obstacle, "the wall." That barrier was nearly impassable for anyone shorter than five feet five inches. That meant the O Course could unfairly wash out women aviators who were, on average, shorter than their male counterparts. Consequently, the navy shut the course down just a month before I arrived. A whole lot of male aviators were none too pleased about that decision.

I was a little conflicted. Given my competitive nature, I wanted to conquer that course. Regardless, I understood that it had nothing to do with flying. The O Course qualification was a long-held rite of passage for aviators, but it was nothing more than a storied tradition. I'm not a fan of tradition for tradition's sake, especially if those traditions hurt people or weed them out for no valid reason.

Many men were vocal about the fact that they thought removing the O Course was a lowering of standards just to accommodate women. That begged the question, what standards? The O Course didn't address flying skills. Women aviators still had to swim a mile in full flight gear to prove they could survive after a water crash. They still had to navigate the disorientation and fear of the Helo Dunker and complete all their flights with passing grades. All those translated to what could happen in actual combat. Mastering those qualifications was crucial to flying any military aircraft. The O Course? Not at all.

The skill of flying was the sum total of what the school was about. That made it a pivot away from the issues of leadership and unit that had been so all-consuming at the naval academy and Quantico. At Pensacola, I had to focus on my own studies. I clicked into competitive mode because it was essential that I score near the top of the class if I was going to earn myself a spot in an F/A-18 squadron. The dream I had held so tightly since I was fourteen was tantalizingly close. I was in the home sprint.

Even so, the workload was lighter than any I'd had in more than a year. I enjoyed the luxury of downtime in Pensacola. There was room to enjoy myself a little, so I decided to rent a place on the beach. It wouldn't be accurate to call the ramshackle, washed-out yellow structure on Perdido Key Drive a house. Sure, it had power and water. But beyond that, it wasn't much more than a shack. It had been divided into two one-room apartments. I plunked down $450 a month for the upstairs unit, a three-hundred-square-foot space with a tiny plastic shower butted up to a toilet. It had no kitchen to speak of, just a sink along one wall with a bachelor's refrigerator and tiny countertop. There was space enough for a mattress and a love seat. Still, there was a porch outside with a stunning view of the waves. Besides, I was twenty-three and not overly concerned with comfort or luxury. I loved that place. I figured it was probably going to be the only time in my life I would get the chance to live right on the beach. I was going to enjoy every night I spent there.

Four guys from flight school rented the house next door. It was a good arrangement. I had someone to hang out with whenever I wanted, but didn't have to put up with living in a frat house. I had other company as well. My time in Pensacola lined up with my father's summer break. He drove down and was as low maintenance as ever. He dropped his suitcase on the floor of my tiny apartment and said, "Don't worry about me. I'll just use your crash pad as my hotel."

During the day, while I was at flight school, he would head out to visit local historical sites and tourist attractions. One day he would explore Gulf Islands National Seashore, the local national park. The next, he'd wander Veterans Memorial Park or Fort Barrancas. At night, he'd settle in with my buddies from flight school, telling stories, drinking beer, and smoking cigars. They loved him. I would inevitably be the first one to fold, getting up, yawning, and saying, "That's it for me, guys. I'm going to bed." They'd stay out there on the porch or the sand, laughing and talking until well past midnight. By the time Friday rolled around, Dad was thoroughly one of the crew. He announced, "I'm taking you and your friends out to dinner." It was a taste of home having him there, comforting and fun in equal measure. I was sorry to hug him goodbye as he headed off on his long drive back to Kentucky.

Fortunately, my classes kept me occupied. Flight school training was organized into phases alternating between ground-school sessions and training flights that were graded. It never ceased to be interesting, and every completed phase seemed like progress toward the goal I had pursued since seventh grade. I saw every single thing I learned in those classes as something valuable that I could eventually take into the cockpit of an F/A-18.

Because of my poor vision, I trained as a back seater, a weapons systems officer. I qualified in navigation, communication, and emergency procedures. Those of us hoping for combat fighter assignments flew in the basic training craft—T-34 turboprops, T-39s, T-1s, and T-2 trainers.

The homework wasn't overwhelming, and it left a good amount of free time. That was a bonus for some and a pitfall for others. Flight school was an introduction to military aviation's drinking culture, and drinks were cheap at the Officers' Club. It was tempting to party to excess. I soon realized that even though I enjoyed a couple of beers with friends, drinking all night wasn't my speed. I had started training for a triathlon, and a hangover was only going to get in the way. I also hated feeling sluggish or out of control. So I avoided late nights at the bars and kept focused on the brass ring of an F/A-18 Hornet selection. I was so close that I had no intention of easing back on that throttle. In my off-hours, when I needed to recharge, I turned to the familiar sanctuary of faith.

I found an off-base Bible study group of retired military members and active-duty military wives and family. They were lovely people, devoted and welcoming. Engaging with the scripture again was deeply satisfying and a comfort. Reading those passages and reciting those prayers as one voice among many took me right back to the pews of St. Mary's Cathedral. In reality, though, the faithful in Pensacola were far different from the congregation I had grown up in. It was my first up close exposure to the Christian Right. They were warmhearted but left no doubt about the strict ideas they held. I felt that many in the group saw my career as a stepping-stone to finding a husband, getting married, and having kids. To me it seemed the thinking was that somehow, as a woman, I was second class. I was grateful for the access to a spiritual community, but the group also felt incredibly restrictive. I wasn't comfortable opening up to anyone there about my long-term goals or my aspiration to fly Hornets and progress through the ranks in the Marine Corps. I kept my career aspirations to myself.

My ambition got a big boost when, after a year, my class gathered in the Officers' Club to hear the flight-school commander read out the aircraft assignments. There was a tense, expectant air as we all gathered there. The commander read the list in alphabetical order, and I felt a thrill when he said, "McGrath, F/A-18." After a year and countless hours hitting the books, performing during training flights, and putting up top grades, I had earned the right to train in the fighter jet of my dreams. Now I just needed my wings of gold to secure the backseat in one.

Others were not so exuberant. Some people who fell closer to the middle or bottom of the class were given aircraft assignments different from what they had requested. Just like in the academy, there were disappointments in the group. Almost all of my classmates started drinking in the Officers' Club—some to celebrate, and some to drown their sorrows. I had a couple of beers and shared congratulations with friends but peeled off when they all headed out to the next bar. I wanted some alone time to process, and I had a long drive to make the next morning.

I had read a classified listing in the *Pensacola News Journal* advertising chocolate Lab puppies. The day after the aircraft selection announcements, I jumped in my Jeep Wrangler and started driving to a trailer park in Andalusia, Alabama. An hour and a half later, I pulled in next to a dusty white double-wide, the sound of dogs barking filling the air.

After a quick exchange of two hundred dollars in cash, I strapped the crate with my six-week-old pup into the passenger seat and started the drive back to Pensacola. I named him Monk. He was my gift to myself for achieving the dream that had been my goal for a decade. He would be my best friend for the next thirteen years.

Alone in the car with him that day, I said, "Hey, you dog. You're in for the ride of your life. I promise to treat you wonderfully and love you, but we're going to be moving." He looked at me and wagged his tail. "There are lots of dogs who spend their whole lives in the same house, with the same backyard, seeing the same people. They don't go anywhere or do anything. You're not going to have that life. But I'll tell you what. I'm going to come home and we're going for runs, and we're going to have fun, and we'll go hiking every weekend." Monk seemed totally game.

He settled right into my beach shack. Labradors love water, and Pensacola certainly had plenty of that. We clocked many, many miles running on the beach in that town, and I was happier for his company.

Monk was almost fully grown six months later, when it came time for the Wings of Gold ceremony. That rite of passage marks the graduation from flight school and the point at which you're truly a Marine—or navy, or air force—aviator. It's as exciting and profound a progression as graduation from the naval academy. My parents drove down, and the ceremony was held in the grand auditorium space at the breathtaking National Naval Aviation Museum. The museum is gorgeous, full of historical carrier aircraft, from World War I biplanes to Vietnam-era jets. After a few speeches, the commander handed out the diplomas and gave each naval flight officer the wings of gold that were the goal all along. I found my parents, and together they pinned my wings on my chest. It was a proud moment for all three of us.

Two days later, I jammed all my worldly possessions into my trusty Jeep Wrangler, settled Monk in as my wingman, and pointed us in the direction of Kentucky. I was eager to show my new best buddy where I grew up. I was happy to have a week to gather myself for the next step in my adventure: Marine Corps Air Station Miramar in San Diego. Monk and I eagerly traveled to whatever adventure lay ahead. I was about to start the coolest job you could ever have, working for the greatest country and military the world had ever seen. The horizon looked pretty damn bright.

6

MARINE CORPS Air Station Miramar and Naval Air Station Pensacola are both military air bases, but they are separated by far more than just two thousand miles of America. Miramar is dedicated to operational Marine Corps aircraft. It is an imposing place, and the first time I stepped on the base I felt a little as if I were crossing the finish line of a race I had started as a young girl. Of course, that wasn't the case. A whole lot of training still stood between me and the backseat of a combat-ready F/A-18 Hornet.

I got settled in as quickly as I could. I rented an apartment in University Town Center, a seaside quarter of San Diego not far from the beach, with a busy shopping district. It was comfortable enough. The truth is, though, a Marine officer doesn't look to get too comfortable at any address. Sooner or later I knew I'd be deployed. I was never under the illusion that my role in a fighter jet would be a nine-to-five job. After all, I hadn't chosen a job; I had followed a passion.

For aspiring Marine combat aircrew, Miramar is the center of the universe. The first time I ever saw a hangar full of F/A-18s was at Miramar, and my pulse sped up. Rows of these fearsome gray warbirds side by side, their distinctive dual tail fins and rounded jet intakes built for speed. I was going to control the weapons and navigation systems in one of those seventy-million-dollar master-pieces of engineering. Me. The girl from Kentucky who wouldn't stop pestering her public officials with handwritten letters and who had once been told to "hang it up."

First, though, there were a lot more hours in the classroom and long days in the simulator to conquer. It felt as if I were learn-ing everything that was worth knowing about the F/A-18, from the operation of the canopy down to the hydraulic system that con-trolled the landing gear. It was the first time that the syllabus I studied was classified. I was learning material and weapons systems that were national secrets. I took that seriously. I was the most junior aircrew on base and one of the first women to get a shot at fighter training. I knew all eyes were on me and a lot more than my career was riding on my succeeding. I was going to follow all the proce-dures to the letter. I was going to do everything right. I keenly felt the weight of responsibility on my shoulders, and I wasn't going to fold under it.

Aviators who train at Miramar arrive as members of what's known as the FRS. Those initials stand for Fleet Replacement Squadron, and the squadron's nickname is the Sharpshooters. It is a fighter aircrew's final posting before being assigned to a combat squadron. Even though I felt an overwhelming obligation to rock my training, FRS was in a lot of ways less stressful than what had come before. I was home. I had earned my wings of gold, and now nobody doubted that I was rightfully due a place in a "gun squadron." There was less competitiveness. We were a smaller, more intimate group, and we helped one another out. The Marine Corps had invested a great deal of time, money, and training in us. Now it was in everyone's interest to support us in becoming combat ready.

Although I was completely accepted within the squadron, I was still pushing back against the timeworn Marine impulse to assume women weren't meant for combat. The idea that Marine Corps and navy combat aviation should be integrated was still a new—and to some a radical—idea. At TBS, I had been in Delta Company. Charlie, the company before mine, had no women. It was a reminder that change in a conservative and tradition-bound institution like the Marine Corps takes time. I had to be patient and understand that outmoded attitudes were bound to persist. That's not a military thing; it's a human thing.

Early in the FRS, I ran into a group of aviators who were returning from a tour of duty to retrain in the F/A-18. I introduced myself to one, and he said, "Oh, you're part of the experimental squadron." I think he truly thought that all the women in the F/A-18 community were going to be put in some temporary squadron where we wouldn't do much harm. I just laughed. I wasn't experimental. I came to fight, and I came to stay.

The way to prove that was the same as it had ever been—performance. Every day was a new challenge, a new weapons system or tactic to master, a new set of procedures to learn. After I got through with the classroom sections of the syllabus, I'd put hour after hour into the domed room that was the simulator. I'd focus on those infrared displays until my eyes hurt. It was all worth it when I was finally ready to move into an F/A-18 cockpit for actual training flights.

The simulator is meant to replicate a fighter jet cockpit as closely as possible, but actually climbing into an F/A-18 Hornet is an impossible experience to mimic. The smell of jet fuel is overwhelming. When you're wearing your G suit, harness, the survival vest called an SV-2, and all your gear, the actual cockpit is much more cramped than any simulator. The noise on a Marine Corps Air Station flight line is tremendous; it's easy for your senses to be overloaded until you get used to it.

As I started flying with pilots and engaging in combat exercises, I got deeper and deeper into the culture of the squadron. At TBS, I had been part of a platoon and a company. At flight school, I had been a member of a small class within a squadron. Marine combat squadrons, though, are unique cultures with their own rules and customs. A big part of my initiation came after one particularly challenging exercise in the air, a situation I fumbled.

We had begun air-to-air combat training. I was learning to track enemy aircraft and how and when to instruct the pilot to fire on them. Although we didn't have live weapons on board, exercises like these meant acting as if you did. I would track "aggressor" aircraft—an F-5 that resembled a Russian MiG—and go through the motions of preparing the onboard radar system to fire a heat-seeking or laser-guided missile. The pilot would then actually "fire" the simulated missile.

On that particular day, though, we had been instructed to track but not fire on the enemy. In the heat of the moment, I locked our radar on the maneuvering F-5 "bogey" and knew I had him squared up perfectly. We were within range for a shot. Amped on adrenaline, I keyed my mic to the pilot and shouted the heading and range of our enemy, "One two zero, thirteen miles, your dot . . . shoot him, shoot him, shoot him." There were only two problems with that. The first was that I was violating the limited engagement order. The second was that I hadn't actually keyed my mic to the pilot. I'd hit the wrong button and broadcast on the radio to all of the aircraft in the exercise.

Every flight at FRS is followed by a long and detailed debrief. In that one, they played the audio of my call multiple times as the other

My mom, Marianne, in the mid-1960s. She was twenty-one and starting medical school at the University of Kentucky.

Before fighter jets became my singular fascination, my love of animals pointed toward a career as a veterinarian.

With Dad and Matt at the 1980 Fourth of July parade in Edgewood, Kentucky. We were a patriotic family in a patriotic town.

A knee brace wasn't going to hold me back from my senior prom. My dad and I posed for this photo before I headed out to the dance.

I could not have been more excited to shake hands with the commandant of midshipmen at my United States Naval Academy graduation and commissioning ceremony in 1997. I had the billet I wanted and was staring down the career I had dreamed of from the age of fourteen.

With my sister, Jane, and her infant son in 2002.
I was between deployments.

My mom was there to greet me when I landed back home from my first deployment in 2002.
She was a welcome sight.

My first official campaign photo, to kick off my congressional run in 2018.

With my business partner in Virginia Beach. Flying an F/A-18C is an unmatched thrill. I loved being in control of that much power and airborne agility, and I've never experienced anything like it again.

Crossing the Atlantic on my first tour of duty in 2001 meant refueling more times than I cared to count.

Monk and I enjoy the California beaches; this spot at Del Mar was one of our favorites.

With my brother, Matt, around my workspace inside an F/A-18D at Cincinnati's Lunken Field in 2002.

The view from my cockpit, while trailing the lead jet during a combat mission over Iraq in 2003.

Sandstorms at Ahmad al-Jaber Air Base in Kuwait made life miserable on the ground. But by 2003, at the start of the Iraq War, I was spending a lot more time in the air.

aviators laughed hard, loud, and long. That's how I earned my first call sign, "Guns."

Contrary to the myth of the military movie, call signs in Marine aviation are not meant to be "cool." In fact, they make fun of the aviators. They are always based on an inside joke. I took my new nickname in stride because it could have been much worse. I would eventually find out how much worse. In the meantime, I focused on avoiding any other missteps.

Nights and weekends, I went for runs with Monk, or hikes with Monk, or just hung out with Monk. Much as I loved him to pieces, I realized that a grown woman's social life should extend beyond a goofy chocolate Lab. I started thinking more seriously than I ever had about meeting someone.

Romance is a difficult proposition for anyone in military aviation. Any potential long-term love interest quickly realizes that you'll be gone for months at a stretch and that the military—especially the Marines—is a far cry from an everyday job. In fact, in many ways, the corps comes first. The sacrifices aircrew in the corps must make inevitably extend to their significant others. It's hard enough for men wearing the uniform to find and keep their better halves. As a female Marine, I found it even more difficult. Meeting someone, getting to know him, and letting him know me usually meant wading through gender stereotypes and pushing against cultural conditioning.

Most nonmilitary guys were intimidated when they learned that I was a Marine, and especially when they discovered I spent my time in an F/A-18. In a military base community like San Diego, most people you come across know the reputation of the Marines. It's not a feminine mystique, and guys weren't sure what to make of a female Marine. Others were just too fascinated with the idea of combat jets and aviators, as if I were a novelty act that should spew *Top Gun*–esque war stories on command.

One of my best friends from flight school, Natalia, was struggling with the same issues. Natalia was a naval flight officer and one of the hardest working people I had ever met. Most men she met were overwhelmed and completely intimidated by her. She was, in most cases, smarter, tougher, and two steps ahead of the guy across the table. As she and I sat in my living room on a Friday night, she had an idea for a whole new approach. "We should go out and not tell guys what we really do."

"What do you mean?"

"We should say we're navy nurses or something. Let's just go out to a few bars and see what happens."

It was an interesting experiment but doomed to fail. The subterfuge just made everything more difficult. We didn't know how nurses acted, but I'm pretty sure that we didn't act like them. Plus, our environment wasn't helping. We were there in San Diego, dropping a twenty-dollar cover charge to get in a bar thick with Southern California women who had their plastic surgeons on speed dial. It was interesting pretending to be something we weren't, but that's all it was. The night was a few hours of wasted time and money. By midnight, we had to admit defeat.

Predictably, I ended up dating Marines.

I went out with two guys at Miramar. The first was an intelligence officer, and the second was another back seater. They were perfectly nice, and I had fun dating them. It was comforting to know that I wasn't going to have to answer any stupid questions about the military or fighter aircraft. The problem was, you simply can't force love. It's not a matter of checking off boxes, that the guy understands what you do for a living and wears the same uniform. Chemistry is always part of that equation. There was just no spark with either guy. I wound up back at square one. It was frustrating, but I always had Monk.

The world of San Diego rentals didn't quite feel the same about my dog. San Diego landlords all seemed to tack on huge surcharges for dogs. I was paying the equivalent of a mortgage to live in an apartment I didn't spend a whole lot of time in. As big a decision as it might have been, it made more sense to buy a place.

I found a small but comfortable ground-floor condo in Sorrento Valley, overlooking a canyon, with a beautiful, well-tended ball field right next door. The peach-colored stucco structure was easy on the eyes, and the construction was fairly new. I qualified for a VA loan at an attractive interest rate, but my father was not impressed when he discovered I was paying $163,000 for a nine-hundred-square-foot condo. I was not entirely successful in explaining to him the vast differences between the real estate markets in San Diego, California, and Edgewood, Kentucky.

My neighbors were an older woman of Middle Eastern descent and her adult son. They were quiet and respectful and unfailingly polite if distant whenever our paths crossed. The neighborhood was quiet and subdued. The condo was close to hiking and running trails, and it was a quick commute to Miramar. The place was as near to perfect as Monk and I could ask for.

I settled into my new digs and got into a steady routine. I studied and prepped for flights, honed my skills in the cockpit, spent a little social time with my squadron in the Officers' Club, and then got home to Monk. Every Saturday, Monk and I would go for a long hike in the canyon or up in the foothills. I kept hoping that the next turn in the trail would reveal the perfect guy taking a breather from his run in the hills. It was a nice daydream, but it was only ever Monk, me, the occasional coyote, and rattlesnakes.

FRS training is challenging, but at a certain point I was itching to get my combat "gun squadron" assignment. Finally, after I came in from one of my last training flights, the squadron commander gathered all of us in the ready room. He called us up one by one and handed us our new squadron patches. Mine was a side view of a green chess piece—the knight—with "VMFA(AW)-121" underneath it. I was officially a Green Knight.

I had two more training flights, but they went quickly. After the last one, during my final debrief, I got a call from my mother that my sister had just had her first child. The officer in charge stopped the debrief. "Are we interrupting your call, McGrath?"

"Sorry, sir. My sister just had a baby. Did I pass the flight?"

He rolled his eyes. "Yeah, you passed. Get the hell out of here." Just like that, without any swelling music or fanfare, I was done with the FRS syllabus and with my training. I was now officially a full-fledged back seater in the fabled Green Knights. I had earned my place in an F/A-18.

7

CIRCUMSTANCES CHANGE amazingly fast in the military. I detached from the Sharpshooters one day, celebrated with a few beers in the Officers' Club in the company of my friends from the squadron, and came back the next day to report in with the Green Knights three hangars down. As a Marine, you learn how to neutralize apprehension because it gets in the way of what you need to do. That first day, though, I had a swarm of butterflies in my stomach. It was something I hadn't experienced since my medical evaluation to get into Annapolis.

Flying with the Green Knights was a wholly different experience from anything that had come before. I was going to deploy with the guys I met in the hangar that day. We were going to put our lives in each other's hands. Most of us would work together for the next three years. I wanted to make a good impression. I was going to be one of only two female aviators in the squadron; another back seater,

Jaden Kim, was the other. Integrating the VMFA(AW)-121 for the first time was a big deal. I wanted to—I needed to—be way better than good.

It was a tall order. The Green Knights is a historic Marine fighter attack squadron, dating from 1941. They had fought valiantly in World War II, producing the most "aces" of any Marine combat squadron. They had flown all the famous early fighter aircraft, including the Wildcat, the fabled Corsair, the Bearcat, and the Cougar. The Green Knight pilot Major Joe Foss even won the Medal of Honor, and the squadron downed 208 Japanese fighters in dogfights over the Pacific. The Green Knights continued to distinguish themselves in Korea, Vietnam, and the Gulf War. I was enormously proud and honored to be part of such a rich legacy.

In the spring of 2001, the squadron had just returned from deployment in the western Pacific. Although I could sense that many men among the aircrew weren't quite sure what to make of Jaden and me, the commanding officer set the tone by treating us exactly as he would men. He was easily the tallest, largest Marine aviator I ever saw. One of the first African American Marine fighter pilots, Colonel Michael "Gumby" Sawyers told Jaden and me, "You're not going to get any special treatment from me. Do your job and prove yourself like everybody else." The other aircrew followed his lead and gave us the hazing that any junior aircrew would have gotten.

Some of that included sexist antics. Squadron life is a lot like a locker room, and rolling with the attitude is a critical part of becoming "one of the guys." Early on, I sat in the ready room with twenty other aviators as another back seater gave a PowerPoint presentation on radar tactics. Every other slide was an explicit picture of a woman taken off some porn site. The men chuckled and tossed out a few rude comments, and the instructor then moved on to the next slide. Many of the guys stole glances to see how I was reacting. It was unpleasant and embarrassing, but I wasn't about to show it. This was the price of admission, at the time, of being a member of this elite group. I had endured endless abuse at the hands of upperclassmen in Annapolis, had struggled through the roughest of circumstances on a few hours of sleep at TBS, and had come through tough evaluations unscathed in flight school. Sitting through some dumb sexist nonsense? It didn't take much to weather that storm.

Underneath it all, I knew that there was a sense of camaraderie. None of these guys disliked me; they were just trying to get a rise. Sure, part of me wondered how they would feel having their sisters, mothers, or girlfriends in the room. In the end, it was immature behavior. But nobody lost sight of the more serious business at hand. What truly mattered was performance in the cockpit. Could you run the radar and sensors? Could you communicate effectively in the air? Could you keep your cool and calculate bombing coordinates on the fly? Did you understand the weapons and how to use them? Could you put a two-thousand-pound bomb exactly where it needed to go exactly when it needed to be there?

When it came to those important questions, I knew the other aviators took me seriously and trusted me. They understood, even if they wouldn't readily admit it, that I had earned my place in the Green Knights. In the air, and increasingly everywhere else, the others treated me as a peer. Yeah, I might be hazed just like every new guy, but I would never be treated as a second-class citizen in that elite group.

The hallmark of acceptance into any combat fighter squadron is earning a call sign. "Guns" was never going to last, because it was way too cool. I knew a new call sign was coming. During flight debriefs and squadron gatherings, the more senior Green Knights tried out different possibilities. The front-runner seemed to be "Krusty," because my hair stuck out of my flight helmet in a way that reminded the others of *The Simpsons* character Krusty the Clown.

The Green Knights conferred call signs during raucous drinkfests they called Kangaroo Court—a perfect description of what went on. We took over a corner of the Officers' Club with the commanding officer presiding as the "Utmost," the judge with the final say. The executive officer served as the "Almost," his bailiff. As the drinking proceeded, members of the squadron shouted out possibilities for my call sign. Each was more silly, stupid, or bizarre than the last. When finally someone yelled out, "Krusty, because she looks like Krusty the Clown," it was actually kind of a relief given the other options. The commanding officer thoughtfully considered for a moment and then said, "Krusty it is!" The crowd broke out in cheers as he brought his gavel down and made it official. I had gone from "Guns" to "Krusty."

Blowing off steam is important to combat aviators. So much of the time, you have to be dead serious with no tolerance for errors. On top of remaining combat ready, every officer in the squadron had what amounted to a second full-time job in the running of the squadron. There are basically seven "departments" in any squadron: administration, intelligence, operations, logistics, safety, S-6 (the fighter squadron version of an IT group), and maintenance. Each aviator is assigned a role in one of those seven departments. In my first year, I was an assistant logistics officer. I was in charge of procuring gear the aviators needed, like boots, flight suits, and desert camouflage uniforms for desert deployment.

I put almost as much into that duty as I did into my role as an aviator. I was constantly aware of being part of a vanguard, the first wave of women in combat roles. The struggle wasn't over; we continued to push against barriers. The military had many positions that still were not open to women, key roles such as forward air controllers. Despite what the regulations said, women were capable of performing all those jobs. I worked hard over the course of my career to drive that point home.

As summer 2001 came to a close, I felt as though I had been

accepted and integrated into the Green Knights. But I had yet to be tested in deployment. That was about to change.

. . .

I was jolted awake by the phone ringing on September 11, 2001. I usually got up early, but the call was early even for me. I picked up on the second ring to hear my sister's voice. Her anxious tone made me think something was wrong with Mom or Dad. I sat up and looked out the window. The sun was just coming up.

"Jane? What is it? What's wrong?"

"Amy, turn on your TV. A plane just crashed into the World Trade Center."

I hung up thinking a Cessna must have accidentally flown into one of the buildings. A tragedy, and unusual, but nothing more. I got up, took a shower, and brushed my teeth. I turned on the TV and watched in disbelief as CNN played the horrific scene of the second plane crashing into the South Tower over and over again. This was quite obviously no accident.

The phone rang again. This time it was the operational duty officer at Miramar. He said, "Mandatory recall for all aircrew. Get in here as soon as you can."

I lived close to the base. Most of the aircrew would need thirty minutes to make it in; I pulled up to the north gate in eight minutes. The Marine sentry checked my ID and waved me through. I parked and headed to the ready room. It was empty except for the duty officer. I asked him, "Where is everybody?"

"Don't know."

He had already written the aircrew's names on the whiteboard, in order of seniority and qualifications. My name was near the bottom. The board showed that the enlisted ground crew was arming two jets to get ready for launch. I waited. Ten minutes later, the operations officer came in and began erasing names until only four were left.

"What's going on, sir?"

"Looks like you're in. Base has locked down the gates, and I can't get any more aircrew in here until those gates open again. I've got to send anyone I can out to the CALA right now. Get your flight gear on. We need you." CALA was the acronym for the Combat Aircraft Loading Area. It was the part of the base where jets were armed with live missiles and parked, ready to launch. The Marines don't arm a jet unless they anticipate firing those missiles. This was as serious as it gets for a Marine aviator.

By that point, we knew that New York had been attacked and that terrorists had also flown into the Pentagon. There were a lot more unknowns. The country had just gone to DEFCON 3. All military installations were locked down as a matter of protocol. No one would be let in or out. That was a problem because almost all the aviators needed to fly jets in defense of the country were off base. It would eventually be fixed, but it took several hours.

The operations officer must have had reservations about putting me in one of the locked-and-loaded jets. It had nothing to do with my gender; I had joined the squadron only four months before. I was young, with no combat experience. In the ideal scenario, the commanding officer would have selected a senior crew. We were far from ideal; I was one of the few available, so it was time to do my part.

The mood of the morning was strange and unnerving. Fighter aircrews are usually briefed for hours before suiting up. The commanding officer—who himself was not able to get on base—wanted us suited up and briefed on the way to the weapons-ready jets. The F/A-18s had been outfitted with six air-to-air missiles—two Sidewinder heat-seeking missiles and four radar-guided AMRAAMs. As

I approached my jet and saw that hardware, the reality of what I might be about to do struck me hard.

It was my first time climbing into the cockpit of a fully armed jet. We were ordered into "ready standby," as backup to the National Guard F-16s that had already taken off from March Air Reserve Base.

Three hours. I sat in the cockpit of a deadly fighter jet on the blacktop of runway 24L, waiting and thinking. It was an eternity, with the magnitude of what had just occurred bearing down on me, along with the seriousness of what came next. Within the hour, we might intercept and shoot down a civilian airliner that wasn't responding to air traffic control's commands. My heart skipped a beat at the sound of every radio call that came in. My adrenaline was off the charts.

We never got the call to launch, but the intensity of that experience would be etched in my mind forever. Those were the longest three hours of my life. I was spent by the time the white pickup arrived to drop off a fresh aircrew and relieve us of our post. The alert status for F/A-18s at Miramar would be maintained for the next twenty-four hours, but my shift was over. As soon as I got home, I called my mother and told her what I had been doing, that I was okay, and that my work for that day at least was over. She and my father were watching CNN, stunned and saddened by what they were seeing.

There was an air of readiness on base from that day forward. Every Marine knew that an assault on America does not go unanswered. Somewhere, someone had planned those attacks. Experienced experts at the highest command level were figuring out who it was and how to eliminate the possibility of it ever happening again. Once they had found the answers to their questions, we were what people called the tip of the spear—the first to go into combat. In the meantime, the Green Knights had a deployment that would proceed as planned.

Operation Bright Star had long been scheduled for October 2001. Although there was an eagerness to be part of a strike in response to the terror attacks, large military campaigns have to be planned and coordinated in detail to be successful. The U.S. government and intelligence community had just identified the role al-Qaeda had played in the attacks. They knew the group's leadership, such as it was, made their headquarters in Afghanistan. The toll from the civil war being fought between the Taliban and the official Afghan government meant that the nation's infrastructure was closer to the Middle Ages than a twenty-first-century network of paved highways and operational facilities. Most pointedly, there wasn't a usable airfield in the country. So, while Pentagon planners worked on the logistics, the Green Knights headed to Egypt to connect with our Operation Bright Star partners in that country's air force.

Joint exercises with allies and partners around the world are crucial and often misunderstood by those outside the armed forces—including political leaders. We have to practice working with friendly militaries so that we can ensure against mishaps. Peacetime joint exercises quite literally save lives in combat. A heated battle is not when you want to discover that your partners are operating on a different and incompatible encrypted radio system.

Deploying means upending your life. I shut up my condo, and my parents agreed to take Monk while I was gone. It was an arrangement we'd repeat for every one of my deployments. The day before I deployed, my neighbors stopped me on the sidewalk. I tensed. America had just been attacked by radical terrorists from the Middle East, and here was this older Middle Eastern woman who obviously had something to say. Mona told me that she and her son, Homan, were from Iran.

"After the fall of the shah, my husband was murdered, and I had to flee with Homan. He was only four. We had nothing. We had to leave it all behind."

I felt embarrassed that I had been concerned.

After several years of moving throughout different countries, Mona had settled with her son in San Diego, claiming asylum. She got a job as a seamstress at a local Nordstrom and enrolled Homan in school. They eventually became citizens, and after saving money for years, she had enough to buy the small condo next to mine. Mona looked me in the eye and said, "You know, we are Americans, too. We love our country and are so grateful to be here. I'm hurt by what has happened. We know you're leaving, and I hope you get the people who did this. Then come home safe."

It was heartwarming to be reminded of the tapestry of America, the ideals and dreams that make it a country so worth fighting for. We smiled and shook hands, and I headed off to deploy.

In short order, I was flying in the backseat of an F/A-18 for the extended evolution to Egypt. We flew to the East Coast and spent a night at Otis Air National Guard Base in Massachusetts. Then we took off for our Atlantic crossing. The quickest way to get a fighter squadron across an ocean is flying behind air tankers, large aircraft such as the DC-10 refitted to carry fuel instead of cargo or passengers. Each F/A-18 took turns refueling, or "topping off," in air to keep the maximum amount of fuel on board in case a mechanical problem caused one aircraft to divert. It's a long, boring, and uncomfortable passage. Twelve hours later, we landed on a runway at Naval Station Rota, in Rota, Spain. We caught a night of sleep, and twenty-four hours later we took to the air again. The squadron traced a path among the clouds that followed the coastlines of Italy and Greece. Finally, we arrived at Beni Suef Air Base in Egypt.

As we taxied to a stop, the ground crew pulled our ladder down below the cockpit. The pilot popped the canopy, and we were smothered with a blast of hot desert air. I followed the pilot out of the cockpit and down the ladder. Then I took off my helmet. The Egyptians had never seen a woman in the cockpit of a fighter jet, and they all stared at me as if they couldn't believe their eyes. I did my best to ignore them and went through the normal postflight routine.

Our days from that point on were dedicated to the joint exercises. When I wasn't flying, I was either passing the time in my quarters or on "tower duty." That meant sitting in the control tower and acting as the liaison between the American pilots and the Egyptian air traffic control. Given the language and cultural differences, it was essential for those of us in the air to have someone on the ground we knew and trusted. The duty would have been difficult in the best of circumstances, but my shifts were even more challenging. The Egyptians wanted nothing to do with me. They avoided talking to me, even though they befriended the other Marines. They would bring food and tea to the male Marines and act as if I weren't in the room. They made a point of sitting as far from me as possible. There was no use getting bent out of shape about it; I wasn't going to change a thousand years of culture overnight.

Over the next month, we flew air-to-air intercept training flights against the Egyptians. Their jets, radar, and equipment were not as sophisticated as ours, and we scaled back our efforts and reined in our natural competitiveness so that the Egyptians didn't see our real capabilities. We let them win over and over again—a true challenge for a group of type A Marine aviators.

As the exercises came to a close, our Egyptian counterparts challenged us to a soccer match. We figured it would be a friendly pickup game, but it turned out that the Egyptian Air Force had a bona fide soccer team. This was a serious competition as far as they were concerned. Our commanding officer accepted the challenge. He knew I had played soccer in college, so he recruited me as a defender. When the Egyptians found out, they insisted that I wear long pants rather than the shorts everyone else would be wearing.

My CO wasn't having it. "If you want a game, she's going to play because she's a good soccer player," he said. "And as Marines, we all wear regulation Marine Corps green T-shirts and green shorts."

The Egyptians backed down. I had played some big games for Annapolis, serious events at the Division I level in front of big crowds. But I had never experienced anything like that game with the Egyptians. We played in a sold-out soccer stadium. The crowd was triple anything I had ever experienced at Annapolis, and everyone in the stands was a man. The Egyptian team was far better than we were and beat us 7–1. But I held my own. At one point, I went up for a header against the Egyptian team's captain, a tall, fast, talented colonel. I came down on my feet, while he tumbled to the grass. The crowd roared.

When the game ended, we all lined up. An Egyptian general walked down the line of Egyptian players, congratulating each one in turn. Then he walked along the line of our players. When he came to me, he stopped. He presented me with the MVP plaque. The crowd roared again. I was by no means the best player on that field. I think it was an acknowledgment of my refusal to back down. That I had played a tough, physical game against men in front of an audience of men had impressed the Egyptians. I walked away thinking that perhaps that was the only way you make inroads against deeply ingrained cultural attitudes—one small success at a time.

We flew home the next day, back over the breadth of the Atlantic. The long hours in the cockpit meant a lot of time to think. My first deployment had been all practice and an eye-opening experience. I had to wonder how much like an actual combat experience any of it was. I also pondered the aftermath of 9/11 and realized I'd most likely get the opportunity to find out sooner rather than later.

It was truly wonderful to finally land at Miramar and know that I was, in the deepest sense of the word, home again. As often as I might return from deployment, it never changed, that feeling. The moment I stepped down from the cockpit onto American soil, I inevitably thought, "This is where I belong. This is who I am, this place and all it is." It always made me feel better, stronger.

Because Mona had broken the ice, she and Homan were no longer polite strangers. They were concerned neighbors, like my neighbors in Edgewood. Mona worried about me and wanted to help in any way she could. It was touching. She would make me dinner when I had late flights. She would bring over a plate of delicious food, still warm, carefully wrapped in aluminum foil. I also think she felt sorry for me, because I worked so much that she felt I didn't have much of a life. Like many civilians, she didn't realize how deeply rewarding military service can be. She wanted to make sure I was at least eating properly.

I embraced the relationship. Neighbors have been so much a part of the richness of my life. Our friendship meant a lot as I anticipated the unknowns of my next deployment. I knew it would be a much greater challenge than a joint forces exercise in Egypt. Mona, too, knew that I would be headed to war. We both understood when I left again, it wouldn't be an exercise. The stakes would be life and death.

8

MARINES ARE TRAINED to be ready. That was good, because I
didn't have long to wait for my first combat deployment. Less
than three months after we touched down at Miramar from Egypt,
our squadron was sent back across the Atlantic as part of Operation
Enduring Freedom. Once again, we made the long, complex flight
to the East Coast, on to Rota, Spain, then to Bahrain, over Pakistan,
Afghanistan, and Tajikistan. The Green Knights were stationed at
an old Soviet "Bear" bomber airfield in Manas, Kyrgyzstan. Given
the lack of runways in Afghanistan, we had no choice but to operate
out of the nearest nation that had a usable air base and would give
us permission to operate. Kyrgyzstan is a tiny country sandwiched
between China to the east and the former Soviet republics Kazakh-
stan and Uzbekistan to the north and west. It is separated from
Afghanistan by even tinier Tajikistan along its southern border.

I'm sure the Russians would have preferred not to have Western military troops camped in their backyard, but it was a diplomatically pragmatic concession. Aiding Western efforts in rooting out and destroying terrorists was in the Russian national interest. Afghanistan was, after all, much closer to Moscow than to Washington. The base wasn't a functioning Russian asset in any case; it needed a lot of work. As "expeditionary" Marine forces, we landed the first day, pitched our work tents, and began erecting more permanent and livable tents that would become a small city. The base needed major repairs; the tarmac was pitted and cracked, and there were decaying Soviet-era aircraft fuselages in the weed-strewn shoulders of the runways.

What started as a U.S. military air base quickly became an international operation. The Australians brought tanker aircraft, the South Koreans ran the medical facilities, and the French added a fighter squadron of Mirage 2000Ds. Base and flight-line security was maintained by a contingent of U.S. Marines, U.S. Air Force, Korean Marine Corps, French Army, and Australian Army. The Danes and Norwegians provided cargo airlift in the form of C-130s, and the Spanish supplied combat search-and-rescue helicopters. With so much of the rest of the world behind us, I felt that Operation Enduring Freedom was the right thing to do and sure to be a success.

The Green Knights' senior aircrew was slated to fly the first combat missions into Afghanistan, in April 2002. The flights were canceled due to bad weather. By the time the skies cleared, those crews had been awake too long; they had run out of "crew day." That meteorological glitch was how I got the opportunity to fly on our squadron's first mission into Afghanistan. Our ground troops didn't need us to drop bombs that day. Instead, we escorted U.S. Army ground convoys along the Afghan countryside. Convoys are exposed and dangerous duty for troops, and our sensors would detect anything in the convoy's path that was large enough to be a threat. Having two friendly fighter jets overhead was reassuring for the ground forces.

After returning to base and debriefing the other aircrew about what we'd seen in Afghanistan, one of the pilots said to me, "Hey, CO says you're the first woman in the Marines to fly a combat mission in a Hornet."

"Hmm, that's interesting. I guess so," I said. I was more excited that I wouldn't be the last. I went back to work setting up tents and getting ready for the next day's flight.

Most of the missions over the next six months were uneventful and even boring. We were in the air five to seven hours at a time. It took ninety minutes just to get to where we needed to be in Afghanistan for our missions. Crossing over the tall mountains in southern Kyrgyzstan and Tajikistan was often the most dangerous thing we did on a flight. If aviators had to eject over mountains, search-and-rescue helicopters wouldn't be able to reach the high altitude. Flying in such a remote area meant radio reception was spotty as well. Pretty much anything could go wrong, and we'd be out of reach of help. Seen from the vantage of the cockpit, the mountains were breathtakingly beautiful. Even so, I was always relieved when we put them behind us.

An older Marine aviator I met described his combat flights to me as "ninety percent sheer boredom and ten percent sheer terror." In Afghanistan, the boredom part of that equation was even higher. Mostly, we flew combat air patrols. They involved circling a region for hours waiting for a call. When ground troops engaged insurgents in a firefight, the forward air controller would call us in. We would support the troops with bombs and—far less often—our onboard 20-millimeter cannon. Whenever we got that radio transmission, everything unfolded fast and intense.

Some situations called for innovative solutions. There were times we simply couldn't drop bombs. On one mission, we were called to a village in central Afghanistan. The locals were unhappy at the presence of American troops on patrol, and an angry mob had surrounded the soldiers. No shots had been fired, but the troops were justifiably concerned that a firefight could break out and civilians be killed. They radioed for air support.

We could see the crowds on our sensors. We would never fire on what were likely unarmed civilians, but we had to defuse the situation. We decided to simply make our presence known. An F/A-18 Hornet is a shockingly powerful machine. Each of the two F404-GE-402 EPEs (Enhanced Performance Engines) is capable of producing seventeen thousand pounds of thrust. The top speed is near twelve hundred miles per hour. The engine noise of an F/A-18 at speed makes a heavy metal concert sound like polite conversation. Couple that power with some simple physics and you have a force that can potentially make people on the ground feel as if they were stuck in the brunt of a hurricane.

We dropped down and flew low and fast right over the town square, circling back and repeating the maneuver several times. Fly an F/A-18 at a thousand feet and the ground shakes with the noise and sheer power of the engines. The roar can be terrifying on the ground. The strategy worked like a charm; the mob scattered as soon as we started our flyovers. The troops went on with their patrol, and we went back to flying in wait for the next call. It was the best kind of day—helping our troops without destroying property, buildings, or vehicles or killing anyone.

Looking down at the Afghan countryside from fifteen thousand feet was like flying back in time to the fifteenth century. Until we reached the capital of Kabul, there were virtually no signs of modern civilization. The routes between one place and another were dirt roads, and the houses were mud huts, while the towns were nothing more than haphazard groupings of ragged huts.

Combat squadrons in the early days of the war in Afghanistan kept jets in the air around the clock, to respond with ground support anytime they might be needed. Every aircrew pulled overnight flights. The Afghan countryside is bleak during the day, but at night it takes on a haunting aspect. Looking down from the sky, you see nothing but a lifeless pitch-black void. No lights, no apparent signs of life. It was reminiscent of desert night training flights over Arizona.

Night flights were incredibly draining. We would take off around 2300 (11:00 p.m.), not returning until sunrise. My internal clock would be a mess. The flying itself took a toll on aircrew. We had to wear disorienting night-vision goggles and be constantly hypervigilant. Flying high enough to be safe meant we ran into weather patterns that added to the feeling of uncertainty. Overnight flights were difficult and dangerous duty even without combat.

Life on the ground was more uncomfortable than dangerous. The accommodations at Ganci Air Base were spartan to say the least. Rows and rows of temporary canvas living quarters defined "Tent City," just about a mile or so from the flight line. The noise was constant. I shared a tent with ten other female Marines and air force officers and noncommissioned officers. Using the head or taking a shower meant a lengthy hike. We slept in sleeping bags on fold-out cots. I taped up pictures of my family and an American flag on the tent wall next to my bunk. Everyone did whatever they could to connect with home.

One of the worst aspects of Tent City was the food. The U.S. military views food as a simple matter of calories, protein, and nutrition. Flavor isn't a consideration. We had what seemed like the exact same meals every single day. There were boxes of dry cereal, with a weird, fake milk in aseptic boxes that didn't need to be refrigerated. The scrambled eggs were dehydrated and then used as needed; when cooked, they were more dirt brown than yellow. Fresh fruits and vegetables were a rarity. We were offered the same chalky coffee cake at every meal.

The French being the French, they weren't about to tolerate what passed for American military cuisine. After a few weeks they abandoned the American chow hall and set up their own. They flew in chefs, who brought with them French bread, aged cheeses, and yogurt. Every night, the staff would prepare a different hot meal; our mess tent would be serving reheated canned chili mac and watered-down peas. The Green Knights' aviators quickly figured out that we needed to walk only a little farther to enjoy the exceptional meals being served in the French chow hall.

More than food, though, a war zone leaves you hungry for spiritual affirmation. I was trying hard to remain a person of faith. I had quickly come to realize that exercises over empty desert with faux weapons were one thing. They were useful for simulation under pressure, and the g-force realities of operating in a fighter jet. But it's make-believe. It paled in comparison to actual combat. Most markedly, the people aspect was missing. The targets were real, flesh-and-blood people. Duty notwithstanding, there was a spiritual reckoning in dropping bombs on humans.

Participating in combat leaves any religious person with a burden that constantly weighs on the mind. It could seem surreal at times. I tried not to think too hard about the reality, the death. Become preoccupied with the toll of that responsibility and it could become impossible to do the job. Faith, though, can't be rationalized. What I was doing every day challenged my religious beliefs, and at some point going to church became a way I could at least act as a person of good moral character—someone who wasn't in the business of killing other human beings.

Dropping a bomb is an awful thing. The sheer destructive force is nearly unimaginable. Every aviator finds his or her own outlet to deal with the inevitable guilt. Some drink; many work out for hours a day. I found relief in the weekly Mass held in Tent City. That ritual reminded me of home and all the people I missed. There were moments I felt lost, but engaging with a higher power, seeking guidance in prayer and faith, were anchors that kept me from wandering off course.

A Catholic chaplain held Mass once a week, and I was grateful for the homily and for the chance to confess. I wasn't alone. There was one tent for all religious services, and it accommodated different faiths at different times during the week. It was always busy.

One Sunday three local nuns attended the Mass. They were Franciscans, and I felt an immediate connection with them. They reminded me of the generous and bright nuns who taught me in high school. My father taught at a Catholic school founded by Franciscans, and he talked about the order often. Those nuns inspired me. I picked up a second daily prayer book and shipped it home to my father. I asked him to read it and say the prayers that corresponded to each calendar day. It was incredibly comforting knowing that Dad and I were reading the same prayers and doing the same meditations each day. It was a simple thing, but it eased the pain of being on the other side of the world, so far away from my loved ones, doing such deadly acts.

Fortunately, Ganci Air Base wasn't all hardship and moral struggles. The international population created an often lighthearted atmosphere. There were fun rivalries and friendly competition that led to a general camaraderie. The World Cup was held during my tour, and the entire French contingent huddled around a small TV to cheer on "Les Bleus"—their national team. The Americans yelled just as loud in support of Team U.S.A. as they took on South Korea in the first round.

We were also given a few hours each week to take a rickety bus into the nearest population center, the town of Bishkek. Those trips were a look into a different way of life and an entirely foreign culture. The Kyrgyz people were gregarious, lovely, and an enigma. They were mostly Muslim, spoke Russian, and looked Mongolian.

It wasn't entirely clear that they understood why we were there, but they were happy to sell us the trinkets and wares they spread out on blankets alongside the road. Those smiling, open, welcoming people were a contrast to the city in which they lived. Bishkek was a former Soviet Union metropolis. The homes were dilapidated, and the city center was bleak in a uniquely Soviet-era way. The large buildings in the "business district" were gray, boxlike, and lacking charm or ornamentation. The one Western hotel was a Hyatt, the only place we ate because all the local restaurants kept making us sick.

As any warriors do, we fought boredom as much as any enemy. Every day seemed the same, like *Groundhog Day*. There wasn't much to do other than work out, have endless conversations, and count the days until the tour was up. I jumped at the chance to break the routine and be detached for a week at Bagram Air Base in Afghanistan as a liaison to special forces "inside the wire." Bagram is just north of Kabul and was a secured zone to which American and allied forces regularly returned for a break from the field. My job was to brief various nations' special forces on the role the F/A-18 could play in support of their operations. In the initial chaos of multinational combat operations, there's a lot that isn't communicated or would not naturally be known from one military to the next. The first group I met with was a Romanian squad. I gave them a list of our call signs, how we worked in support, how to call us, and more.

I had the opportunity during my time in Bagram to venture out and see some of Afghanistan from the ground. Kabul was the nation's capital, and it was devastated from fighting. The condition of the city was shocking. There wasn't much in the way of municipal services, and trash was piled everywhere. The stink was overwhelming. The citizens would go out only for food, but most of the city was cordoned off into makeshift enclaves defined by barriers of craggy concrete slabs, sandbags, and concertina wire. Even though it was a secure military installation, the service personnel at Bagram never went anywhere on base without a loaded weapon. There was a heightened sense of alert all around me, and the combat readiness was palpable. Ganci seemed almost luxurious and safe by contrast.

My deployment came to an end in the fall of 2002, and my squadron returned home. It had been a long time. I was indescribably happy to see my parents as I climbed down from my F/A-18 and set foot back on American soil. They had flown out to meet me and deliver Monk.

The local press had picked up the fact that Jaden and I were the first women in the Marine Corps to fly combat missions in the F/A-18. A small number of media outlets showed up right as we got home. The teasing by the rest of our squadron would far outlast the modest and short-lived celebrity status Jaden and I enjoyed.

As part of settling back in at Miramar, I checked in with our squadron's flight surgeon. He told me that photorefractive keratectomy— better known as PRK—had finally been approved as a treatment for Marine aviators. The moment had come: I could have my eyes fixed. That meant there was a path for me to move from the backseat to the front seat of the F/A-18. It was an incredible piece of news.

I requested the PRK. I got the green light to have the procedure over the Christmas holidays, when we wouldn't be scheduled to fly much. I would have to be out of the cockpit for a month while I healed.

A friend gave me a ride to the doctor's office. I went in for the procedure and in forty minutes walked out with what amounted to a new pair of eyes. My vision instantly went from 200/800 to 20/15—the perfect vision for a pilot. After forty-eight hours of no TV or sunlight, I was well on my way to healthy new sight. By the end of the month, I applied for one of two slots available to train as an F/A-18 pilot. Before I heard back, though, I had to answer a more pressing need for my skills in the backseat. The Green Knights were being deployed to Iraq.

9

EVERY COMBAT DEPLOYMENT is challenging, but Iraq would be much more intense than Afghanistan in almost every way. It would test my fortitude and leave me with greater demons to wrestle. It was somehow fitting that the deployment started with doubt. I was skeptical of the reason we were being sent to Iraq—the claim that Saddam Hussein had weapons of mass destruction. I didn't trust the politicians. Not Vice President Dick Cheney, Secretary of Defense Donald Rumsfeld, or even President Bush. But I trusted Secretary of State General Colin Powell. He was one of us, someone who had worn the uniform. The Marines I knew shared my belief that he would never send us into a frivolous fight. So, when he gave a speech to the United Nations stating in no uncertain terms that there were weapons of mass destruction in Iraq, every single Marine I knew was ready for the fight. In any case, we were going to follow orders. The truth was, we wanted to do our jobs. If there was going to be a fight, we wanted to be in it. After 9/11, all of us Marines wanted to do something. We had trained long and hard to be the tip of the spear, and we were ready.

As an experienced squadron that had flown combat missions in Afghanistan, the Green Knights were designated to be part of the first wave sent to the Gulf. The military buildup in Kuwait made a conflict with Iraq seem imminent. Squadrons from multiple American bases—Miramar and Camp Pendleton in California, and the Marine Corps Air Stations in Yuma, Arizona, and Beaufort, South Carolina—were transported to two bases in Kuwait. It took just forty-five days to transplant almost every jet, helicopter, and Marine from those bases to the Middle East. The Green Knights' new home was Ahmad al-Jaber Air Base in Kuwait.

We arrived in February, into the teeth of harsh conditions. Once again, we had to build our camp from scratch. The days were warm, but at night the temperatures plummeted. We had no electricity or heat in the tents. I'd wake up most nights shivering. As a Marine, you learn to eat discomfort for breakfast. I quickly got used to working on little or no sleep.

The Kuwaiti air base didn't have the international camaraderie we had enjoyed at Ganci. Except for a small coalition of our staunchest allies, America was going it alone. The French chow hall would be badly missed. The base was also bigger than Ganci had been. I shared a tent with eight other female Marines of all ranks, and ours was just one of hundreds, most of the rest full of men. The air base was incredibly busy, full of rushing green troop trucks, Humvees, and other vehicles. The flight line was crowded with F/A-18 Hornets and AV-8B Harrier jets. Hundreds of laser-guided and GPS-guided bombs were stored right off the flight line. You didn't have to be a part of strategic command to know it was all preparation for a big fight.

Some days, we'd live in our mission-oriented protective posture (MOPP) suits. MOPP suits are meant to protect against chemical weapons. We knew Saddam had chemical weapon capabilities. He had used sarin and mustard gas on his own citizens. That made MOPP gear essential, but nothing could make it comfortable. It is tedious to put on and extremely bulky and clumsy. Nobody went without, though, because the idea of enduring a chemical or biological weapon attack without protection was terrifying.

The MOPP suits were just one of many unusual aspects of the Iraq War. For the first time in my experience, reporters embedded with our air wing. One female reporter even slept in our tent. There was a certain amount of distrust between the reporters and the Marines. We had no control over what they wrote or the pictures they took and published. War zones are messy, chaotic places, and no Marine wants to walk around watching everything she says, or think that someone is lurking with a camera, just waiting to catch her at her worst. At the same time, the reporters thought we were hiding things from them. We weren't. They all thought we knew exactly when the war was going to kick off and that we knew how everything was going to happen. Unfortunately, we were just as in the dark as they were. All we could do was wait for orders.

Initially, the Green Knights flew missions north into Iraq, enforcing a no-fly zone for what was called Operation Southern Watch. Although we were tasked with "patrolling" the Iraqi skies, we would occasionally be ordered to bomb Iraqi anti-aircraft and communications sites. I felt as if we were being used as bait, testing the Iraqis to see if we could draw fire that would be justification for a full-scale conflict. When I read or listened to the words of our American leadership, it became more and more evident that war was inevitable.

Marines aren't fond of saber rattling. At some point, you get on with things. I was eager to do what we did best and then get home. We had no idea what the leaders in Washington were waiting for, because it was obvious that the plans had been laid. Finally, in mid-March, the war formally started. It was called Operation Iraqi Freedom and would consume my every waking hour for the better part of three months.

Saddam's troops had different capabilities and were better armed than any of the enemy fighters in Afghanistan had been. Most pointedly, Saddam had Scuds—deadly surface-to-surface ballistic missiles produced by the Soviets. Scuds were truck mounted, so it was difficult for intelligence officers to determine exactly where and when they would strike. The only way we had of knowing a Scud was coming in was when radar picked up the missile in flight and set off the base alarms.

My air section of two F/A-18s was scheduled to fly our first mission in support of Marines crossing the border from Kuwait into Iraq. Just getting off the ground turned out to be an adventure. The four of us—my pilot "Cherry," me, and the second aircrew of "Jason" and "Gomer"—were headed toward our fully armed jets for our preflight checks when a deafening alarm sounded. The Iraqis had launched a Scud at our base.

We had just a minute or two to make it to the nearest bunker before the Scud landed. There was no way of knowing if this was a barrage of Scuds and if one or all of them would be armed with chemical or biological weapons. It was a Catch-22 for us; we had to be suited up for flight, which meant we couldn't wear our MOPP gear. The timing left us incredibly exposed. It made no sense to race back into the equipment tent, take off our flight gear, and don the MOPP gear.

Instead, we pushed ahead, running to the jets. Scud or no Scud, the mission went on. We fired up the engines and went through our preflight checks as quickly as humanly possible. Unfortunately, the final step involved arming our bombs and onboard 20-millimeter cannon. Arming had to be done by ground-ordnance Marines.

Just when we thought we would have to climb out of the cockpit and arm the weapons ourselves, a Marine ran out from one of the side bunkers. He armed our bombs, missiles, and guns, then scurried back to the cover of the bunker. I would never know who that brave Marine was because he was covered head to toe in MOPP gear. He knew as we did that we had to launch if we were going to protect the Marines on the ground. I'm sure he also realized that without MOPP gear, the aircrew were safer in the air than on the ground. It was a dramatic start to my time in the air over Iraq.

Once we got airborne, the sky seemed to fill with anti-aircraft fire. Night-vision goggles have poor depth perception. Although we took pains to fly above the maximum altitude for the anti-aircraft weapons the Iraqis were using, the explosions looked as if they were close enough to touch.

We saw a lot of action on that first flight, bombing targets that were in the path of the advancing Marine battalion. The terrain beneath us was sparkling with the flash of artillery fire, automatic weapon exchanges, and isolated explosions. We returned with our munitions largely exhausted. It would set the tone for almost all our missions.

The flights over the next month were the most intense I had flown. Ground troops were encountering heavy resistance from Iraqi forces, and air support was crucial. I flew at least two and sometimes three missions every day. The pace was relentless, and one day blurred into the next with a repetition that tested my endurance. I would wake up at 0300 and be in the sky by 0530. Bomb, return, refuel, and take off (sometimes doing it a third time). Grab some food, a long debrief, and then sit down to my second job around 1300 (1:00 p.m.) as flight schedule officer. That was its own mental test. It was like an intricate, complex puzzle every day. If I were lucky, I'd be in my rack at 2000 (8:00 p.m.) trying to grab a few hours of fitful sleep before it all happened again.

The hectic pace masked the pure physical discomfort that was life at al-Jaber Air Base. We all quickly accepted that it was going to be constantly loud, dusty, dirty, and hot. Kuwait is a desert country, one of the hottest and least hospitable places on earth. As spring wore on, the heat became nearly unbearable. Air conditioners were a rarity; we had one in the mission planning and operations tent and one sleeping tent that aircrew rotated into when it got so hot that we couldn't sleep in our own tents. The heat was so oppressive that the men finally rolled up the sides of their tents to create more air-flow. They stopped caring about anyone seeing them change clothes. Those of us in the female tent managed to be a bit more modest; we lasted two days longer than the men. At some point, though, any sense of modesty goes out the window. No one cared about how anyone looked changing clothes when the temperature topped 115 degrees.

The boredom that marked many of my flights over Afghani-stan was a distant memory. We dropped bombs every single day. It was the rare moment when we landed with bombs left on our jets. Nasiriyah was typical of our combat flights.

We received a radio call at 1200 local time that Task Force Tarawa from 1st Battalion, 2nd Marines, was under attack and taking heavy fire from enemy-held buildings in Nasiriyah, a town on the banks of the Euphrates River in southern Iraq. Those Marines were part of a contingent headed north toward Baghdad. The pressure they were applying was crucial, and they were pinned down, unable to advance. My pilot, "Mongo," and I were flying Zami-48, one of two F/A-18s on the mission. The aircrew in Zami-47 were "Virge" and "Tuck." We had been diverted from a reconnaissance mission to assist the Marines on the ground. The brigade's forward air control-ler went by the call sign "Mouth." The situation on the ground had become so serious that he had to cut radio contact several times to take cover from overwhelming incoming fire. We were dealing with a lot of confusion over the airwaves—radios going off and on and the pure deadly chaos on the ground. The fog of war was thick.

Because the original mission was reconnaissance rather than attack, each of our F/A-18s was equipped with only two two-thousand-pound GPS-guided bombs. Mouth helped us identify the Marines' location on the ground, and we quickly isolated the GPS coordinates of the enemy building from which our Marines were taking fire. Mouth gave the lead F/A-18 the go-ahead to bomb the building.

"Zami-47, you are cleared hot."

Mongo and I listened intently to the communications between Mouth and Zami-47. Their first bomb hit the target but skipped off the side of the building without exploding. It was a dud. We followed Zami-47 as it banked into a steep turn to take a second run at the target.

All four of us in the air were keenly aware that we had only enough gas for one or two more runs before we would have to fly back to base. There wasn't a lot of room for another dud or any misses. Mongo and I didn't realize that Virge and Tuck were having problems with their weapons system. The GPS wasn't accepting the coordinates for the second bomb. We were both approaching the target at around six hundred miles per hour at seventeen thousand feet. Lots of things can go wrong flying at those speeds with equipment that is incredibly complex.

Virge, a lieutenant colonel and our squadron's executive officer, abruptly handed the mission to Mongo and me with about three and a half miles to go to the drop point. That left me about twenty-five seconds to get my bomb prepped and ready to drop. Mongo and I had been captains for less than two years. We were still a junior aircrew. Although we were on our second combat tour, most of the other aircrew in the squadron outranked us. We had flown a lot of missions, but only rarely had we been given the opportunity to lead one. It didn't matter; our coordination in the cockpit was as good as any experienced aircrew, and we knew it.

It's a back seater's job to be prepared for moments like these, and I was. I had our GPS-guided bombs ready to go. I took over the radio communications with Mouth and read the coordinates and required calls as clearly, smoothly, and quickly as I could. We had five seconds' leeway to the drop point.

Mouth confirmed my coordinates: "Zami-48, cleared hot."

Three seconds, two seconds.

Mongo pressed the bomb-release button.

One second. Thunk. I felt the two-thousand-pound bomb coming off our right wing, rocking the jet slightly. Now we waited. The F/A-18's system showed a countdown from when the bomb was released to the moment it would hit the target. We alternated between watching the countdown and checking our forward-looking infrared (FLIR) video feed focused on the enemy's building.

The radio silence seemed to go on forever. It was an incredibly long thirty seconds. Suddenly Mouth came back on the radio and said matter-of-factly, "That was a shack."

We'd hit it dead on. Virge asked Mouth if he needed another bomb on target.

"No need," he replied. "The building is gone. Zami-48 leveled it."

Normally, we were extremely professional, but there are brief moments that call for irreverent celebration. That day, seventeen thousand feet above an Iraqi battlefield, the hot mic in our cockpit erupted with unusual shouts of triumph. Our Marines on the ground had been pinned down under heavy enemy fire, and there was no time to waste. Just like that, in the shock wave of an explosion from one of our bombs, they were safe. We had helped them, and maybe saved some lives. We were also happy that as a junior aircrew we had shown our combat readiness.

The whole thing was textbook. That moment was exactly why we had dedicated hour after hour to training, study, and prep. All that time in the simulator; all that painstaking effort poring over the minute details of the F/A-18 Hornet and its advanced weapons systems. The training flights, the living in tents, the shitty food, the dirt and dust of the desert, and the lack of sleep had all been worth it. We had performed in combat when our fellow Marines' lives were on the line. For fighter aircrew, it doesn't get any better.

A few weeks later, I was working at a computer in the mission planning tent when a captain tapped me on the shoulder. I turned to see a battle-weary warrior wearing camouflage fatigues covered in fresh field dust. His name tag was obscured, and I didn't recognize him. He said, "Krusty, I'm Mouth. Do you remember me?"

It took a minute for it to click in, that he was the voice over my radio. I stood up. "Yes, of course. Nasiriyah, right?"

He smiled and stuck out his hand. "Right. I wanted to shake your hand and thank you."

"You're more than welcome. How did you find me?"

"Well, I remembered the call signs from that day. And I just asked around for the weapons officer with a 'chick voice.'" We both had a good laugh at that.

It was the first time I had met a Marine who had been on the ground during one of my air-support missions. It was a special moment for me and helped me connect what we did in the air with the people we were defending below. It gave me a little bit of relief from the guilt I was increasingly dealing with. Mouth and I spent some quality time together that afternoon. We shared two hard-to-get ice-cold Coca-Colas, talked briefly about the mission, and discussed how good it would be to get home. We reminisced about our time at the naval academy. Mouth had been a year ahead of me. We pondered what we'd do after the war.

Feel-good moments like that were few and far between in Iraq. The crisis of conscience is something that plagues all warriors in combat. As much as it buoyed me to know we had helped protect Mouth's battalion from the enemy, many of our missions were not so black and white. Our orders were often to destroy anything that looked to be a military vehicle in a certain location. That put me in the position of making life-and-death decisions based on whatever sketchy information I could pick up in a few seconds from a grainy video or FLIR image.

We used our best judgment and took the duty as seriously as it merited. There was a Wild West aspect to Iraq, much different from the more controlled rules of engagement that would be enforced in theaters of war over the next decade. Mongo and I flew missions in which we destroyed Iraqi Republican Guard barracks in the middle of the night. There were times we could see Iraqi soldiers running— some crawling—to get away from the onslaught of our bombs. We bombed bridges with cars and trucks on them. Military personnel? There was no way of knowing, but our orders were clear and it was essential to cut off supply and attack lines. We took every precaution to avoid civilian deaths.

The upside to the blistering flight schedule was that I didn't have much free time to ponder the reality of dropping all those bombs on actual human beings. But you don't get to escape that reality. It's just a deferred payment. Sooner or later, every warrior grapples with what happens in battle, with what he or she has been called upon to do. It's a terrible burden, one that led me again and again to my faith. I kept looking for some relief, some way to make sense of what was increasingly making very little sense to me. Whenever I could, I attended Mass on the base. It was held once a week in a battered green tent. For half an hour, the folding chairs would hold Catholics—right after the Protestant service. I sat there hoping I could remain attached to the person I used to be before the war. I'd follow the sermon and say the prayers. I'd go to confession but feel no better for it. A few hours later, I'd be in the air with six thousand pounds of bombs on my wings. It all seemed surreal.

I couldn't spend a lot of energy wrestling with the humanity, or inhumanity, of what I was doing in Iraq. It was war, and the country had called on me to do my duty. There was no option. I would have to make peace with the contradictions between my obligations as a warrior and my humanity as a person some time in the future. That is the nature of going into battle. Perhaps we fight a war many times. In that moment, in that place, I held tight to the fact that I was doing the right thing as a Marine, even if I knew as a Catholic that killing is never truly "right."

I flew every mission with my dog tags and my military ID card should I ever need to be identified after a crash. I also flew with a silver cross blessed by a Catholic priest, an American flag patch my mother had given me right before I left the States, and a Marine Corps patch. Faith, family, country, and corps, held close to my heart.

Between missions, I was sustained by letters and emails from home. My family wrote to me regularly, and I received weekly letters from Mrs. Eck, the woman who cared for me as a child. She was, by that point, very old. It didn't stop her from writing letter after letter. I would later learn that she dictated letters to her daughter, who would write them for Mrs. Eck when she became too frail to do it herself. She managed to spread sentiments of love and support across pages of cream-colored stationery. She offered a shining example of love and faith embodied.

The letters and emails I exchanged with everyone back home fed my need to stay connected. I wanted to experience as much of home as I could get. I turned to my father for updates on how the University of Kentucky Wildcats were doing in the NCAA tournament. I traded passionate theories with my brother on what the Cincinnati Reds should do with their lineup for opening day. I eagerly read my sister's heartwarming descriptions of managing her toddler and her current pregnancy.

Not all the communications were upbeat. In the middle of the deployment, I heard that I had not been selected for the transition to pilot. It would have been a bigger disappointment if I hadn't been so busy and preoccupied with the serious job at hand. I still held out hope because I was designated as an alternate in case one of the candidates dropped out. I knew there was a good chance that I'd eventually have an opportunity to become a front seater. I focused on what I could control: my flying, my work on the base, and successfully completing missions.

One afternoon, a forward air controller radioed for air support over the center of Baghdad. Masses of people were flooding into the city's main park, a gigantic expanse called Firdos Square. The square was dominated by Ramadan Mosque and a huge statue of Saddam on a towering concrete pedestal. We were in constant communication with the Marines on the ground, who nervously stood by as the crowd quickly swelled into the thousands.

We circled "on station" for an hour until we ran out of gas. After we returned to base, we headed to the ready room tent. The TV was playing a taped feed from Fox News, covering Firdos Square. The jubilant crowds were throwing ropes and guy wires over the statue of Saddam, slowly pulling it down. It was stunning to watch that statue fall as the crowd scrambled to get out of the way. They cheered wildly.

Mongo and I looked at each other. I said, "So that's what was happening down there." We had been directly overhead when everyday Iraqis had brought down the statue that signified Saddam Hussein's repressive regime, in one of the most powerful gestures we could imagine. Sitting there, we thought we had won. We felt we had helped the Iraqis achieve their independence and that now the country would be fine.

A few weeks later, in May, the Green Knights got their orders to return home. Almost all the squadrons would be joining us. There wasn't much need for air support anymore. The fight was supposed to be over. Now the operation was into a "stabilization" phase; the goal was to support the Iraqis as they went forward in freedom. Little did we know. I was just so happy to be going home.

This homecoming would be different from the last one. I wavered on asking my parents to meet me when I flew into San Diego. I knew I wasn't in the best of places mentally and thought I might need some time to adjust back to noncombat life and work through everything that had happened in Iraq. I wrote my mother an email telling her that I thought I might need some time to digest everything before I could see family. But as we packed up for the long flight home, the thought of arriving in San Diego made me anxious. I asked my mother to meet me there. It turned out to be a good idea. I would need her steady presence more than I ever had.

10

HOME. That word carries such weight and power when you serve in the military. I landed in San Diego on a beautiful early summer day. I couldn't have imagined a more welcoming sight than my mom there to greet me. I hugged her tight and held her for a long time. It was so gratifying to connect with the person who had always been such an anchor in my life. After all I'd seen and done in Iraq, it was a gift just to see her smile. Finally, I let go of her and we piled my three beat-up, dingy green seabags into her car. We drove to my condo as I processed being back on American soil once again.

I unloaded my bags from the car and carried them up to my front door, where Mona and Homan were waiting. She was holding a sign that said, "Welcome Home Amy," and he proudly held up an American flag. They were both smiling and excited, as if I were family returning. They knew better than most the special feeling of being home, the place you know that you're safe, secure, and welcome. I hugged them and thanked them, fighting back tears.

It was a perfectly timed reminder. For all my internal conflicts about what had gone on in Iraq, this was the America I loved and fought for. Serving your country can be an abstract concept lost in the chaos of strapping yourself into a cockpit day after day, completing a mission, and going to sleep, only to repeat the process the next day. But serving a country takes its truest form when you can relate your duty to those for whom you're doing it. I went to Iraq not to protect oil, or because some politicians wanted to project American power as a message to the rest of the world. I went there for my parents, for my brother and sister and Mrs. Eck, and for everyone I knew growing up in Kentucky. I went there for people like Mona and Homan, refugees and newcomers who embraced the American dream as their own. Those two were as American as anyone I had grown up with. The country I fought for was a beacon of hope for so many like them. Having flown all those miles over the Middle East, I had seen firsthand what the citizens of those countries dealt with. I understood just how special America is to the world.

I introduced them to my mother, and then she helped me get my condo squared away. It seemed so comfortable and even opulent after months in a ragged, dusty, brutally hot tent. My mom bustled around the kitchen, looking for anything resembling food. I had gotten rid of everything before I deployed.

"So, do you want to go out to eat, or would you like me to make you something?"

She knew perfectly well that I adored her cooking. It was more than just delicious. It was the taste of home, of happiness. A restaurant meal couldn't possibly compare.

"Your spaghetti would be the best thing in the world right now. Would you mind making dinner?"

"Of course not."

We headed out to the grocery store. It was a disorienting experience. At one point, I stopped mid-aisle and just processed the overwhelming number of choices, the mind-boggling bounty. When we got to the checkout line, the woman in front of us began arguing with the cashier over an expired one-dollar-off coupon. I thought, "Does she understand we're at war, bombing people? Does she even care?" I became unreasonably angry. It was the first sign that something deeper was troubling me. It dawned on me that as much as I might have wanted to, I had not left Kuwait and Iraq behind.

I had a pervasive feeling that all the people around me simply didn't get it. The war didn't touch them. It didn't impact their pocketbooks. It wasn't going to hit them financially, because the war was put on our country's credit card. That debt would be kicked down the road to future generations. I had signed up and willingly fought, willingly sacrificed. Shouldn't everyday Americans sacrifice at least a little too? Shouldn't they have some skin in the game? The ones I resented most, though, were the leaders, the politicians. I would remain deeply disappointed in the president and Congress and in the casual way they treated the war and the world post-9/11.

After a week, my mom flew home to Kentucky. I followed her a few weeks later, to pick up Monk and just be home in the best possible sense. My family and friends threw me a party where I got to physically embrace all those people who had written and sustained me over my months in the Middle East. It was heartening to see my brother and sister right there in front of me, instead of on the address line of an email. I held my infant nephew, Charlie. He was an affirmation of all that is good and worthwhile in the world. I spent time with Mrs. Eck, now elderly and frail, but as positive, faithful, and loving as always. Those people offered food for my soul, a wonderful respite from the intensity of the war. The truth was, though, my combat experiences and the issues they created lingered.

I became aware of how much those issues were bothering me

about a month after arriving home. Fighter aircrew constantly push for more qualifications, working to build on their knowledge and skills and to prepare them for promotion. That's why I jumped at the chance to attend the weeklong ground school at TOPGUN, the navy's elite air combat training course made famous by the Tom Cruise film named for it. The shortened, ground-based course included about fifty pilots and back seaters. The purpose was to review the latest navy and Marine Corps fighter tactics. Several Green Knights attended with me.

The TOPGUN instructors made a point of welcoming the Green Knights. We were the first aviators they had hosted who had flown in Iraq. We all gathered in the main auditorium for the introduction to the week, and the instructors identified those of us from the Green Knights and thanked us for our work in Iraq. Then they showed a "motivational" video.

The Green Knights in the room had no idea what was coming. Suddenly a montage of bombing footage from our missions started playing on a big screen at the front of the room. It had been over-dubbed with a heavy metal soundtrack. I spotted clips taken from video sensors on jets I had flown in. My missions. My bombs. My targets. Dead people. I felt sick to my stomach.

In Iraq, debriefs only reviewed bombing footage right after a mission. It was a clinical approach. We were providing intel to our ops and intelligence Marines. During those sessions, I was still in flying mode. I never wanted or needed to process anything other than the technical aspects of target destruction. Did I perform everything by the book as my training had taught me? It was academic. But in that auditorium far from a war zone with an irreverent soundtrack, the footage and the memories it brought back shook me to my core. That video glorified what was a lot of death. Enemies or not, those bombs killed real people with lives and families and hopes and fears. When there was a particularly big explosion on the screen, the other people in the room cheered. That only made me sicker.

I wasn't alone. Another Green Knight was sitting next to me. He quietly got up, walked to the aisle, and left the auditorium. A second Green Knight followed him. I was the third to leave. In the hallway, we stood there looking at each other. One of my squadron mates shook his head. "I don't need to see that shit." A huge sigh of relief came over me. I wasn't alone. At least one other Marine felt the way I did.

Those feelings surfaced in other less obvious settings as well. A month after my TOPGUN experience, I attended my cousin's wedding in Colorado. It was an incredibly beautiful setting, a purely optimistic, enjoyable event. My extended family treated me like a hero. Inside, though, I felt like a mess. This amazing group of people, so happy and cheerful, and here I was trying to process a confusing mixture of guilt and anger. I felt like an impostor. I left the reception because I was close to crying. Those wonderful people had no idea what I had done just two months before. I had killed people, lots of people. "Thou shall not kill." It's a big commandment. No one I knew growing up had committed that sin. Not in the Christian world of northern Kentucky. So, who was I? Did my sins define me? Was I some sort of killer now? The questions haunted me. They were the types of questions that never have easy answers, if they can be answered at all. Certainly, there aren't any satisfying answers.

I was most comfortable burying myself in work, and there was plenty to keep me busy. Shortly after I returned from Colorado, I began air combat tactics instructor (ACTI) training. ACTI is a grueling qualification to earn, but it was a critical achievement for aircrew, especially a woman; the qualification would give me access to the top jobs in the community and would allow me even greater opportunities to mentor aviators who came after me. The "workup" for the certification took months and was intense. It was a process of digging down into ever-finer details of air combat, of learning to teach those details rather than just internalize them. The rigorous training couldn't have come at a better time, because it kept my mind from pondering my combat experiences.

ACTI culminated in a three-day certification test overseen by two instructors who flew in from Marine Corps Air Station Yuma, in Yuma, Arizona. No woman Marine aircrew had ever completed ACTI up to that point. The pressure was tremendous. Getting that certification was a big accomplishment for me and would allow me to fulfill an important role: teaching less experienced, junior members of the squadron. I was proud when I passed the certification.

It wasn't long before I got another golden opportunity to advance my skills and abilities even further. Marine Division Tactics Course (MDTC) is an air-to-air training course. It is the Marine version of the navy's TOPGUN school. Every year, a certain number of openings are available to be filled by squadron commanding officers. The Green Knights' commanding officer put me up for one of the slots, and I was thrilled at the opportunity to take the course.

The training is the equivalent of earning a master's degree in air-to-air tactics—the particular strategies and techniques for flying against and shooting down enemy fighter jets. Over five weeks I would engage in some of the most intense tactical flying I had ever done outside combat. The flights held every day and night were complex air-to-air missions against multiple types of enemy fighter aircraft. In a theater of war, combat preparations over time become repetitive. In a place like Iraq, the enemy doesn't suddenly start using different weapons or develop a whole new set of skills and combat approaches. You cover the same things in briefings over and over. But during MDTC, every day was an entirely new and unique scenario. Different enemy aircraft. Different capabilities. We had to plan for all of it. Preparations for each flight took hours of work.

There were six of us in the course, and we operated as a team. The pace was relentless.

Time constraints were our biggest enemy. We would complete a day of flying and the subsequent debrief, and only then be given the scenario for the next day. That would leave us a scant hour for planning because the material was classified and could be studied only in a Sensitive Compartmented Information Facility (SCIF); we couldn't take it back to our rooms. The Catch-22 was that we were limited in how much time we could spend in the SCIF; crew day regulations required that we be back in our quarters by a certain time each night.

I was fortunate to be teamed with "Peepers," a pilot who was easy to work with and a sharp thinker. The final step in MDTC is a detailed debrief that students give in front of a large group of seasoned aviators in the air base's auditorium. It's a nerve-racking experience. The guys who make up the audience are older seasoned fighter pilots, some with decades of experience. They were, without a doubt, the best fighter pilots in the world.

Standing in front of the filled auditorium, I was more nervous than at any point in my career. Their swagger and confidence filled up the room and was more overpowering than the smell of their sweat and chewing tobacco. I had to recap the day's flight event and then go through and pick apart everything that had happened in our final fifteen-aircraft engagement. The audience was there to assess and test me, not only for my performance in the air, but to determine how much I understood of what had transpired during the hectic combat exercise. As critical audiences go, they don't get much more brutal.

Completing that debrief and successfully getting through the course were big accomplishments and an even bigger relief. I was ready to unwind by the time the graduation ceremony began. It's held in the same auditorium, and my entire squadron had flown in for it. Each student is given a ritual shot of whiskey from a 30-millimeter Harrier cannon shell casing before stepping out to get a diploma and a handshake from the colonel who serves as the commander of the Weapons and Tactics Squadron. I don't remember much after that because the post-graduation celebration became a typical Marine Corps fighter squadron drinkfest. I woke up with an epic headache and the satisfaction that I had passed another milestone. Hand me the patch.

Work all you want, but life continues apace. Back home in Kentucky, my father had been dealing with ongoing dental problems. I hadn't given it much thought, other than to empathize with him. Then, suddenly, his doctor made a devastating discovery. The cause of his problems was cancer of the jaw. The cancer was aggressive, and the prognosis was grim. The doctors had no way of knowing, short of the actual surgery, how far the cancer had advanced. It was possible that it had passed through lymph nodes, into soft tissue, and possibly even into the brain. There was a chance that the diagnosis was actually a short-term death sentence. The call from my mother was like a punch to the gut.

As the situation developed and my father prepared for what would be a traumatic and possibly fatal surgery, I planned a special event for him. The year before, on leave and home in Kentucky, I had gone with my brother to a Cincinnati Reds game. It was the last day of a losing season. The game was my first time in the team's brand-new home, Great American Ball Park. As we sat in our nosebleed seats, I asked my brother if there had been a flyover for the inaugural game.

"Yeah, a C-130."

"A C-130? Are you kidding me? That's terrible. A slow flyby?"

That seemed ridiculous. A C-130 was vital to military operations because it was big enough to transport heavy equipment and large numbers of troops. That said, it was anything but fast, exciting, or graceful. It was the lumbering elephant of military aviation. A proper flyover involved jets screaming overhead, leaving everyone in awe at the display of sheer power. A C-130 simply didn't inspire that same feeling.

Matt, ever the teasing older brother, said, "Well, you couldn't do any better, could you?"

"Is that a bet?"

"Yeah, sure, it's a bet."

Game on. I had taken his challenge seriously and contacted the Reds' front office, who were delighted at the prospect of an F/A-18 flyover. I began working through military channels, helping the team make a formal request to the Pentagon for a four-jet display.

My father's illness made it an even more pressing matter. As we got Marine and FAA approvals and I finalized the planning, I could have handed over the actual flying to another aircrew. But my father was going to be in the stands, so I was going to be in one of those F/A-18s. In fact, Dad delayed his surgery by forty-eight hours just so he could attend the Reds' 2004 home opener and witness his daughter fly over the stadium in a fighter jet. I had planned for the jets to pass right over the stadium on the word "brave" in "The Star-Spangled Banner." My goal was that with four low-flying F/A-18s, the crowd would never hear that word sung, and that's exactly how it happened. It was one last jubilant moment before the stress and worry of my father's surgery. I was ecstatic when it worked out precisely as we had drawn it up.

The surgery was both a success and a harsh new reality. The surgeons found no evidence that the cancer had spread to my father's brain, but they had to remove one side of his jaw. He was irreversibly disfigured and would never again be able to speak or eat normally. The experience changed my father. He had been an orator, a teacher with a booming, majestic voice. He was the reader the congregation wanted to hear at Christmas Mass. He had been the guy who loved to talk to people, and he always relished eating and drinking.

All that was now lost to him. He faced a still-uncertain future, with more surgeries, radiation, and complications. For the first time, he was marked by a deep and obvious sadness.

I was torn. I badly wanted to be there for him, to help him however I could. My parents, though, were true to form. They weren't having it. My mother made that absolutely clear in a phone call to me a month after my father's surgery. "We don't want you to stop your life, Amy. Your father doesn't want you to come home during this time. He wants you to stay, and train, and fly. Do your job."

I understood, but it hurt. It was frustrating that this man, someone who was a giant in my eyes, should lose so much, and there was nothing I could do for him. I did as my mom had requested. I continued working, flying, and training. I did my job. Shortly after the phone call with her, a pilot in the ready room tapped me on the shoulder and said, "Have you checked the messages?"

He was talking about the official online messages, distributed to all personnel. Official messages from Headquarters Marine Corps were distributed system-wide.

"No, why?"

"You're on it. You got the transition. You're going back to flight school. Check it out."

I headed to the closest computer and checked the official messages. Sure enough, I was one of two Marines to have been given a slot to go from backseat to front seat. My orders would be to Corpus Christi, Texas. I was in. I was going to sit in the front seat and fly an F/A-18. I was about to realize the goal I had dreamed of since I was fourteen years old. A few days later, the Green Knights' commanding officer, a crusty combat veteran named Colonel Earl "the Pearl" Wederbrook, called me into his office.

"So, you got flight school."

"Yes, sir."

"Do you know what you're doing to your career?"

"Yes, sir, I'm going to be a front seater."

He leaned back in his chair and scowled. "It's tough for back seaters to transition and then get back on the ladder. You're starting all over. Right now, you have some salt. You've earned your place, and you have a reputation. You go back to flight school, and you're nobody to those instructors. You start fresh. Your combat experience doesn't mean anything. You understand?"

"Yes, sir."

"I just want to make sure that this is really what you want."

I looked him in the eyes and said, "I do. I know what I'm getting myself into. It's something I've always wanted to do, sir. And I'm going to do it."

"Okay." He put his pen to the paper. Just like that, I took my eighty-nine combat missions, my months in the Afghanistan and Iraq wars, and my ACTI and MDTC qualifications and headed to Texas, where I would be nothing more than a new green student pilot. I couldn't wait.

11

I F I HAD HARBORED any illusions about what going back to flight school meant for me, the no-nonsense advice I got from Colonel "Gumby" Sawyers when I checked in would have cured me of them. He had been my first commanding officer in the Green Knights. Now he was the commander of Training Air Wing Four, Naval Air Station Corpus Christi. He was a blunt man and got straight to the point.

"Look, Krusty, you're going to know a lot more than any other student and many of your instructors. When some of these guys want to tell you how it is, just shut up, nod your head, and get through the syllabus. Get your butt back to the Hornet community as fast as possible. Don't make waves. Get through the program. That's all."

His words and everything my Green Knights' commanding officer had said to me before I checked out of my operational squadron were an indication of just how unusual what I was trying to do was in Marine Corps aviation. I had flown in some of the most intense combat flights a back seater can encounter. Now I was headed into a year of primary flight school, much of it repeating what I had learned in Pensacola nearly four years before. It was like returning to an undergraduate degree program after graduating with your master's. As a captain, I would be the same rank and age as most of my instructors. I would likely have more flight hours and experience than many of them, and certainly more combat flight hours. It was reasonable that my command-level superiors were concerned about how I would handle the transition. Other aviators attempting the same change had struggled with their egos, and their careers had never recovered. I knew this.

I went in clear-eyed. If I had to take grief from people who had flown less than I had, hadn't seen combat, and were my equals in rank, so be it. The reward was well worth whatever I had to do. Ultimately, I was going to strap on an F/A-18 and fly that incredible machine myself. I was going to fulfill the dream of a fourteen-year-old girl who had heard "you can't" more times than she could count. I kept that in mind every single day I was at flight school.

For all the warnings, flight school the second time around had its upsides. It was a pleasure adjusting to the more leisurely pace of a student. After several intense years of either being in combat or working flat out to earn one advanced qualification or another, I found the lighter workload a welcome break. I was looking forward to having a little time to myself and to diving into life outside the military.

My condo in San Diego had almost doubled in value, so I decided to buy in Corpus Christi. It would be a better investment than renting, and I didn't want the hassle of dealing with landlords who penalized me for having a chocolate Labrador roommate. I rented out my condo and bought a small house in a quiet neighborhood about twenty minutes from Naval Air Station Corpus Christi. The house was a modest little place, a single-level ranch house just big enough for Monk and me. It had a nice backyard that he could run around in and was a short drive from the beach. I was looking forward to settling in for an extended period, which for me meant more than a year. It would be nice not handing Monk off to my parents every few months.

The coursework in the first year was familiar; it was much the same as what I'd studied in Pensacola. That meant I didn't have to spend a lot of time studying and had more free time than I ever had enjoyed in my military career. I decided to try new things and the first was golf. My uncles all played, but I had never even stepped on a fairway. I headed to a local driving range to slice and shank my way through a bucket of balls. As I was hacking away, a stooped, white-haired man in his eighties showed up behind my driving tee. I was aware that he was watching me and thought he might be lost.

Finally, he spoke up. "You need lessons."

It was a blunt assessment, but you couldn't argue the truth of it.

"Thank you, sir. I know that."

"Well, I'll give you lessons." He handed me his card. He was a golf pro. An extremely old golf pro. Knowledge doesn't always come packaged the way you think it should. He turned out to be an excellent teacher, patient and precise. To start with, he went with me on a shopping trip to buy clubs. He helped me find the right set, perfectly sized and well within my price range. After that, we met once a week for lessons. Within six months, my scores were coming down, and I was confident that I could hold my own in any foursome. More important, I loved the game. The pace, the course, the sunshine, were all a wonderful break from anything military and represented an entirely different world from anything I had known before. There was a meditative element to the sport. I could lose myself in driving a bucket of balls or even working on my short game, my mind focused only on small motor movements. It was relaxing but also a never-ending competition against myself, which intrigued me. With golf, there was no end point; you had to be absorbed in the process as much as the goal.

As simple as it was, golf was part of a bigger exploration for me. I had a desire to find pursuits and places where there was no moral ambiguity. It was a relief to walk a beautiful golf course knowing that my next shot had no life-or-death implications. I would come to realize it was all part of working through what I had done in Iraq. More than anything else, reflecting on those experiences created a deep need within me to do something purely good. I wanted to help people as I had done in volunteering through the church when I was younger. There was a moral logic and calculus to it, almost as a counterbalance to all those bombs I had dropped. I realized that I needed to be of service. I decided to train Monk as a therapy dog so that we could help patients in hospital settings. I found a three-month training program in Corpus Christi offered by the Delta Society. As usual, Monk was game.

It took a lot of work, but Monk finally passed the course and got his service vest and ID tags. We started a schedule of service work that same week. Because I was ahead of the curve at school, weekends were all ours. Every Saturday we'd head to the beach for a run and a swim. On Sunday, I would dress Monk in his vest and tags and we would head to a nursing home or hospital. Room by room, we'd visit Alzheimer's patients or others who were bedridden. Sometimes we would go to a children's hospital. He and I would check in at the nurse's station first, to get our schedule. The nurse would tell us which rooms wanted a visit, and I'd start knocking on doors, saying, "Monk here is a chocolate Lab. He would love to visit with you if you're up for it."

The kids were always excited to see Monk, no matter how sick they were. He would sit there patiently, like the good, kindhearted dog he was. He had been trained to be careful of IVs and to ignore the odd whirs, clicks, and beeps any machines might make. A sick little boy or girl would pet Monk and talk to him and play with his ears, while I talked to them about the TV programs they liked or their favorite flavor of ice cream. The kids loved Monk, and they'd be all smiles by the time I had to say, "Okay, Monk's going to go see a couple of other people now."

After an hour spent visiting, Monk and I would head home. He would be wiped out, as if he had absorbed the worries and stress from the patients we visited. He'd fall asleep in the car on the way home, more tired than when we made the trip back from an afternoon at the beach. For me, those hospital visits were therapeutic. They helped me deal with what I'd done and seen in Iraq. Our time in hospital rooms and nursing homes confirmed to me that I could be a good person, that I could tap into the compassion and love I held in my soul. Those moments next to Monk, him in his vest and some smiling child petting his soft brown fur with adoration, returned me to the profound peace and calm I enjoyed as a young girl in church. I felt as I had sitting next to my father, reading the same prayer or singing the same hymn. It was a feeling I was struggling to find in the pews of my local church.

I had a deep need to help. It was beyond the obligation of my religion. It was a way to define myself to myself. I mentored young flight students, especially women. I was in a unique position because I wasn't one of their instructors but I had a lot of intense experience both in the military and in combat. I'd have the woman student pilots over to my house for dinner once a month. We would talk about what life was like for a woman in a squadron. We discussed what they could expect working with male aircrew and explored all the things that no one had ever talked to me about.

At school, though, I was all business. I was careful to mind the advice Gumby had given me. I got along with all my instructors, but some made more of an impression on me than others. Lieutenant

Erik Henderson was a navy guy, laid back with a solid reputation. He was easy to talk to. Between flights, as the ready room emptied out, I found myself trading stories with him about our families, hometowns, and a shared love of history. Although I wasn't going to admit it to myself, I was drawn to him for other reasons as well. He had the most amazing blue eyes and a wonderful strong feeling about him. I was human; I noted that he wasn't wearing a wedding ring and never mentioned a girlfriend.

I put those thoughts out of my head. I couldn't think about him in that way. There were strict regulations against instructors dating students, even if we were the same rank. I never flirted with Erik, because I didn't want to introduce that sort of tension into our relationship. Getting through the syllabus and not making waves were the most important goals. I was so close to my lifelong dream, and I wasn't going to mess it up by breaking the rule about fraternization.

The primary syllabus in flight school focused on flying T-34 turboprop aircraft. Each student was assigned an "on-wing," a flight instructor who flew with the same student for several key flights and mentored the student. Near the end of the primary syllabus, after about seven months, each student had to take a three-day weekend cross-country flight with his or her on-wing. It was essentially the final for the first school year.

My on-wing was Lieutenant Fritz Fitzgerald. He got orders and left the squadron halfway through my training year. That meant my cross-country flight was up for grabs for any flight instructor. Erik volunteered. Traditionally, the student decides the destination for that particular flight. Usually, he or she picks a vacation spot— a reward after the rigors of the school. I really wanted to go skiing, so I asked Erik if he knew how to ski.

"Sure, of course."

That settled it. I picked Vail, Colorado, as our destination.

That weekend was easily among the top ten most fun of my life.

We flew low-level training flights, landing in small airfields along the way, from Corpus Christi, to Lubbock, Pueblo, Eagle County, Grand Junction, and eventually back to Amarillo and Corpus Christi. Along the way, we maintained our professionalism, even though we had long talks that had nothing to do with aviation. Erik graded me on my flight maneuvers, visual navigation, and instrument approaches. Finally, on our off day in Vail, we rented skis and purchased all-day lift tickets. It quickly became evident that Erik had grossly overstated his skiing ability. In fact, he didn't have a clue. At the top of the mountain, he fell off the ski lift and struggled to even stand up.

In the moment, I was amazed that he couldn't even get down a green run. I taught him the basics, starting with snowplowing, but he still fell down about every ten seconds. The day before, he had ordered me to redo a flight maneuver again and again. I felt strongly that I was doing it perfectly. It had been frustrating to hear him say, "Not good enough. Try it again." I had gotten a little ticked off at that. So the skiing was a tiny bit of payback, and I took an inappropriate amount of pleasure watching him struggle, covered head to toe in powdered snow. Time and time again, as he struggled to recover from a fall, I would say, "Not good enough. Try it again." Finally, he looked at me and said, "You're really enjoying this, aren't you?"

I couldn't help but smile. "Yep."

He was worn out and frustrated after an hour. I told him to go have a drink in the lodge. After a couple of runs, I found him finishing up a beer and a burger, and we headed out to try another run together.

There was no getting around the fact that we just clicked. Everywhere we went that weekend, people treated us as if we were a couple. It was awkward, but also felt as though the world understood something we weren't owning up to. I think we both knew it, but we were both dead set on maintaining a professional distance. Being a woman in a military aviation community, I knew the rules. After having been in a fighter squadron, I also knew that my personal life was something everyone wanted to know about, and I knew how the rumor mill could crush a reputation and career.

The final flight, a month after my cross-country trip, was a night check ride. My instructor for the flight was an old reserve navy pilot who flew for a commercial airline in his civilian life. I completed the flight with no issues, and we wrapped up the debrief in a window-less room around midnight on a Wednesday. We assumed we were the only ones left because the duty officer had locked up and gone home. But as we came out of the debrief room, we found Erik on a computer, still working.

My instructor packed up his things. He congratulated me, shook my hand, gave me my final grade sheet, and left. I looked over at Erik. He got up from the computer and asked me, "That was your last flight, right?"

"Yep," I said, smiling.

"Want to go out for a drink to celebrate?" Even though he didn't say it, we both knew that my primary training year was over. Erik could no longer be considered one of my instructors, nor did he outrank me. Fraternization rules no longer applied.

"Yep."

I told him we had to stop at my house so I could change clothes. Regulations prohibited officers from going out in town wearing a flight suit. We drove to my place, but never made it to the bar that night.

I had dated before, but I had never dated someone I was so comfortable with out of the gate. I wasn't alone. Monk loved Erik. Admittedly, chocolate Labs are easy to bribe, and it never failed that Erik showed up at the house with a pocketful of dog treats. I wasn't so susceptible to bribery, but it became obvious that we had the elusive chemistry I had heard people talk about but never experienced myself. Without realizing it, I fell hard for Lieutenant Erik Henderson.

Wrapped up in my other feelings for him, I just respected and admired Erik. He had earned everything he'd achieved through hard work and diligence. He grew up in a blue-collar family that lived in a row house in Hagerstown, Maryland. His father was an air force veteran who had started his own business selling and repairing farm equipment, while his mother raised their sons and then went to work at the DMV. While I was playing after-school sports at Notre Dame Academy, Erik was working his way through high school. He'd go on to be the first one in his family to attend college and fought mighty hard for his place in Officer Candidate School. He was rightfully proud, honest, and no stranger to facing down and conquering huge challenges. The relationship continued as I started commuting to Naval Air Station Kingsville in Kingsville, Texas. That would be my home base for the second year of flight school. I was finally learning to fly jets.

Kingsville was more challenging than Corpus Christi had been, but I was still ahead of the class thanks to a lot of intense hours spent in the backseat of an F/A-18. We flew T-45 Goshawks, sleek trainer jets painted a distinctive bright white with fire-engine red nose, wingtips, and tail. The training was invigorating and interesting, but I knew the real challenge was waiting for me at the end of the school year—carrier landings. Everything up to that point was just prelude.

The school workload still left time for me to spend a lot of nights with Erik. I wasn't ready to think about the rest of our lives, but we had a connection unlike any I had ever known. I knew it was special, even if I didn't yet understand how special. So halfway through the syllabus in my second year of flight school, I decided to take him as my date to the Marine Corps Ball. The Marine Corps Ball is a long-standing tradition, a celebration of the establishment—the birthday—of the Marine Corps. The balls are held around the country for units large and small. The ball is a big deal for any Marine in uniform.

I made an appointment to meet with my direct superior at the flight school, a Marine major. I told him, "Sir, I'm dating a navy lieutenant, and I want to bring him to the Marine Corps Ball. I wanted to make sure you were okay with it. He was an instructor in my last squadron, and even though we didn't date while I was there, I just wanted to make sure it's all okay and that we're good to go."

The major brushed it off. "Yeah, that's fine. No big deal. Hope you guys have a great ball."

That would have been that, if the major had not inexplicably felt the need to pass on what I told him to the new senior Marine in South Texas, a colonel who had replaced Gumby. The colonel, a former AV-8B Harrier pilot, blew his stack. He told the major, "She has to break up with him. I'm not going to stand for this. He's an instructor and she's a student. I have a zero-tolerance policy for this."

When the major told me what the colonel had said, I was angry. We were Marines. According to the unwritten code, the major should have had my back and should have stood up for me. You protect those who report to you. There was simply no reason to take what I told him up the command ladder, because Erik and I weren't breaking any regulations. I had done everything by the book. Unfortunately, the colonel was a short guy with a small man's complex, the type of officer whose only goal is to climb the command structure. It was a power trip, plain and simple. The more I thought about the whole thing, the angrier I got. I decided to keep dating Erik.

A week after the ball, the major reluctantly told me that the colonel had ordered me to go to Naval Air Station Corpus Christi and report to his office. I knew that wasn't good news. I put on my service alpha uniform and headed off to Corpus Christi. As soon as I walked into the colonel's office, he lit into me while I stood at attention. He finished up by ordering me not to see Erik for the rest of my time under his command.

That left me with a big quandary. He had given me an illegal order. I could have hired a lawyer and fought it; I had met with a JAG on base. There would, however, almost certainly be blowback. Some officers in the command structure would see me as a complainer or a troublemaker, and it would make problems for other women who followed in my footsteps. Sometimes, you have to accept that people get to be wrong even when you know they're wrong. There were two months left until I got winged. I told Erik that we couldn't date until I finished the advanced flight school and earned my wings. Understandably, he was not happy. We were in a routine of seeing each other and were having nothing but fun. We would continue to text and call each other, but we couldn't be together.

Much as I adored him and was slowly coming to understand that he was my future, I wasn't going to jeopardize my lifelong dream of flying F/A-18s. I knew that if Erik and I were the real deal, we'd be able to last two months apart.

I spent those months in the classroom, the simulator, and the cockpit of the T-45. Finally, the VT-21 Redhawk training squadron headed to Jacksonville, Florida, for daytime carrier qualifications. We would be landing on the USS *George Washington*. At least any of us who had a future as fighter jet pilots would.

Carrier landings are the summit of a pilot's technical skills. They are incredibly technically demanding, but also a test of pure nerve and self-confidence. As we flew out over the Atlantic, I focused on what I had been taught. My first thought as I flew over the carrier was how incredibly small a target it was from the air. A carrier landing starts with an amazingly precise approach. The "flight" of jets passes over the carrier in formation at eight hundred feet. Each jet in the formation performs what's called a break, essentially peeling off to the left of the formation in order—from left to right at five-second intervals. The maneuver itself involves a 180-degree turn pulling multiple g-forces. It takes you back in the direction of the carrier, flying head-on to the ship.

You have to throttle down to idle in the turn, "bleeding" energy and speed, in a process of getting down to "gear speed"—an acceptable air speed at which you can lower your landing gear without fear it will be ripped off. You fly by the carrier at a low altitude (about eight hundred feet—it feels as if you could reach out of the cockpit and touch the water) and then execute another turn about a quarter mile behind it. Now you're on the landing approach, when the pressure becomes intense and an aviator can easily get inside his or her own head.

There is a plus-sign-shaped light bank off to the left of the carrier's runway. As I flew the approach, a horizontal line of green lights illuminated on either side of a vertical line of yellow lights. The green lights represented the ideal level of my approach. Whichever yellow light was illuminated represented my jet's vertical position; the yellow light had to line up with the row of green lights to indicate a safe approach and landing. The yellow light is "the ball." When you can see the ball, you radio to the landing signal officer (LSO), the person who controls the deck of the carrier. My pulse was pounding as I heard the radio crackle to life and the LSO say, "Call the ball." I keyed my mic and said, "Two forty-five, Goshawk, ball, 2.2, McGrath." The communication gave the LSO the pertinent information of who I was, how much fuel I was carrying, and that I actually had the ball.

In response, I heard, "Raaaawwwger, ball."

I was cleared to make my first carrier touch-and-go pass. The process happens quickly. Unfortunately, on that first approach I was still a little transfixed by the sight of the carrier heaving in the open ocean. Landing on a carrier involves lowering a hook on the rear of the plane. If you've positioned yourself correctly, that hook will catch one of four heavy steel cables strung across the deck and numbered 1 through 4, from the back to the front of the carrier. The perfect landing catches wire number 3. Mesmerized as I was, I missed all of the wires in what is known as a "bolter." I was waved off and had to immediately throttle back up and fly out into the landing pattern.

After I executed a few touch-and-goes on the deck, the LSO radioed for me to put my tailhook down and make a landing pass. I tried to calm myself as I executed the second turn and approached the aft of the carrier. I lined the ball up, which was almost like playing a video game, but with much higher stakes. After the initial radio exchange, I approached in the calm of radio silence. Silence is good. It meant the LSO saw no problems with my approach. I only realized that I had caught the wire after I came to an abrupt halt—150 miles per hour to 0 in just over a second. My mind was still flying, but my eyes were looking out over the deck. The air boss (observing from the bridge and a much higher rank than the LSO) had to radio an embarrassing transmission I thought the entire ship could hear, "Throttle back, 245, you ain't making the ship go any faster."

I slowly pulled the throttle back; my arms and hands were shaking uncontrollably. I had done it! Which proved to me that I could do it. I could do it again and again. As many times as I needed to.

I raised the tailhook and followed the hand signals of the deck personnel as they guided me over to the ship's catapult. I reset all my controls from a landing configuration to preparation for takeoff. Once I was positioned over the catapult, I put my hands up in the air to show the deck crew I wouldn't move any flight controls that could hurt them. They ran under the jet, hooked the catapult wire to my nose gear, and then gave me the thumbs-up signal. I felt the jet subtly sink as the catapult line pulled taut, compressing my nose gear. After running through a final check of all my controls, I saluted the catapult officer, signaling I was ready to go. I grabbed the hand grips on either side of the cockpit. He dropped to one knee and signaled to a deck operator to push the button that fired the catapult.

A catapult launch from a carrier is almost the exact opposite of a landing. A second's hesitation and suddenly I was shot forward, from 0 to 150 miles an hour in the blink of an eye. My knees slammed up into my chest as I let out an involuntary grunt, and then the carrier disappeared out of my peripheral view and I was airborne and flying once again, ready for my next landing approach. It was exhilarating.

I got better with each landing, and my hands stopped shaking. After my tenth landing, I realized I had qualified—I didn't need anyone to tell me. I had passed the final hurdle to becoming a naval aviator. I could barely process that reality on the twenty-minute flight back to Cecil Field in Jacksonville.

There were only a couple more flights before graduation, and they were anticlimactic after the carrier landings. It wasn't long before I found myself getting dressed for the winging ceremony that signaled the end of my time in flight school. The ceremony awarding the naval wings of gold was similar to my first winging ceremony. It was smaller, with only six pilots being winged, but it seemed just as momentous. My mom and dad came, as did Captain Coward and his wife, Croom. Captain Coward had retired but remained a trusted mentor and a reliable sounding board anytime I needed advice. He did the honors of pinning on my wings.

I was touched that several of my fellow Green Knights made the trip for the ceremony. Erik was there as well, dressed in a suit rather than his dress uniform. His presence made clear that although we had abided by the letter of the colonel's order, we had rejected the spiteful spirit of it.

The next week, I received orders to the F/A-18 training squadron in Virginia Beach, Virginia. VFA-106, the Gladiators, would be my home for eleven months. It would also be the final step in my

F/A-18 training. It was an emotional time. Processing the fact that I was now a certified F/A-18 pilot was exciting and overwhelming. A dream held for so long takes on a life of its own. Achieving the dream leaves you looking forward with anticipation, eager for and anxious about what comes next.

My relationship with Erik was part of the excitement and anxiety. I quickly sold my home in Corpus Christi, and because I had two weeks before I had to report to Virginia Beach, Monk and I moved in with Erik. It was a wonderful, all-too-short moment in time. Leaving him for my new assignment was painful and hurt in a way I hadn't experienced before. There was simply no option, though. Erik had received orders to Joint Reserve Base New Orleans, where he would train as a C-130 pilot. We both understood the reality. If we were going to continue as a couple, we'd have to do it long-distance. We would wrestle with that for the next four long and difficult years. There was nothing to be done about it. We both still had goals to achieve and a country to serve. We said our goodbyes and set out for our new challenges.

12

C HECKING IN at Naval Air Station Oceana in Virginia Beach felt
a little like coming home. For the first time in two years—an
eternity in a military career—I would be strapping into the cockpit
of an F/A-18 Hornet. Different seat, but the same magnificent aircraft. I was so familiar with the F/A-18 that much of the syllabus was
redundant to me. The one entirely new challenge would come at the
end of the training: night carrier landing qualifications. I had landed
a T-45 on a carrier, but only during the daytime, and the F/A-18 was
a faster, more complex, and more responsive aircraft. More important, night on the ocean redefines the depth of blackness. Flying
low at night, even without having to land on a ship heaving on the
waves, is the very definition of dangerous. Night carrier landings are
as much about overcoming your own fear and trepidation as about
mastering the technical proficiency.

I've always taken challenges as they come. I knew that experienced pilots with all the necessary skills sometimes washed out of the night carrier landing qualifications simply because they couldn't get beyond their own mental blocks. I wasn't going to worry about that until I was pointing my nose at the back end of a carrier. In the meantime, I was determined to enjoy my second time through the F/A-18 training squadron. It was easier than the first time. I knew the plane. I'd seen the amazing things it could do in the air, the extraordinary combat ability. Now the stick was in my hand, the beast entirely under my control. It was everything my fourteen-year-old self could have possibly imagined and then some.

I knew it would be a quick eleven months, but I wanted Monk and I to enjoy our free time as much as we could. I found a nondescript apartment in a huge complex at the northeastern tip of Virginia Beach, just south of First Landing State Park and a stone's throw from the beach. Monk and I got into a daily routine of running a mile and a half along the bike trail that wound through the weather-beaten spruce and pine trees in the wooded parkland. We'd slow our pace as we crossed the main road headed toward the Chesapeake Bay, then walk back along the beach.

Fall changed to winter almost in the blink of an eye. Monk and I continued to run our route along the now-deserted trail, returning along a windswept, driftwood-strewn shore in bracing cold. Erik was busy in New Orleans, but he flew up every chance he could. The damage from Hurricane Katrina was still apparent everywhere, and decent rentals were nearly impossible to come by. Erik ended up bunking in a trailer. It wasn't well suited to a couple's weekend, but it was great for him because it was on base and close to the squadron and the gym. Still, I had little desire to fly down and spend time there.

The Lockheed C-130 Hercules is a lumbering, reliable turboprop workhorse of an aircraft, essential to transporting troops and cargo all over the world. It is not a terribly complex plane to learn, but it is huge and difficult to handle in actual practice. That's why C-130 pilots largely train on the job. Erik was so busy flying actual missions around the world that we didn't have a lot of opportunities to spend time together. That meant my birthday that year was a special occasion for both us, a chance to share a long, leisurely few days together.

The one luxury in my apartment was a fireplace. So aside from walking Monk, we spent the whole time in my living room. Erik showed up with an unusual present—an M1 Garand. He knew that I had inherited a love of history from my father. The Garand was the standard-issue infantry rifle for American armed forces in World War II and the Korean War. The Department of Defense retired the weapon in the late 1950s and stored the remaining stockpile in Europe, in anticipation of future conflicts. The rifles were coated in a thick waxlike substance to prevent rust, wrapped in oilcloth, and boxed. By the Vietnam era, though, the M1 Garand was antiquated, having been replaced by the much more powerful and practical M4. The Pentagon decided to liquidate the inventory of M1s in 2006 and launched a program in which select veterans and active-duty personnel could apply for one of the rifles. Erik had filled out the paperwork and been approved. He didn't realize just how well prepared the weapons had been for storage. We spent some pleasant time together relaxing and cleaning the M1—letting the metal parts soak in aviation gas and running the wood stock through the dishwasher on cold cycle.

It was a lovely, low-key break that ended far too soon. Erik headed back to New Orleans, and I returned to honing my radar tactics and practicing "within visual range" dogfights. I learned the geometric precision of dive-bombing—flying at a steep thirty- or forty-five-degree angle toward the ground to bomb a small ground-based target. The classroom, simulator, and cockpit work kept me busy and engaged. All the while, I could feel the ultimate challenge lurking in the background. Finally, we wrapped up our training at Oceana, and it came time for night carrier landing qualifications.

Flying a fighter jet out over the ocean in the middle of the night is an ethereal experience. I pointed the F/A-18 to a bearing out in the imposing dark expanse. The sea was distinguishable from the night sky only because it lacked stars. It was utterly beautiful, mesmerizing, and—for a fighter pilot—incredibly dangerous terrain. I was headed to the USS *Enterprise*. The ship was the first nuclear-powered carrier ever built and was coming to the end of its life. The *Enterprise,* like all carriers, was absolutely massive. It could accommodate more than forty-five hundred crew members and featured a deck that was longer than two football fields laid end to end. Sixty aircraft could fit comfortably on the topside. For all that, the mighty vessel seemed toylike from ten thousand feet, an impossibly small landing strip in the dark. The sky around me was clear, but a waning moon shed little light. Piloting a jet screaming along at almost four hundred miles an hour, I was amazed at how quiet and mysterious the world outside my canopy seemed. The darkness was profound. I felt excited, but prepared. In reality, though, there is no way for a pilot to be completely ready for his or her first night carrier landing. There's no experience like it. It is the most intense and unforgiving challenge in combat aviation.

An F/A-18 pilot relies on navigation systems to get the craft lined up properly with the carrier and close enough to land by sight. The jet's onboard nav electronics sync with companion systems on the carrier. The primary system is called the automatic carrier landing system (ACLS). It is amazingly sophisticated, able to precisely guide a pilot through the dark into an appropriate glide slope until the pilot can actually see the "ball." The troublesome truth about complex systems like the ACLS is that they sometimes break down. The backup is called the instrument landing system (ILS). Cruder in practice, it is just as effective. Both systems require electronic communication between the jet and the carrier.

I had done night carrier landings in the simulator many times. After one of those sessions, I asked the LSO overseeing the training what would happen if the unthinkable occurred and both those systems went down.

"It's extremely unlikely."

"But what if it did?"

"You'd get lined up using the ship's TACAN, and you would use a step-down approach to find the ship."

TACAN, or tactical air navigation system, is an ultrahigh-frequency navigation system. It is not as user-friendly or as useful as either ACLS or ILS is for lining up a pilot's landing approach. It's not specifically meant for carrier landings; it was developed to establish the jet's bearings in relation to a stable, fixed point on the ground—not a moving aircraft carrier. It was designed as an approach system but not a precise landing system.

"Okay, but what if the TACAN went down, too?"

The LSO laughed.

"You wouldn't have any navigational aids at all, but that never happens."

"But if it did?"

He shook his head. "If it did, it would be a real emergency. You'd have to fly back to shore and land the plane using a ground-controlled radio approach. But I've never seen all three go down."

That night, as I flew out to the "boat," I realized that the ACLS (called needles) in my F/A-18 wasn't functioning. It didn't worry me, because I had the backup ILS (called bull's-eye) to rely on.

Having a navigational system is crucial in the dark. It's like having someone guide you through a pitch-black living room to the one easy chair. If they can get you there, you can discern enough to sit your butt down. At night, on the ocean, there is virtually no depth perception. All the visual cues I might have used in the daytime as I got in position to line up the ball were impossible to see. It was so dark that I couldn't make out the horizon line. Flying in on a landing approach, it would be incredibly difficult to visually discern between the back edge of the carrier, the water, and the sky.

Using my ILS, I made my first few "traps," landings in which I caught the wire. It was going well, and I was building confidence. I had three more traps to do for the qualification. The catapult shot me off into a black hole of nothingness, and I flew around into an approach run when I suddenly realized the ship's ILS was not linking with my onboard system. I switched to the third-string TACAN (called father), but that wasn't giving me any indication either. I turned it off and back on, hoping to "reboot" it. It still didn't come up. I calmed myself. Panic is never a pilot's friend.

I broke into my final approach, my nose pointed directly at the aft of the ship. I radioed the deck: "Negative father." The carrier's LSO didn't seem to totally grasp that what I was saying was that all three of my navigational systems were now inoperable. It was exactly the situation I had asked the LSO about after my simulator session, the one he assured me could never happen!

I radioed again. "Roman 35, negative father, negative needles, negative bull's-eye." That got the attention of the controllers in the carrier air traffic control center, and I was immediately vectored onto a carrier-controlled approach. The ship controller talked me down just like a precision approach, until about three miles out. From there, I maneuvered into the best glide slope I could with the radio help of the LSO, using what I had memorized as far as numbers for checkpoints. No one waved me off, so I continued. I approached the ship, got lined up, and could see the ball. I made the radio call, "Two oh one, Hornet Ball, 4.5, McGrath." The LSO came back, "Roger, ball." A few seconds later, I touched down and felt the jet come to an abrupt halt. I had hooked the wire.

There are judgment calls those in the military chain of command must make on the fly. How far do you go in testing warriors or pilots? What do you demand of them? How much risk is acceptable? Sometimes, the training that involves these calls is preparation for the fog of war. No situation is ideal, and you can't run from bad circumstances. The commanding officer of the training squadron had to make just such a judgment call in my case. Waste a lot of precious time, break my rhythm, and send me back to shore to switch jets? Or just allow me to continue and hope that I rise to the occasion?

As I was being moved to the catapult, I radioed the ready room and reiterated the fact that I had no navigational aids to the duty officer, who was an experienced F/A-18 pilot. He told me to stand by. A minute later, he came back on the radio. "Skipper copies. Launch and finish your final two traps." The "skipper" was the commanding officer. He was making a fog-of-war decision to let me prove myself under one of the most challenging situations a carrier pilot can face.

The catapult hurled me off the ship and into the pitch-dark sky. I was flying with no visual reference, relying purely on instrument readings and my own sense of where I was in space. I requested headings and distances from the ship's controller, which got me into the ballpark. I had no choice but to keep going, hoping I'd see the ship and get myself visually on the appropriate glide slope. At last, I saw the ball, called it, and was able to make another trap.

I had just one more trap to make to qualify. I got the go-ahead to catapult again into the darkness and make another approach to the "boat." All my nav systems still came up negative, but I had the confidence of already having done this before, twice. I was vectored into the approach by the ship and found the ball. I was so occupied with everything I had to process inside the cockpit that before I knew it, I felt the whiplash of the two wire catching my hook. It wasn't a perfect trap, but for strapping on a seventy-million-dollar jet and successfully landing it on a heaving carrier at 140 miles per hour, at night, in degrading weather, with no navigational aids . . . I'd take it. As quickly as I landed, I followed the plane director's night wand signals and taxied into the total darkness that would be my parking spot. As I powered the jet down, I took a moment to just breathe and let my adrenaline level come down. I climbed out of the cockpit, helmet and gear still on, and made my way belowdecks to the ready room for my debrief. My commanding officer was waiting for me.

"Krusty, I thought I was going to have to send you back to the beach to get another jet. Normally there is no way I'd let a nugget land without ACLS, ILS, or TACAN, but you kept managing to get yourself on board somehow. So I just let you keep going to see if you could get the qual. And you did! Nice work."

It hit me that if I had screwed up, lost my bearings and the horizon, I would have no normal cues to warn me and could have drilled my F/A-18 right into the back of the carrier or even crashed on the deck. I thought, "Should I be mad at this guy, or hug him?" Ultimately, though, I had the qualification. I had just put the finishing touches on my transition to the front seat of the F/A-18. I was a legitimate fighter pilot and done with carrier quals. I felt like King Kong.

I stayed the night on the carrier and flew back to Virginia Beach the next morning. I was still buzzing from qualifying, but there is an anticlimactic nature to the end of the F/A-18 training syllabus. There was no graduation ceremony. I had conquered a huge challenge and achieved a lifelong dream, but there was no fanfare. I quietly packed up my apartment and waited for my orders. When they came through, I was happy to be going back to familiar terrain: I was assigned to Miramar once again. Before I could head back to

San Diego, though, I'd have to handle yet another challenge—one of the hardest I would ever face: SERE training.

SERE stands for Survival, Evasion, Resistance, and Escape. Also known as survival school, it tests the individual in ways no other military training does. The school is meant to train service members who may see frontline combat and potentially be captured by the enemy. When I was first sent to Miramar, SERE wasn't mandatory. Back seaters were in such demand at that point that it was more urgent I get up to speed and combat ready than it was for me to attend survival school. After 9/11, though, SERE became mandatory for all combat troops.

The school teaches students methods and strategies for evading capture while staying alive in a hostile environment. You learn to navigate and return to friendly forces without starving to death or being killed by the elements. The school involves roughly a week of classroom training, followed by a week in the field. The second week is the toughest experience many students will ever face. It means going days without food while burning a lot of calories. The week ends with students doing a stint as prisoners of war in the school's mock POW camp (which is purposely made as close as possible to a real prisoner-of-war experience).

As the senior ranking officer (SRO) among the forty-five students in my class, I had responsibilities far beyond just getting through the course in one piece. I was in command of the platoon and had to set the example for others to follow. As usual, I was also keenly aware of my status as one of the precious few women in that class at SERE; I needed to set a good example for all the women who would come after me.

During an early classroom session, the instructor showed us how to field dress a rabbit. Because I was the SRO, he invited me to demonstrate eating the eyeball out of the skull. It wasn't really a request. I can tell you from experience, the texture of a rabbit's eyeball is even worse than the flavor. That early incident was a good indicator of what I was to expect from my SERE experience.

As we moved into the second week and out into the field, we organized into four squads. I commanded squad one, the next most senior officer commanded squad two, and so on. Each squad had to complete daily goals and exercises without giving their presence away and without the benefit of shelter or a ready source of food. Each student had a knife. Catch something crawling through the underbrush in the hot, scrubby California mountainside, kill it, and you could eat it. Otherwise, you went hungry. A lot of useful information is passed along, but the more powerful lessons you learn yourself. Who are you at your core? How far can you go before you break? How do you function when you're deprived of those most fundamental needs—food, water, and sleep? When you're stressed every moment? It was fascinating that in ways I would have said that I was strong, I was actually weak. In other areas where I thought I might lag, I surprised myself with reserves of strength and endurance. Such is the eye-opening nature of the SERE experience.

Other people surprised me as well. One of our first field exercises was night navigation to a tire that had been placed in the mountains. The tire was meant to represent a dead drop or evacuation point a downed pilot might have to reach. Although I'd gone through night navigation in TBS (including a remedial session after I failed the first time), I decided to delegate leadership of the exercise to someone I thought would be better suited to lead us.

My squad included an enlisted Navy SEAL. Although he was a lower rank than I was, SEAL training is the same for enlisted men and officers. It's legendarily difficult and encompasses many of the hardships students face in SERE. He seemed like the obvious choice to get us to that tire. I came to regret that decision.

The SEAL used a navigation method called terrain mapping, which basically involves running all over the place, covering a grid of potential locations until you find what you're looking for. The squad had already gone two days without food, and we were all weak. The hours of wasted effort, and the fact that we never found the tire, destroyed morale. A lot of heads were hanging by the next morning. I knew I had to do something different. Our instructors gave us a second chance to find the tire the next night. Rather than turn to the SEAL again, I decided to use what I'd learned in TBS. I opted for "straight-line" navigation, using a compass and crude map to draw a straight line to the objective. It would mean going over or through whatever lay between the squad and the tire. It took us three hours of painstakingly slow progress—largely because we had to be as silent as possible to avoid detection—but we finally found that cursed tire. The group was suddenly buoyed. More important, I cemented my legitimacy as a leader.

Although the training is a personal challenge, group cohesion is essential in SERE. The difficulty of going without food and being constantly uncomfortable and pushed to your limits often overwhelms the individual and gets inside a person's head. It is so easy to sink into yourself, to wallow in your own misery. The second-highest-ranking officer in my squad fell victim to that trap. He, too, was a Marine. In fact, he could have been a poster boy for the Marine Corps. He was tall, fit, and good-looking. I assumed he would ace survival training. Instead, after two days without food, he completely shut down. I had platoon responsibilities that required I leave him in charge of the squad for several hours. I briefed him on what needed to be done and expected I would come back to a squared-away squad. But when I returned, I was shocked to find that the squad had done nothing. My second-in-command, that picture-perfect Marine, was sitting under a tree with one boot on and one boot off, staring at the ground. He had simply switched off. I had no choice but to "fire" him. In his place, I put the responsibility on a slightly overweight, crusty, older navy chief. He was a civil engineer in the Seabees, the group in the navy that builds bridges and constructs military camps.

I told him, "Chief, the lieutenant's fired. He's checked out. He can't lead an ant to an anthill. You're in charge of the squad. Questions?"

He said, "No, ma'am, I'll get it done." And by God, he did. The lieutenant didn't seem to care. He had lost the ability to motivate himself, and we would have to drag him along as deadweight through the rest of survival school.

SERE wraps up with "capture" and imprisonment in a crude prisoner-of-war camp. It's meant to replicate the experience of being held by someone like the Taliban. Students have no idea how long the POW part of survival school will go on, which increases the psychological stress. There is also a modest amount of physical abuse. SERE school was the first time I'd ever been hit in the head, and it was an eye-opening experience. I had done well managing the lack of food and pure exhaustion and was proud of that. I assumed I could take physical punishment. I was, after all, larger than the average woman, and I had already completed brutal Marine Corps training. I had been in combat, and I had lived in harsh conditions in the middle of a desert. I had dealt with people yelling at me, berating me, challenging me. That was just about the sum of my first year at Annapolis. But that punch? It dropped me to the ground and filled my field of vision with tiny white explosions; I was literally seeing stars for the first time in my life. It dented my pride and made me feel weak. Nobody had ever before dominated me like that. The captor stood over me spewing insults. Weak from lack of food and heightened stress, I couldn't shake off the repeated blows. Finding out that I was not quite as tough as I had thought was yet another surprising discovery. It humbled me.

By the time we were all prisoners of war, our mental states were so compromised that it was hard to keep in mind that our captors wouldn't seriously harm us or even kill us. It was the culmination of survival school in every way. The point of SERE is not to train troops to hold out information or resist captors to the point of death. We learned that the goal was only to resist until you can't resist any longer. The instructors—and, more important, the actual former POWs who lectured the students at the end of SERE—were adamant that we were to come home alive with honor. If that meant you broke down and read something awful in front of a camera, the military and the country would forgive you provided that you resisted long enough. There is no extra badge of honor in coming back inside a body bag or never coming home at all.

Although SERE was only two weeks long, it had a profound impact on me. I came away from the experience with a new understanding of who I was in those dark places we rarely probe. There are questions we don't naturally ask of ourselves: How much pain, suffering, and discomfort can I stand? How will I hold up in the worst of circumstances, challenged to my very limits? Am I the person I believe myself to be?

Most people never go there because they don't particularly want to know the answers and because testing ourselves in extreme ways is unpleasant. But it was useful to discover my limits and find reserves of strength I hadn't known I possessed. My experience at SERE was one of the most intense I would have in the military. What I learned there would help me in future challenges as a Marine and with tribulations far beyond the military. At the end of those hellish two weeks, however, I was happy to be through it. I was happier still to head back to San Diego and return to doing what I did best—flying.

13

CHANGE IS A CONSTANT in any life. The change inherent in military life, though, is thoroughly unpredictable. You never have full control over the future, over what comes next. That's why career military officers look to create small pockets of stability in their lives, safe harbors they can legitimately call home. It can be a civilian husband or wife waiting patiently for you to return from deployment. More often, it's a physical structure that means so much more than wood, bricks, nails, and mortar. When I knew for certain I'd be headed back to Miramar, I hired a professional to redesign and remodel my condo in San Diego. I wanted someplace that felt like home, a comfortable sanctuary Monk and I could treat as our own safe haven.

I ached for somewhere quiet where I could work through everything I had experienced. It was the rare opportunity to press pause on life. I spent the first month back at Miramar on desk duty, at the Air Group's safety department, moving paper from here to there. I was waiting to be assigned to an operational squadron. My two possible landing spots were the Green Knights and the Red Devils. Both squadrons were deployed, so I wouldn't be given my orders until they returned. Whichever I wound up in, I would be there for three years. The office job afforded me the luxury of time to transition and to ponder life in general.

Iraq was still on my mind. It was becoming painfully clear that the reason for the United States going in there, the reason the Green Knights and the rest of the military had risked their lives—some dying in the effort—had been a lie. President Bush, Dick Cheney, and Secretary of Defense Don Rumsfeld had all misled the country. Worst of all, Colin Powell had aided them. I had no idea if it was an intentional mistruth or simply misrepresenting incomplete intelligence, but it was a bitter pill to swallow. It weighed on me, and it wasn't the only thing bothering me.

I was becoming increasingly frustrated that Erik and I couldn't be together. Holding together a long-distance relationship was much harder than I would have thought. I questioned what we were doing. Were we moving forward? Just treading water? I was thirty-two, old enough for it to feel as if a certain part of life were passing me by. Anyone who chooses a career in the military knowingly accepts a different day-to-day reality, a life of sacrifices. That doesn't mean you're not human, that you don't still hold the hopes and dreams anyone would keep in her heart. I knew that eventually I wanted a family and a partner in life. I wasn't sure Erik and I would ever get there.

Like so many puzzles in life, there were no clean and neat solutions for the thoughts that filled my head. At some point, I decided it would be best to just put them out of my mind and get down to business. That meant flying, so I was thrilled to receive my orders to the Green Knights once the squadron returned to Miramar. The posting was perfect. It was such a wonderful squadron with an amazing, storied history. I was proud to wear the knight chess piece badge once again. It was also a comfort; I was already familiar with the hangar spaces and the squadron's culture, and I was returning to the two-seat F/A-18 community. The other option had been a single-seat carrier squadron.

A month later, our commanding officer cycled out, and a new one took his place. Lieutenant Colonel Mark "Rosie" Palmer would wind up being one of my favorite commanding officers. I always appreciated strong, smart leaders, and he was an exemplary leader and communicator. He let everyone in the squadron know where he stood on any given issue that mattered. That was important because there were ongoing problems involving gender and the Marine Corps. Shortly after Colonel Palmer took command, a Marine Corps aviator in a sister squadron was accused of sexually assaulting a civilian woman. The Marine had met his accuser at a Marine Corps Ball; predictably, there had been a lot of drinking. What had actually happened was in dispute. The woman alleged date rape, and the case came down to he said, she said. The Marine was eventually acquitted, but it wasn't a good look for the corps. He was formally reprimanded for showing poor judgment and conduct unbecoming an officer. Colonel Palmer wasted no time in holding a squadron-wide meeting and laying out his take on the situation.

"I don't know all the details, but I'll tell you this—you wear this uniform. You're all officers. That means your behavior needs to be at a higher level than everybody else's in the world. I won't tolerate this type of thing in my squadron. Don't put yourself in that position, a place where it becomes 'he said, she said.' Because if you do, I ain't going to back you. You'll know what's coming, because I stood up here and told you."

The talk rubbed some of the aviators the wrong way, but the Green Knights would never deal with that type of problem after the colonel's speech. Whether they appreciated the sentiment or not, everyone knew where he stood. It was a good lesson, an example of how to be honest with people under your command. The hard truth is that as a leader you inevitably make decisions and take positions that someone under you doesn't agree with. It doesn't matter. You do what you believe is right, and you effectively communicate why. Above all else, you are honest, clear, and you don't waver. Leaders are strong and decisive about any serious matter.

Colonel Palmer wasn't taking a side, or saying anything in particular about that individual case or the Marine's guilt or innocence. He was just telling everyone exactly how he expected things to be. If any aviator decided to behave in a certain way, that officer wouldn't have any illusions about what was coming.

That moment in history was part of a long arc of change in Marine Corps culture. Although integrating women in combat forces was still relatively new, the corps had dealt with similar course corrections before. Right after I was first assigned to Miramar, there had been several high-profile DUIs involving Marines. The corps began to clamp down with severe penalties for any Marine caught drinking and driving. Despite a lot of grumbling, the policy drastically reduced the number of DUIs. I have absolutely no doubt that it saved lives and careers.

Change in a culture as rigid as the military happens quickest when it is championed from the top down. If high-ranking superiors champion a new direction, it happens quickly; otherwise, it tends to happen more slowly. I had to accept that from the very beginning of my career, right from my time at Annapolis. Day-to-day squadron life, on the other hand, was the opposite. It changes in the blink of an eye. You can establish your own routine, but you have to be prepared to upend it and attack a new mission. Shortly after I got my orders to join the Green Knights, we left Miramar once again. We began a string of exercises. Most were "red flag" joint forces war games we conducted with other squadrons and other countries in different areas of the United States and abroad.

We traveled from Nellis Air Force Base in Nevada to Eielson Air Force Base in Fairbanks, Alaska. In every destination, the exercises were all about combat readiness and cooperation. A red flag exercise is the opportunity to become intimately familiar with how allies and partners operate, to head off any mistakes or wasted effort that could occur in actual combat. Each exercise was a new challenge, different from any other.

It was a year of flying mock battles one after another. I saw Erik whenever I could, which was rarely. He was flying too, piloting C-130s carrying navy equipment like the navy's dolphins, military working dogs, vehicles, missiles, and personnel such as Navy SEALs all over the world. Our schedules left less and less time to see each other, and my frustration with the relationship continued to build. Erik would fly out to spend long weekends with me in San Diego on the rare occasion we both had leave or a break in our schedules. Those brief connections were not satisfying. It felt to me as if we were in some weird permanent holding pattern, never actually moving the relationship forward. I increasingly doubted whether we had a future together. During our rare time together, we talked and talked about the difficulties of the distance separating us. Talking didn't help; there were no easy answers.

I was promoted to major. I was proud of the achievement because the higher an officer goes in the command structure, the more stringent the requirements for promotion. Where the first two promotions a Marine officer gets—to first lieutenant and captain—are primarily awarded for time in grade, the ranks beyond are earned through a combination of time, qualifications, and achievements. Combat experience, performance reviews, and new training challenges all enter into the equation. I felt as if making major set a good example for the women who would come later. If I could do it, so could they. I was proof.

Each time an officer is promoted, he or she gets to decide on an appropriate ceremony. When I made captain, I had chosen to take my oath of office in flight, inside the cockpit of my F/A-18. The squadron's executive officer read my oath of office over the radio, and I repeated it back in a radio transmission. Then I had pulled the "1st Lieutenant" patch off my flight suit and slapped on a captain's patch.

I wanted to do something a little more traditional to mark my promotion to major. We held the ceremony in the squadron "Heritage Room" (the bar) at Miramar, with all the other Green Knights in attendance. The night was presided over by Colonel John "Pappy" Rupp, a senior pilot I'd flown with in Afghanistan and Iraq. I respected the colonel and was grateful he agreed to lead the ceremony. I took my oath once again, and then the colonel removed my captain's bars and replaced them with a major's gold oak leaves. Then, being Marine Corps aviators, we raised a glass or two.

My first order of business as a major would be a new and exciting adventure. After a year of flying various exercises, the squadron would deploy to Japan. It was an incredible opportunity to work with America's allies in the Pacific and to see parts of the world I'd never explored. I still didn't know what to do about my relationship with Erik, but I knew that in all likelihood, we wouldn't be seeing each other for the six months that I would be away. The more I considered it, the more it looked a lot like a natural point of resolution.

I took a week of leave to close up my condo, get my life in order, and fly Monk to Kentucky, where he'd stay with my parents. I also wanted to spend some time with my father, who was still dealing with the aftermath of his cancer and the surgery to remove it. I was relaxing at the end of the day when my cell phone rang. It was Erik.

"Hey."

"Hey. What's going on?"

"I'm in Cincinnati, at the airport. Can you pick me up?"

I had a flash of irritation. I wasn't in the mood for a surprise visit.

I was getting mentally prepared for Japan and was on the fence about what to do next in our relationship. Him being there wasn't going to make my thinking any clearer. My frustration had peaked, and it had begun to seem obvious to me that the only way forward was to break up. There in my childhood home, with my parents and Monk, I simply wasn't ready to face Erik and have what was surely going to be a brutal conversation.

"Sure. I'll see you in half an hour."

The ride from the airport back to my parents' house was awkward. I was preoccupied and couldn't bring myself to fake enthusiasm. I was so confused about my feelings. My faith had been of little help in figuring it out. If there were answers, they didn't lie in scripture and prayers. Really, though, I was beginning to suspect nothing about relationships was easy. I hadn't sorted out exactly what I wanted and was angry at Erik for showing up and forcing my hand. I didn't want to have "the talk" at my parents' house. I realized it was going to be uncomfortable and painful. When we got to the house, Erik asked me to go out in the backyard with him.

Having visited before, he knew perfectly well how special the backyard was to me. It was a large rectangular yard that abruptly sloped down into a steep hill from the back porch. I had broken my arm sledding down that hill. I played many games of tag there. As a kid, I sat out there dozens of times, staring at the star-filled Kentucky sky, just thinking about things. When I was facing a particular challenge or upset about something, I would head out back to sit in silence and pray. The backyard of my parents' house somehow felt closer to God, a place where—in my child's mind—He would hear me more clearly.

As Erik and I walked down the back porch stairs, he stopped and turned to me. He got down on one knee and pulled out a box. He flipped it open to reveal a gigantic diamond ring, sparkling even in the dim light.

"Amy, I want to spend the rest of my life with you. Marry me?"

My feelings and thoughts jumbled together—what I had been mulling over about ending the relationship, the frustration, and the surprise of a proposal I thought was long overdue. I was silent for much longer than Erik would have liked. I was seriously ticked off at him, dropping this bomb on me at my parents' house, right as I was getting ready to deploy. A minute turned into two. Still, I hadn't answered him or made a move to put on the ring. His smiled faded and he began to fidget.

Finally, I nodded. "Yes."

The relief washed over his face. I hugged him and then slipped the ring on my finger. It was audacious and it wasn't me; I'm not a fan of jewelry. But it was a gesture of Erik's love and now a sign of our bond. I thought, "Okay, this feels right. This is the right thing to do." We went inside and told my parents, who were as surprised as I was but delighted.

There was precious little time to process such a big life change. I was leaving for Japan in a few days, and Erik had to return to New Orleans the next night. We agreed on a date for the wedding the following year. I'd be back from my deployment, and we'd have a better idea of where we would both be posted. In the meantime, my mother and sister graciously—and even enthusiastically—took on the burden of planning the wedding in Kentucky. It was a good way to leave. Erik and I were no longer in limbo. I was headed to my first noncombat international deployment. I was suddenly upbeat and confident about everything.

Japan is a part of what is known as a UDP—Unit Deployment Program. Some troops are permanently stationed in places like Japan and South Korea, but their numbers are constantly supplemented by troops that cycle in and out. It's part of that exciting promise on recruitment posters across the country, to "see the world."

We would be based out of Marine Corps Air Station Iwakuni in the south of the mainland. We spent several months there, eventually moving to Okinawa and Kadena Air Base, where we would celebrate the Christmas holidays.

Iwakuni was an ideal spot from which to go sightseeing. It's a small city perched on Hiroshima Bay, about thirty miles from Hiroshima. Although my squadron duties and flying took up most of my time, I had the occasional weekend to see historical sites like Hiroshima itself. Walking through that city, one of only two to have ever been struck by a nuclear weapon, was a profound and moving experience. I wished that my father could have joined me, because he would have deeply connected to the historical and moral significance of the city.

I made a trip to Tokyo as well. It is a far different city from Hiroshima, more akin to New York City. Tokyo is incredibly crowded, hectic, and noisy. It is full of neon signs and traffic and pure sensory overload. It rivaled any of the world's big cities for sheer spectacle and wasn't really the type of place a Kentucky girl would be drawn to. Kyoto, with its craggy, ancient shogun's castles, was more my speed. Kyoto and Iwakuni offered a natural beauty that never grew old. Everywhere I went in Japan, the streets and public spaces were clean, neat, and orderly. The people were gracious and kind, even if I often felt like an Amazon around them. I can only imagine what they thought having a five-foot-eight-inch woman fighter pilot in their midst.

Christmas that year was the first I had ever spent on deployment. I had been fortunate that my deployments in Afghanistan and Iraq had all ended before the holidays. I was determined to make a Christmas away from home an enjoyable holiday for the Marines who reported to me. My parents, sister, and nephews joined forces to send me a small fake Christmas tree, along with a set of ornaments they had made by hand. I roped all my Marines into trimming the tree and decorating the squadron's shop. After we were done, we had the most festive space on base, and a lot of smiles came out of that. On Christmas Day, I took the junior Marines out for a five-course dinner at a cool local Japanese restaurant. The Sapporo and saki flowed freely, and everybody had a good time.

It wasn't long before the Green Knights were once again on the move. We headed to Guam for exercises, flying once again over the amazing emptiness of the Pacific Ocean. The sheer vastness of the water was at once awe inspiring and humbling. Even in a fast, powerful F/A-18, I felt small. If I went down in the endless ocean, the unfathomable deep and the ceaseless waves wouldn't care that I was a fighter pilot or an officer or engaged to be married. The ocean just *was*. It was a stunning reminder of the almost inconceivable breadth and scope of God's creation. It put faith in perspective to see so vividly how large the world was and how small and fragile we truly were.

We spent a lot of time over the ocean, eventually flying all the way to RAAF Base Tindal, in the Australian outback. The base was home to a Royal Australian Air Force F/A-18 squadron. It was the first allied F/A-18 squadron I'd ever flown with, and it was incredibly interesting to see the different techniques and approaches the Australians used in flying the jet with which I was now so intimately familiar. The air base is located in Katherine, in the Northern Territory. It's a desolate place. The location is incredibly remote and a hostile natural environment. The Northern Territory is populated mostly by bats, wallabies, and eight of the ten most poisonous snakes in the world. I tried to keep in shape by running in the cool dark of late night rather than the oppressive heat of day. I quickly ended that routine after I learned that the snakes came out at night by having some up close and personal moments with a couple large specimens.

The flying was some of the most enjoyable I had ever done. Much like Alaska, the outback has virtually no airspace restrictions. I could fly as fast, far, high, and loud as my jet would allow. I could break the sound barrier, which is prohibited almost everywhere in American airspace. Unlike the skies over a place like Nevada, I could fly and fly, without having to constantly turn back at the imaginary border of airspace. It was pure joy from a pilot's perspective.

I got to work with valued allies and fly over incredible places. I met wonderful people and did interesting work. Halfway through, though, I was struck by how much Erik was on my mind. He meant everything to me. I missed him terribly. Here I was doing what I had always dreamed of—flying the F/A-18 day after day. Still, I found myself focusing more and more on the magic of starting a life together with Erik, of growing old side by side. He was my future. Together we would build a family. I cherished the regular wedding updates my mom and sister sent me. One week, they decided on a marble cake that Erik and I loved. The next, they emailed images of the invitations and flowers they had picked out. The wedding became a reality, even though I wasn't there to do anything about it.

The wedding loomed large, but I increasingly thought more about the period right after, when we would have to figure out a way to be stationed near each other on our next tours of duty. Military bureaucracy has a way of complicating simple logistics, and the structure isn't built to accommodate couples. We'd have to move mountains to get what we wanted. Erik had already contacted his "detailer," the officer in charge of cutting orders for navy officers. As soon as the Green Knights returned to Miramar, I reached out to my "monitor," the Marine equivalent of a detailer. I had applied for a congressional fellowship that would take me to Washington, D.C. I knew that even if I didn't get it, there were several other options for me in D.C. I could go to Marine Corps headquarters in Quantico and to the Pentagon. I just needed to be sure that Erik would be wherever I was stationed.

Unfortunately, the different branches of the military sometimes don't play well together. Erik's detailer was set on sending him to

Pennsylvania or Texas, far from where I would be. Neither one of us wanted to give up a career just so we could be together, but we also weren't willing to give up each other for the sake or our careers. I had been singularly focused on my goal and on serving for so long, but now Erik meant more to me than the military. It seemed silly that we couldn't figure out a way to both serve the country and stay together. Finally, I asked my commanding officer to intervene. He put in a call to Erik's detailer and explained that it made no sense to lose two well-respected officers because of military bureaucracy. The detailer then made Erik a less-than-perfect offer.

If Erik was willing to do a nine-month tour in Afghanistan on what's known as an individual augment—essentially boosting troop levels for another arm of the military—he could come back and do a three-year tour flying out of Joint Base Andrews in Washington, D.C. We would be together. He agreed to a deployment with the army in Kabul. Shortly afterward, I was awarded the congressional fellowship. The plan was set. All he had to do was survive Afghanistan.

All things being equal, I would have spent the next nine months completing my tour with the Green Knights. I wanted to be nearer to Erik, though, and I saw a way I could do that and get more combat experience. I met with my commanding officer to discuss my idea.

"Sir, I know Third MAW [Marine Aircraft Wing] is going to Afghanistan, and I'd like to volunteer to deploy with them. If you can release me, I'll do the rest of this tour in Afghanistan."

"You sure that's what you want?"

"I'm positive, sir."

"Okay, Krusty, we can make that happen."

With that, it was set. Erik and I would return to the States within weeks of each other, find a place in Washington, D.C., and start the rest of our lives. We just had to make it through nine months of combat in Afghanistan. The only loose end left to tie up was the actually getting married part.

We were married on a beautiful, chilly December day in 2009. The service was held at St. Agnes, a Catholic church in Park Hills, Kentucky, near my old high school. It was a special church where my high school graduation ceremony had been held so many years before. Erik was in his navy formal white-tie mess uniform, and I wore a simple and stunning white bridal gown. It was a Catholic wedding ceremony, including biblical readings that Erik and I had selected together and that were read by our friends and family. A string quartet played beautiful classical music prior to the ceremony and the navy hymn—"Eternal Father, Strong to Save"—at the end. We actually had two priests presiding: Buddy, my mother's cousin; and Father Warren, a longtime close friend of my father's. My sister, Jane, was a lovely matron of honor, and Erik's best friend from high school, Chris, was his best man.

The reception was held at Drees Pavilion, a large reception hall atop a hill in the center of Covington's Devou Park. The view was breathtaking from the pavilion, overlooking the Ohio River and the Cincinnati skyline. My mom and sister had honored my request to decorate in red and gold, a nod toward the Christmas season and the Marine colors. Our family members far and wide made the trip to celebrate with us, and it was a huge gathering. Despite his difficulties speaking, my father gave a wonderful speech at the rehearsal dinner, and the reception capped a happy whirlwind of a day. It was as close to a dream wedding as it could be and was the best day of my life.

We had precious little time for a honeymoon. We were married on the nineteenth, and I desperately wanted to spend Christmas with my family—something I had missed the year before. Erik had to check in with the army at Fort Jackson in South Carolina right after New Year's to get ready for deployment. But he surprised me with a three-day trip to Wyoming. He splurged on a resort called Amangani, the most beautiful place I'd ever stayed. We snowshoed for long hikes across fields of virgin snow, took a snowmobile trip through Yellowstone, which was impassable by car, and had a wonderful time. All too soon, we were back in Kentucky for a quick Christmas, followed by a rushed goodbye at the airport. The next time we would see each other would be in the dusty, dangerous provinces of Afghanistan.

14

HELMAND PROVINCE, Afghanistan, looked a lot like Al Jaber, Kuwait, from the air base tarmac. The brutal sun and gusts of sand-filled hot air blowing through the flat grid of tents had a familiar feel, but my time at Camp Leatherneck would be a world apart from my previous deployment. To start with, I wouldn't see the inside of an F/A-18 cockpit the entire time I was in Afghanistan. Instead, I would be a ground-based problem solver. As a major who had seen two tours of combat, I was a seasoned veteran and an experienced military asset. Officers rising up the ladder of command are called upon to tackle increasingly complex assignments and higher-level responsibilities. I had to go where I was needed and do what was best for the military. So rather than flying missions one by one, I'd be planning and coordinating air attacks. Instead of sitting in briefings, I'd be briefing ground unit planners. In place of the cramped confines under a fighter canopy, I'd be parked on a folding chair in a sweltering operations tent in front of a laptop. I didn't have just one mission; I was given multiple overlapping responsibilities that kept me busy every moment.

Erik had a similar workload. He was stationed at Camp Eggers, four hundred miles to the north. He had already been there for a month before I arrived, and had his hands full managing search-and-rescue operations. He had a tougher time than I did because beyond his responsibilities he had to fit into the much different culture of the army. In contrast to the navy, army structure and protocols were much more rigid. The hectic pace we shared ensured that although we were only separated by a short, quick flight, we wouldn't have a lot of opportunities to spend time together. Newly deployed trumped newly wed.

Although I had a boss who lobbied for me to be sent to Kabul anytime a Marine aviation liaison was needed there, Erik and I saw each other a grand total of four times during the six months I was in Afghanistan. They were all quick meetings. We grabbed either dinner in the chow hall or a latte in the coffee tent next to Kabul International Airport. It was nice to at least get the chance to talk to him face-to-face, but we both were looking forward to the moment when we could sit down across from each other and eat a leisurely dinner in our own home. That magical moment seemed far away.

Home was a topic that was always on my mind in Afghanistan. I was getting rid of one even as I did my tour of duty. It didn't make sense to hold on to my condo in San Diego if Erik and I were going to start a new life in Washington, D.C. So I contacted a real estate agent who specialized in working with deployed military members. I had a moment of wistful nostalgia but quickly got over it. As an active-duty officer, I knew it wasn't wise to become too attached to any one place. In any case, home for me would ultimately always be Kentucky. More important, home meant people, not a structure.

Although I wasn't seeing the person who would become my flesh-

and-blood embodiment of home, we were able to regularly talk over the Secret Internet Protocol Router Network. The network is a classified communications system military members use; it allowed us to speak openly about what we were working on, something that most deployed personnel can't do with their spouses. As frustrating as it was not being able to spend more time with Erik, I had to remind myself that we were luckier than most military spouses. We were in the same time zone and could discuss anything we wanted to talk about. If either one of us had been a civilian, much of that would have been classified and out of bounds for discussion.

We certainly had a lot to talk about. My primary role was to act as a liaison between the air wing and ground units. Military and combat operations often look orderly from the outside, but on the ground in a foreign country it's a constant struggle to ensure that everyone knows what everyone else is doing. I would eventually log thousands of miles traveling to forward operating bases to meet with ground forces. I briefed ground Marines and operations officers on the air-attack resources available to them and the best ways to use those assets. I assisted in planning fixed-wing and helicopter missions in support of ground troops and offered my expertise on air combat capabilities. All that was just one aspect of what I was called upon to do.

The more frustrating responsibility that had landed on my shoulders was coordinating logistics for the Afghan National Army. Afghanistan had nothing that could be called an air force. Moving Afghan National troops anywhere was an ordeal, made even more so because regulations strictly limited how the American military could assist in transporting allied troops. There were Catch-22s aplenty.

At one point, I needed to get a unit of Afghan troops from a forward operating base back to Kabul so they could take leave and see their families. Unfortunately, the rules clearly required that anybody setting foot on a U.S. C-130 in a war zone be outfitted with a helmet and body armor. Other regulations prohibited U.S. soldiers from lending or giving their armor or helmets to partnered forces. That meant we couldn't get the Afghan fighters from the front lines because they weren't allowed on a transport flight without full-body armor, and we couldn't lend them the body armor they needed because other rules prohibited that. These guys had been in the fight a long time, sometimes months or years. Many hadn't ever had a break to see their families. It was a matter of morale to try to get them home for a week or two, and I almost couldn't pull it off. Nobody in the chain of command wanted to violate regulations, so I spent a lot of time trying to create work-arounds.

Hour after hour I sat at my crude desk in the operations tent working a battered phone to craft solutions. It was equal parts challenging, frustrating, and rewarding. As with every assignment in a combat zone, the long hours were made more pleasant thanks to Marine camaraderie. I sat next to Lieutenant Colonel Mario "Sugar Bear" Carazo. Sugar Bear was a helicopter pilot who regularly flew AH-1W Cobras on missions out of Camp Bastion.

Everyone liked Sugar Bear. He was a solid Marine, with a wrestler's build and an infectious smile. He was more politically conservative than I was, and we had spirited but respectful arguments about issues of the day. He was down to earth and commonsensical, and one of the hardest-working Marines I had ever come across. Not all officers were comfortable working next to a woman, but Sugar Bear never made me feel like anything but a fellow officer. I respected his work ethic and decency, and I used "sir" when I addressed him, even though he was not my boss and only a rank above me and he addressed me with my call sign. Friendships with fellow Marines are crucial to keep your bearings in a place like Helmand Province. I valued those relationships and was thankful to have three or four Marines like Sugar Bear that I worked with every day.

When work took me out of the tent, I was exposed to the complexity of day-to-day life in Afghanistan. Like so much that happens in the Middle East, that war was no simple conflict. We were bogged down in something halfway between a conventional war and building a nation-state from scratch. The American military is the best in the world in conducting warfare. War can be, in a way, simple. Identify the enemy, plan an attack using your available resources in the best possible way, and destroy the enemy. However, the American military, for all its might and superiority, is not well suited to the various imprecise demands of statecraft and nation building. We were not especially effective in securing civilian populations and nurturing the Afghan government's ability to provide services to its citizens. We had no answer for endemic corruption and a centuries-old tribal system that made regional warlords more powerful than the national government. That's not even considering the great stumbling blocks of vast and deep cultural differences. My assignments in Afghanistan gave me the opportunity to see firsthand the damaging effects America's actions had on everyday Afghans.

One of my best friends from flight school, Natalia, was running the military hospital at Camp Bastion. Camp Bastion was right next to Camp Leatherneck, so I visited her often and saw the heart-wrenching cases she dealt with. Most of the injured were seriously wounded soldiers. Many of the patients had lost limbs in explosions or were fighting to survive multiple gunshot wounds. Because U.S. forces are bound by strict ethical rules of engagement, the hospital's patients included some enemy combatants. Even knowing that, it was odd to see some local recovering from surgery handcuffed to his gurney.

The hospital was a stark accounting of the actual human cost of war. Most of the patients were Afghan, British, and U.S. military. There were, however, many civilians who had gotten caught in cross fire or been blown up by IEDs. They were people who had simply been in the wrong place at the wrong time. I tried to help Natalia

etting my pilot's wings in 2006 was a high point of my military career. My mentor and USNA onsor, Sandy Coward, was able to attend the ceremony.

y pilot's winging ceremony would not have been complete without my parents by my side.

My wingman took this photo as I flew over Denali, in Alaska, during red flag exercises. There are moments in a fighter jet cockpit when you get to experience the astounding beauty and wonder of the world from 25,000 feet above it.

The sword arch is a tradition for military weddings, and ours was conducted by friends from all four branches of the military.

Newlyweds!

Erik and I on our honeymoon in Jackson Hole, Wyoming, in 2010. It was way too short, but we managed to pack in a lot of snowy fun.

Erik and I got to see each other several times during our Afghanistan combat tour. Here, we spent a couple of hours together in Kabul, in 2010.

The women Marines of the Green Knights in 2009, out of more than 130 aircrew and maintainers.

My work at the Pentagon left me free time to enjoy a few long hikes with Teddy.

Getting my master's degree while working full-time at the Pentagon meant long nights and weekends studying . . . often with my infant, Teddy, for company.

One of the first family photos we took after I retired from the Marine Corps and we moved back to Kentucky, 2017.

Teaching a class in national security and WMDs to a room full of midshipmen at the U.S. Naval Academy in Annapolis, Maryland, 2015.

Christmas 2016 was a holiday full of family—Ellie, Teddy, and George.

Vice President Joe Biden was gracious in meeting Erik, the kids, and my mom backstage at my Bath County, Kentucky, campaign rally in 2018.

I was honored to have future president Joe Biden speak at one of my campaign rallies, in Bath County, Kentucky, during my 2018 congressional campaign.

With Mark Putnam, the producer of my campaign video ads. Behind us, the nose of an F-4 Phantom—not the aircraft I flew, but a spectacular fighter jet in its day.

A Senate campaign event, pre-pandemic. Here a meet-and-greet at a coffee shop in Bowling Green, Kentucky, with a café table as an impromptu stage.

The sheer beauty of the Appalachian Mountains wasn't lost on me on this rare vacation with Monk and Erik in 2007.

process all the pain and suffering she was seeing, but I had my own mental struggles.

Four months into my tour, I was sent to Bagram Air Base to join a review board charged with evaluating the status of Afghan detainees being held at the Parwan Detention Facility. Parwan was part of the oddness inherent in the Afghan conflict. Prisoners were not classified as prisoners of war, but they also weren't considered civilian criminal offenders. They were trapped in between, and the particulars of each case reflected that ambiguity. Reviewing detainee files left me frustrated and conflicted. There was a profound disconnect between the Afghan population and the U.S. military presence in the country. That gap created untold suffering.

The three-member review board was supposed to impose something resembling a system of justice, but the process was backward. The detainees had already been caught and imprisoned without trial or due process. We were giving them a hearing after they had already spent significant time behind bars. There was precious little time for anyone to properly prepare for hearings, and only cursory representation for the detainees. None of us on the board were JAGs (military lawyers); we were all operational officers using our best judgment and intentions. Prisoners sometimes had family members and local imams appear and speak up on their behalf but more often had nobody to testify for them. I spent a month at Parwan and reviewed about eighty cases. None were clear-cut. I'm not sure that we ever achieved true "justice," or that it was even possible in that time and place.

One of the first cases I reviewed was a seventeen-year-old boy who had been arrested and imprisoned the year before. On its face, the case seemed open-and-shut. Investigators had received a tip that led them to an unexploded IED under a bridge. They were able to recover the explosive and run forensic tests on it. They found the boy's fingerprints all over the tape used to bind the device. The boy, who had lost both his parents when he was fourteen and had no siblings, was arrested and incarcerated at Parwan.

As I dug down into the background paperwork, the complexity of the case became obvious. Orphaned at an age when many of his peers were getting married, he faced an uncertain future. He was scratching out an existence, and all he had to his name were two goats. He was desperately trying to pull together the money to buy a wife and start a family. One day, someone came to him and told him that if he planted the device under the bridge, they would give him enough money to buy a wife. They were offering him a future. This boy wasn't trying to kill Americans. The fact was, he didn't understand what America was or what the conflict in his country was about. He was just desperate, and someone offered to pay him a great deal of money to do something simple. On the other hand, he wasn't trying *not* to kill Americans either. To all outward appearances, he wasn't concerned about what would happen after he planted that device. I think he fully understood that it was a bomb. He was just focused more on improving a hellish life than on what damage that IED would do.

Like so many of his countrymen, he could think only of survival. That had become the overarching goal for most civilians in Afghanistan. It was an unbelievably hostile place. If cooperating with American authorities meant survival, so be it. If doing a small favor for someone you knew to be Taliban meant survival, so be it. The whole goal was to make it through the day and wake up the next day. Another day, another week, another month. What would any of us choose to do in the same circumstances?

It was a question that haunted me throughout my time at Parwan. There were precious few viable options open to Afghan civilians. They had become a nation of survivors. They didn't really understand, most of them, what America stood for. They weren't craving democracy. They were hungry and scared and often had only the hope that tomorrow would be slightly better. They knew that the Taliban hated America and that America—and other countries like it—had come into their country to eradicate the Taliban. That was the sum of what most people on the ground in Afghanistan understood. More important to them was just to get by and avoid getting killed.

Unfortunately, the hardest question we had to ask ourselves, those of us sitting on that board, was what happens if we release this person? It was easy to have compassion for a young, foolish kid who did something stupid out of desperation but without malice. The harder duty was to determine if, given the chance, he'd do the same thing tomorrow. Was he a risk? After all, now he had no goats, and he still needed to buy a wife. We had soldiers to protect.

There wasn't an easy choice to be made at Parwan. Each case presented a new moral quandary, another soul-searching ethical question. The decisions we made one way or another could easily result in the loss of life. It constantly weighed on me.

This was a key difference between Afghanistan and my previous deployments in Kuwait and Kyrgyzstan. Flying missions in an F/A-18, I was singularly focused on the target. A building, a bridge, an enemy base camp. I'd drop a bomb, fly back to base, and debrief. Now I had a broader, more personal, and more troubling set of responsibilities. I was seeing in person the grief and misery that was Afghanistan. I was struggling with a reality, a problem that had no easy resolution if it had a resolution at all. You can't bomb your way out of a moral quandary. You can't shoot through cultural differences that many military commanders didn't even understand, much less acknowledge.

I felt an obligation to be conscientious in my work at Parwan. I wanted to provide some semblance of justice, some dignity and honor. I kept a journal of all the cases I reviewed and what I came to know about each prisoner. I couldn't record their names or specifics such as locations because that information was classified, and I couldn't have it floating around in a journal. But I wanted to capture the stories as best I could to at least acknowledge that each prisoner was a person and had a right to his story. The Christian in me had to pay due respect to the belief that each person's life mattered, even as the Marine in me had to ensure that no individual went free who posed even a modest danger to U.S. forces.

Returning to Camp Leatherneck and visiting Natalia—and seeing a new crop of horribly injured Marines and British soldiers— I found it increasingly difficult to make sense of what we were doing in Afghanistan. My time on the review board, the endless cases I read through, had convinced me that the Taliban were just hiding and waiting for us to leave. They had been there long before we arrived, and no matter what we did, they would be there when we left. The only option seemed to be not leaving at all. The idea of staying in that brutal country, sending Marines on endless patrols down dusty dangerous streets in one more hostile small town or village, risking getting blown up or shot, seemed so pointless. We could execute countless raids, take over thousands of villages, but to what end? Sure, we could spray herbicides or unleash fields of fire to destroy the poppy industry and undercut the Taliban's drug revenue, but who was going to help the Afghan families who would lose their only source of income? Most Afghans knew nothing about America or democracy. Most couldn't read or write. How were we to give them the gift of freedom, of a modern representative government? How did we know they even wanted it or would accept it?

Parwan stayed in my mind as I returned to my desk in the operations tent, planning the next briefing and then the next. Day after day, I sat there still bothered by the paradox of that awful prison. I was sitting at my desk one morning when another Marine major I worked with came into the tent and stood there staring at me, a worried look on his face.

"Sugar Bear's not back."

"So?"

He had a haunted look in his eyes. "No, you don't understand. Sugar Bear's not back. He hasn't landed. He should have been back by now."

It dawned on me exactly what he was saying. Sugar Bear had been out on a mission, and he was late returning. Everyone in the tent began to worry, but I thought, "Missions sometimes take longer than expected. Helos break down all the time. There might be an easy explanation."

An hour later, we received word from Sugar Bear's squadron that a helicopter was missing. The tent became quiet. We all tried not to think the worst. Then we got news that an AH-1W Super Cobra had been brought down by a rocket-propelled grenade. We knew. Shortly thereafter, we got the news no one wants to hear.

"Sugar Bear's gone."

Sugar Bear and his co-pilot had been killed in action. I got up from my desk, walked out of the operations tent, and made my way to the chapel tent. I went in and knelt and prayed. What else could I do at this moment but pray to the God I knew, to honor the Catholic that Sugar Bear had been? We were Marines, and Marines died doing their duty, but that thought provided no relief and did not help me make sense of Sugar Bear's death. So I prayed and prayed.

Late that night, far after midnight, I went out to the tarmac to bear witness as they loaded the box with Sugar Bear's remains onto the C-130 that would carry him home for the last time. Inside a plain, utilitarian coffin lay the remains of Lieutenant Colonel Mario "Sugar Bear" Carazo. Like me, he was a graduate of Annapolis. He was a proud Marine officer who served his country with distinction and did his job and his duty well. He was a no-nonsense man who could be tough but often flashed a thousand-watt smile. Although he could be gruff and didn't shy from an argument, his voice would change noticeably when he made his nightly call to California. He would speak softly, gently to his wife, Jennifer, and to the children he so clearly adored. Sugar Bear was a family man through and through. He was also the first member of his Costa Rican immigrant family to be born in the United States, and he didn't speak English until after he began elementary school. He was enormously proud to serve the country he loved and hoped to follow in the footsteps of John McCain, a man whose values he held dear. He was my friend.

Now everything he ever was or ever would be was contained in a simple flag-draped box. I couldn't help but ponder those questions that eventually haunt every warrior in a combat zone: Why? Why did he have to die? What are we even doing here?

Sadly, in a misbegotten country of relentless heat, sand, blood, and ancient hatreds, there are no satisfying answers to those questions. Just as I had struggled with all that I had done in Iraq, I was having a hard time coming to grips with the war we found ourselves in, the conflict that was laying waste to an already godforsaken place. I had learned a lot about Afghan culture, and I knew that the population was going to do whatever was necessary to survive. It wasn't about ideology for those people. It was about getting to tomorrow. I couldn't reconcile why that meant that Sugar Bear had to die. It was so utterly pointless.

The next morning, I returned to my desk and struggled to focus on my work. I felt sadder than I ever had in uniform. Two Marines came in with brown boxes. They cleaned out Sugar Bear's desk, carefully separating anything that might be classified from his personal possessions. They packed up everything that was distinctly his. They sent those boxes, the last traces of Sugar Bear, off to his widow and children.

Afghanistan wasn't Vietnam or Korea. It wasn't Normandy. It couldn't even be called a proper war. We took far fewer casualties, but that didn't mean some didn't die. Those casualties were just largely invisible to the people back home, unless you were the one who got the box of belongings or the call from the casualty officer or chaplain. In country, though, we were all aware that every day presented deadly risk. We carried that awareness and worried about one another. Erik worried that I would be shot down by a rocket-propelled grenade on my way to a forward operating base. I feared that he would be blown up by an IED as his convoy traveled through Kabul, which it so often did. In the end, our fear didn't matter. We had our duty to do, and we did it. We were thankful when the tour came to an end and we headed home, keeping those we had lost forever in our hearts and minds.

15

SHIFTING GEARS from the ever-present danger of a combat zone to the familiar safety of America should be a welcome change, but it is psychologically disorienting. I had been in a heightened state of alert for more than six months. You rewire yourself to be ready to react at any second to the worst of circumstances. Many veterans returning home from combat deployments are often jumpy and impatient, even when they are processing their experiences in a healthy way. The sad truth is, though, all too many don't have the tools to properly work through everything they've seen and done. Self-medication is common. Divorce and suicide are serious problems.

I wasn't immune to that stress. Although I had my faith and a strong support system in my family and friends, my third combat tour had been the roughest emotionally and spiritually. I had seen so much suffering, such frustratingly intractable problems, that I was a little overwhelmed. It's easy to fall into the trap of feeling as if the bad in the world blots out the sun. I was also still grieving Sugar Bear. Saying a final goodbye to someone you've served alongside, someone you shared a profound sacrifice with, is brutally hard. Sugar Bear's death had been the very definition of senseless, but it's only human nature to try to find some sort of logic in traumatic events. I badly wanted an explanation. I knew I had to make my peace with that death, but it wasn't a process I would get to rush.

I flew home on a chartered commercial flight. We stopped to refuel in Pease, New Hampshire, at the Portsmouth International Airport. As we got off the plane to stretch our legs, we were greeted by dozens of well-wishers who just about filled the tiny airport. They applauded and shouted their support for all of us service members. It was a moment of tremendously mixed emotions. I was wrestling with the contradictions of being proudly American yet knowing that we were responsible for some of the desperate conditions in Afghanistan. It had been so hard to find anything hopeful in that country. Suddenly, though, there were these people, these bighearted American citizens giving me and my fellow service members the most wonderful gift I could have imagined. They were offering us the compassion, humanity, and generosity that was in woefully short supply in Afghanistan. It could not have been a better boost for my morale.

I thought about the reception Sugar Bear must have gotten for his return. I could only imagine that homecoming, so full of devastating pain and heartache. My eyes filled with tears. I avoided talking to anyone for fear I would break down. I had to hold it together, but I was more grateful to all those well-wishers in Pease than I could have ever expressed.

As we flew the last leg of the flight home to San Diego, I felt a tangible ache. I wanted to be coming home to Erik, to know that both of us were safe. I wanted to get started on our life together. A new beginning would put Afghanistan behind me and start both of us on a path to something brighter and more positive. Unfortunately, Erik was still finishing his tour in Kabul. I made an effort not to think about exploding IEDs and RPGs, not to let the danger he was still facing every day worry me. Instead, I told myself over and over—almost like a mantra—that he would be home soon. I walked off the plane to the sight of my mother and father waving like crazy. I held them both tight for the longest time. We posed together under a banner welcoming my unit back to Miramar. If I couldn't be with Erik, it was the next best homecoming.

The following day I turned in my combat gear and began the reintegration process. The military has learned from bitter experience to be careful with individuals returning from combat zones. They do everything they can to head off potential problems, from substance abuse to suicide. I was required to go through a standard protocol that included medical and psychological tests. The process would take almost two weeks. I took the opportunity to get my new orders squared away and to say my goodbyes to my neighbors in San Diego. I visited Mona and Homan and my other San Diego neighbors, and took one last look at the condo that had been such a great home for Monk and me.

Once I satisfied all the integration requirements, I took a few days of liberty and flew to Baltimore to be at the airport when Erik landed. I wanted his homecoming to be special, something memorable that would put the war behind us and focus on our future together. The best way to do that was to embrace the role of military spouse. I went to the local Macy's and bought myself a dress. I'm a Marine, not someone who normally wears dresses, but I knew that Erik would love it. I picked out an understated pink-and-peach number. His parents, brother, and I gathered at the airport. Seeing him come off the plane in his army fatigues was a tremendous relief. I could let my guard down and officially stop worrying. Our life together could now begin.

We spent the next two days unwinding and enjoying being together after so long. Then Erik had to fly to South Carolina to turn in his combat gear and process through his own return protocol. I flew back to San Diego and wrapped up all the details that go into a cross-country move. Erik joined me when he was done processing back into the navy. We packed up my forest green Nissan Xterra with what little luggage we'd need for a lazy, meandering road trip. We had taken almost a month of leave and planned on driving across the country to our new postings in Washington, D.C. I was looking forward to a short break from the military and thoughts of Afghanistan. I wanted to rediscover the wonders of America, to have an adventure that would rival the memorable family vacation we had taken when I was ten.

We weren't in a rush and drove a winding route across the breadth of America. We didn't fret about the next mission or the last. We simply focused on the moment, the day ahead, and the road right in front of us. We car camped more often than not, ate some not terribly healthy but thoroughly satisfying diner food, talked to people everywhere we went, and were happy. We packed in every scenic location and attraction we could visit. After so long in a war zone, we wanted nothing more than to be tourists. We had no demands other than a date we had to report for service in D.C. It was a one-of-a-kind chance to indulge my love of wild spaces. We hiked the dusty, rust-colored paths of Arches National Park, took in the breathtaking views offered in Utah's Canyonlands, and wandered among the spiky rock formations that mark Bryce Canyon National Park. We crossed the majestic Rockies that seem to touch the sky in places and visited relatives in Breckenridge, Colorado. We kayaked, hiked, and rode bikes to town. We attended Breckenridge's Oktoberfest celebration and took away souvenir beer mugs.

We drove to Milwaukee, Wisconsin, where we toured the Miller brewery and spent a night so that I could catch the Cincinnati Reds play the Brewers. It was a losing effort, but it was good to see my favorite team in person. In Chicago, we sat right behind home plate at Wrigley Field, something I had always wanted to do. We had drinks on the ninety-fifth floor of the John Hancock Center, taking in a horizon that I could have sworn included the curve of the earth. We even found time to tour Frank Lloyd Wright's Robie House and visit the Rockefeller Memorial Chapel.

That month offered us the chance to tick item after item off our "bucket list." It was also the opportunity to reconnect with the familiar. We made our way to Kentucky, where we picked up Monk and stayed with my parents for the better part of a week. Then we drove to Hagerstown, Maryland, to give Erik's family equal time.

We ended that glorious trip in Arlington, Virginia, at the doorstep of a modest two-bedroom furnished rental apartment in Pentagon City. It would be the launchpad for our new life, and I was even more excited than I had been when we first set out. It was a new beginning with untold promise stretching out before us.

I assumed my new role as a congressional fellow, while Erik reported for duty at Joint Base Andrews Naval Air Facility. We ate dinner together almost every night, finally able to have leisurely conversations face-to-face rather than quick chats over a secure line. Although our jobs kept us busy, we had more free time than we had ever enjoyed in our military careers. We were keenly aware of how unique that particular point in our personal history was. We knew that we were going to have kids, but in Arlington we were a newly married couple with two incomes and time to spend the money. We took advantage of all that D.C. had to offer. We split Nationals season tickets—choice seats right behind home plate—with three other couples. We made a point of going out to eat a couple times a week; we tried to hit all of the restaurants on *Washingtonian* magazine's top 100 list. I rediscovered my golf game, and Erik and I made a group of new friends.

We also splurged on a real, honest-to-goodness honeymoon in France. We started with a biking tour through the incomparable Loire valley. Each day for a week, we would enjoy a light breakfast of croissants, fresh fruit, and incredible coffee. Then we'd jump on our bikes and ride mile after mile through a lush, picturesque country-side, passing loamy fields full of cream-colored cows under a cloudless sky, stopping at a medieval castle, or a museum, or a winery. We pedaled and pedaled. Fifty miles later, bone tired and incredibly happy, we would end up at a new hotel or château right at cocktail hour. We'd have just enough time to get cleaned up and sit down to yet another in a string of four-course meals. We'd linger over espressos, planning our sightseeing for the next day.

It would have hardly been a French honeymoon without a few days spent in Paris, and we tacked on a few days in Normandy, where the D-day troops had landed and fought so valiantly. We ventured to Mont Saint-Michel, the incredible island commune where an ancient abbey stands. It was a memorable, once-in-a-lifetime trip.

We found a wonderful house to buy in Alexandria. Erik and I were drawn to the idea of a permanent residence and all the security it implied for someone in the military. We found a small, redbrick Georgian well within our price range. It sat at the top of a hill in a quaint tree-lined neighborhood. The property wasn't huge, but it backed up to a quiet wooded area. Monk was showing his age, so he wouldn't be exploring the woods or anything much beyond our living room, but the trees made for a lovely view.

The house was tiny, cozy, badly in need of repair, and ideal for us. The location couldn't have been better. We were close to the Pentagon and Old Town, and our neighborhood had a warm family feel. We quickly made friends up and down the street. There was something almost tangibly satisfying about having a true home once again. That undersized brick three bedroom would serve as a happy, comfortable place we could come back to each night and simply enjoy our life together. It was the ideal calm, restful sanctuary to balance my time in the Capitol. That was essential, because Congress was a strange and oddly intense place, unlike anywhere I had ever worked before.

I was assigned as a fellow to Congresswoman Susan Davis's office. She represented California's Fifty-Third District in San Diego and was a high-ranking member of the House Armed Services Committee. She also turned out to be one of the finest public servants and people I ever had the privilege to meet, as well as the first and only female boss I would have as a Marine. She cared about "doing the right thing." Even when it was the hard thing to do.

I saw the fellowship as a unique opportunity to not only exercise my expertise in service of Congresswoman Davis but also learn and grow in exciting new ways. The congresswoman wasn't quite sure what a fellow could do for her, and I didn't have a brief to go on. That left me a lot of latitude. I was intensely curious about the workings of the federal government. I still felt the sting of Iraq, of the political nature and reasoning behind that war. I continue to puzzle over how we—my country, my leaders, my military—could have begun a war where real people lost limbs, did awful things, and even died, all based on a callous lie. How could a nation that was supposed to be so transparent and righteous do that? I wanted to find the point of breakdown, to root it out at least for myself. I wanted to discover if any of our leaders, in Congress or the executive, understood how traumatic it was to kill someone. Did they have an idea what it meant to go to war? I still nursed feelings that ranged at times from naive disbelief, to ferocious anger, to a pressing desire to influence policy making. I came at the fellowship with a fairly new and strident skepticism. I had lost the blind faith I had in our leadership early in my military career. No longer would I just believe the four-stars or the political leaders. No longer would I assume they had more or better information than I did, or that their intentions were always pure and right. I was determined that when life-changing decisions were being made, the country's leaders would have someone in the room who had been there, had been a part of war, and had been duped before.

Working for Congresswoman Davis was a lucky break; she allowed me to define my role. In a broad sense, I would gather and distill insight and data that would help her make key decisions regarding legislation and committee actions. I attended every think tank discussion, every Congressional Research Service lecture, and every hearing I could possibly fit into my schedule. I was the only one in the congresswoman's office with a security clearance, so I was able to attend briefings nobody else on her staff could have attended.

It was an amazing education and an opportunity to delve into issues that were intriguing and mattered to me personally, from military procurement procedures to nuclear weapons policies and the struggle for women's rights in Afghanistan. There was a lot of ground to cover, and I wanted to absorb as much as I could. I never lost sight that it wasn't learning for learning's sake. I had an obligation to summarize information that would be crucial to the congresswoman's role on the Armed Services Committee—and beyond. I occasionally helped draft legislation but more often sat in on meetings where my expertise could be helpful. Sometimes those were with high-ranking military officials where I could translate military-speak on the fly. More often, they were with lobbyists.

One afternoon, three lobbyists working for a defense contractor met with the congresswoman. I sat quietly off to the side in her office, taking notes and listening. The lobbyists were seeking her support to back an unnecessary project that would involve the fighter jet community in the navy and Marine Corps. The lobbyists had no idea I was a fighter pilot. In fact, I'm convinced they thought I was some sort of career pencil pusher because I was a woman. They rattled off a polished spiel that was almost complete BS. As soon as they wrapped up, the congresswoman thanked them and turned to me. She smiled and introduced me.

"This is Major McGrath and I'll lean on her for her expertise. She's an F/A-18 pilot and has done three tours of duty, so I'm sure she can shed some light on the subject."

The three men looked sick. They knew their pitch was dead in the water. More to the point, we all knew it was a pitch no one should have been making. They might as well have been selling snake oil. That type of blatant nonsense was the worst part of the lobbyist-Congress dynamic. It was one more lesson in a year jam-packed with them.

I had been in the Marine Corps for so long that without realizing it, I had come to see the world through a Marine officer lens. In the halls and meeting rooms of Congress, I was exposed to the roles of other services and to the part other departments—and even other countries—played in U.S. foreign and military policy.

Congress being Congress, my education wasn't limited to the issues. I learned about how "the Beltway" operates, real-world truths that brought to mind the saying "no one wants to see how the sausage is made." I found myself shocked at how little members of Congress and their staffs understood about military operations and the waging of war. They were often surprisingly poorly informed about the issues affecting military conflict and troop safety in messy places like Afghanistan and Iraq. Then again, how would they know the realities of the armed forces, such as how long it would take to deploy a small squad or unit from an aircraft carrier in the Gulf to some place like Libya or Syria? To make matters worse, the critical staff who served members of Congress were usually younger and far less experienced than I think most people might imagine.

More predictably, much of what went on in the Capitol was pure politics, often to the detriment of American interests. I came to the Hill as an independent; I wasn't interested in being guided by

Republican or Democratic talking points. I was surprised by how important those points were to everyone around me—often more important than issues of national security. I was disappointed that, at times, many of the politicians and political staffers I met in briefings, meetings, and hearings had lost sight of what was in the best interests of the country. They were, instead, focused on political gain or finding a way to hit the other side somehow. It was upsetting that people in power were making crucial, sometimes life-and-death decisions with too little information and too much political bias.

The Emerging Threats Subcommittee of the House Armed Services Committee was a good example of many basic flaws in the congressional committee structure. That particular subcommittee was incredibly important. It was tasked with oversight of all cyber operations, special operations, and special forces. Its purview included several other areas of oversight as well. For all that responsibility, the subcommittee had a grand total of four professional staffers. On the Democratic side, one staffer was in his mid-thirties and the other in his mid-twenties. Those four people were supposed to provide oversight for entire military commands, major areas of operations within the executive branch. It was shocking. The lawmakers on the subcommittee were not going to dig in and do the actual work, much less educate themselves to a degree that would allow them to make wise decisions. They had other responsibilities, more than there were hours in the day. In any case, members of Congress were forced to spend the bulk of their time on the phone to donors, building war chests essential to reelection. Committee assignments, for many of them, were little more than badges of honor or lines on a résumé periodically sold to voters.

I respected Congresswoman Davis, and she grew to value me as a trusted member of her team. I dedicated myself to helping her and her staff understand the key issues affecting the military, overseas operations, and the particulars of our conflicts around the globe.

I briefed her regularly and tried to anticipate what she would need to know for any pending vote or upcoming hearing. I even drafted questions for her to ask during hearings. I'd give her five or six to choose from, and she might pick one to ask a witness. To be honest, although they were questions about things I thought Congresswoman Davis needed to know, they were often also about something I wanted to know.

At one point, Secretary of Defense Robert Gates was scheduled to testify before the House Armed Services Committee. It would be his last time on the Hill; after serving both Republican and Democratic administrations, he was stepping down. I gave Congresswoman Davis five questions in advance of his appearance, and near the end of her allotted time she asked him what I felt was the most important of them: "Now that you're on your way out, can you tell me what threat you're most worried about? What keeps you up at night?"

As if he had been anticipating and perhaps even hoping for the question, he answered without hesitation. "Congresswoman, actually, what keeps me up at night is you, and the dysfunction in this body, and what it will mean for our future defense." I understood that he meant the entire committee system. He had seen, as I had, that the structure didn't reward deep knowledge. If members of Congress who held positions on a committee lacked essential knowledge about the committee's topic, how could they even hope to ask the questions they needed to ask to get to the truth? How could they hope to make the right decisions when it came time to decide between war and diplomacy? Between risking military lives and projecting American power?

I think Secretary Gates was referring to that entire environment, to all those factors that were really dysfunctional on a grand scale. He knew all too well from experience that the problems in the institution led directly to defense budget chaos and uncertainty. Real people got hurt. Wars were started for the wrong reasons, for lies.

Making matters worse, the Tea Party had just risen to prominence, and Tea Party legislators were taking their election as a mandate to oppose any government spending. They took that position to ridiculous extremes, bragging about sleeping on their couches and refusing to fully staff up their congressional offices. I think they honestly felt that they were somehow saving money, but it was proof positive of the truth behind the adage "penny wise, pound foolish." The more members of Congress slashed their own budgets, the fewer and less experienced staffers they could hire. That meant they got less and less high-quality information and advice and were less able to make informed decisions about pending legislation or committee motions. There was a notable lack of seasoned staff, because experienced experts demanded much higher salaries. The advisers and assistants those congresspeople wound up with were too green to even begin to offer wisdom, much less practical advice on key issues. Most were glorified office help. As the trend continued, congressional staff salaries failed to keep up with the cost of living in Washington, D.C. Young, smart staffers who might have blazed careers on Capitol Hill or elsewhere in government had much greater incentive to do their time, pad their résumés, and get out. Instead of improving government, they wound up as lobbyists or moving into the private sector. It was a vicious cycle that continues to this day.

That leaves us, the American people, saddled with lawmakers and congressional staffers who simply don't have the knowledge they need to make insightful, informed decisions. They become increasingly susceptible to being swayed by powerful, well-financed outsiders. Those lobbyists and influencers use their access to push narrow agendas, often to the detriment of the country's interests.

In few areas was the influence of special interests as apparent as in military committees on Capitol Hill. President Eisenhower didn't have it entirely right when he coined the term "military-industrial complex" in his farewell speech to the nation. It's really the "military-industrial-congressional complex." The Joint Strike Fighter program was a perfect example of how that machine conducts business. The program's goal was to replace a variety of existing attack assets with a multifaceted fighter aircraft. As the name implied, the fighter was to be developed for the fighting forces not only of the United States but in conjunction with many of our allies. As a Marine aviator, I saw a number of challenges and problems with the program. Perhaps most devastating was the role members of Congress played.

Working for Congresswoman Davis, I discovered that the Joint Strike Fighter was supposed to be constructed from parts made in more than forty-eight states. Landing gear would be fabricated in one state, while the cockpit was constructed across the country. From a cost-efficiency standpoint, that didn't make sense. However, Lockheed Martin knew what they were doing when they decentralized the plane's assembly. By spreading construction around to factories across the country, the program gained a large group of champions in Congress. Individual legislators are forever looking to keep or create jobs in their districts, something that translates to votes. The program was, almost from the start, predictably plagued by cost overruns and other inefficiencies. Unfortunately, lawmakers charged with oversight weren't about to make a decision that would cut jobs in their own districts.

The clash of personal legislative agendas with the greater interests of the country is seemingly intractable in Washington. Call it politics or compromise, or just the way things are, I found it purely frustrating. It's not that the system is broken; I don't think it is. But there is a shocking lack of experience and knowledge on the Hill, and it's getting worse. That deficit, and the personal agendas of individual lawmakers, are putting our national security interests—the safety of flesh-and-blood American citizens—at risk. The more I worked on the Hill, the more I saw that in action.

As my fellowship year came to a close, I had a decision to make. I was coming to a point in my life where my priorities were evolving. I had seen combat and served my country for almost two decades. I'd been involved in America's center of power and experienced politics for myself. I knew that I could probably fill a position as a Marine liaison to Capitol Hill, but that would have entailed narrowing the scope of my brief. Liaisons were essentially champions for whatever legislative policies and positions the Marines were trying to advance. It would have been a similar role to a lobbyist. Marine liaisons were also, at the worst of times, little more than glorified travel agents for members of Congress. The Marine liaison to a senator or representative sets up transportation for official trips and junkets based on security concerns. I didn't think that carrying a senator's luggage would be a productive use of my time and effort. I wanted to do more, not less.

I had enjoyed my time in the Capitol, and I liked working for Congresswoman Davis. It was challenging, fast paced, and thought provoking. Unfortunately, though, Congress at that time was almost entirely reactive. I wanted to get back to a place where I felt I had a real mission, a proactive goal. That place would be the Pentagon.

We had a new commandant of the Marine Corps in the Pentagon, General James Amos. He had just released, as all new commandants do, a new Planning Guidance. The guidance is a document that outlines twelve to fifteen goals the commandant wants to see the Marine Corps achieve during his command. Ninth on the list was this: "The Marine Corps will integrate better with other government agencies." That particular objective naturally fell under the Plans, Policies, and Operations Directorate. It was the responsibility of Brigadier General Michael Rocco, the head of the International Affairs Branch, to figure out how to achieve the objective.

I was, at the same time, trying to figure out what I wanted to do next. As my fellowship drew to a close, the Marine Corps needed to find a new assignment for me. I wanted to control that process, so I began emailing and calling around to different departments where I thought I could be effective and could grow. I called a colonel in International Affairs and asked him about possible assignments in his group.

"Do you have a master's degree?"

"No, sir, I'm going to be starting a program at Johns Hopkins."

"Well, I can't put you to work with foreign countries, because you need a master's. But there is a new position, something that just fell in my lap. It's dealing with the other agencies of government, like the State Department or USAID. I don't know exactly what it's going to entail, but Brigadier General Rocco has tasked me with this thing, and I've got a lot on my plate right now. I need somebody who could take it on."

I read the description and didn't have to think hard about whether I wanted it. It played right into the experience I'd had on Capitol Hill, and I felt strongly that there was a blind spot in operations between the military and all the other departments in the government. War had gotten much more complex, but the military was still conducting actions in places like Afghanistan in the same ways as we had fought World War II. The job would entail an almost three-year posting to the Pentagon, working in one of my passion areas—international affairs. I called the colonel back and told him I'd love to work with him on the guidance.

My new position was called interagency policy coordinator. Being based in the International Affairs Branch was perfect because I was in close contact with other Marines who could get me into the State Department, USAID, Treasury, the CIA, and the other partners I'd be working with to draft a new strategy. It would be a new, exciting, and challenging opportunity. It wasn't the only opportunity for personal "growth" that came up. After a quick trip to a drugstore and fifteen minutes with an over-the-counter kit, I got a life-changing piece of news: I was pregnant.

16

THE MOST IMPORTANT MOMENTS in any life, the ones that change everything, are beginnings and endings. They define our lives, clarifying what matters. They are the most traumatic, exciting, heart-wrenching, fun, sad, and instructive moments we experience. They test our faith, teach us about ourselves, and often set us off in surprising, new directions.

As my congressional fellowship ended and I learned I was pregnant, my life was packed with exhilarating new beginnings. There was a challenging adventure awaiting me at the Pentagon, the center of the military universe in America. I could feel the baby inside me growing, and Erik and I were excited to start a new family. We didn't really know what to expect. Does any soon-to-be parent? Having a child is one of those things in life that you only truly understand after you've done it. It was already clear, though, that things were about to change radically.

So many beginnings. Then, as always seems to happen, there was an ending, too.

Monk had already been showing signs of age when we moved to Alexandria. At thirteen, he was a senior citizen in the dog world. By the time I got my orders to the Pentagon, he was dealing with overlapping health problems. He had become diabetic, and I had to give him two shots of insulin a day. He had tumors growing throughout his body, and he moved slower and slept more than he ever had. He was just as wonderful, dopey, and loving as he had ever been, even if morning runs, vigorous hikes, or even long walks were out of the question. Erik and I tried not to think about the reality of Monk's deteriorating physical condition. After all, he was still a happy dog, and he was so deeply embedded in our hearts. The very notion of his not being with us was almost inconceivable. He was the greatest dog I'd ever known. Accept it or not, life's clock never stops.

One morning as I hurried to get ready for work, I came downstairs to find Monk in a bad state. He didn't seem himself. He didn't want to move from the spot in the hall where he had spent the night. His breathing was labored, his nose was dry, and his eyes were cloudy. The more I watched him, the more concerned I became that something was seriously wrong and that he might be in pain. Erik was flying a C-130 on a turnaround to Hawaii, so I bundled Monk into the car by myself and drove him to the vet. The news wasn't good.

After taking a few X-rays, the vet met me in the waiting room. "I'm sorry to tell you this, but the tumors are really advanced. I'm worried that one of them could burst at any moment. He would bleed out in excruciating pain. The most humane thing to do is to let him go."

"Can we wait for my husband to get home?"

The vet frowned. "It's risky. With his symptoms right now, it could be as quick as a couple hours. But it's definitely going to happen, and sooner rather than later."

"Let me call my husband and we'll figure it out."

I got a call through to Erik and told him what was happening. He was as devastated as I was. He was on a refueling stop for the return flight to Andrews. He said, "I can be there in four hours. Can you wait?"

"I don't think we can, honey."

"Just hold on until I get home, and I'll meet you at the vet's. Please."

I talked to the vet, who agreed to keep Monk sedated and out of pain. Finally, Erik arrived and we sat with Monk as the doctor gave him the shot that would end his life. Erik and I each held a paw, and I looked into Monk's eyes. It was such a painful moment, but I knew it was the right thing to do. My fun, beautiful, loving friend had come to the end of his road. I had to say goodbye and let him go.

I've heard people describe their dogs as "children." That has never made sense to me. We don't need to call them our children to acknowledge the special place they hold in our hearts. Having a dog in your life is unlike any other relationship. Monk was one of a kind and was at the center of some of my favorite memories. He had been my reward to myself for earning my first set of wings. We had traveled across the country together to a new and exciting future at Miramar. We had hiked or run or walked hundreds if not thousands of miles, sharing a simple joy and companionship. He had been adored by everyone he met, from Mona and Homan, to Erik, to my parents and the rest of my family. He was always a comforting presence. Picking up Monk after a deployment was one of the ways I knew I was truly home.

He left a big hole in our lives. It was a small mercy that I was far too busy to indulge my grief. In addition to my work at the Pentagon, I started a master's degree in global security at Johns Hopkins University. Night classes and weekends spent hammering out a thesis made my schedule incredibly hectic, but it was worth it. The work

I had done during my fellowship had driven home to me just how much I enjoyed untangling the intricacies of international policy. Understanding how America interacted with and was perceived by the rest of the world was quite obviously key to making sense of an increasingly complex picture, one in which our concerns were never confined within the shores of our own country.

My real-world experiences brought everything that was covered in the classrooms at Johns Hopkins to life. I knew firsthand how the theories and ideas we were studying and discussing impacted people's lives around the globe. The program also gave me the chance to take advantage of the GI Bill—a major benefit of any career in the military—and it was the best opportunity I'd ever have to go to a top-tier university. Short of Harvard or Stanford, the most prestigious schools for international studies were located in the D.C. metro area. Johns Hopkins was at the top of that list.

I tore into my studies and sank my teeth into my work at the Pentagon. It was all satisfying and invigorating. Unfortunately, I was not as comfortable with all the changes my body was throwing at me. Pregnancy was the first time in my life I had so completely lost control of what was happening to me physically. Even when I'd been injured, I knew that the damage was a blip on the screen. Injuries could be fixed with surgery, and my body would respond predictably if I was willing to dedicate hours and hard work to physical rehab. Pregnancy, though, was something else again. The most unpleasant part of it was that I felt overwhelmingly vulnerable. That wasn't a feeling I enjoyed. I was used to my body responding to anything I asked it to do. I had always been an athlete, moving around with ease. It was a shock to suddenly have trouble climbing a long flight of stairs or even getting up off a sofa. I often couldn't get comfortable enough in bed to put in a much-needed night of solid sleep. I was more tired than I had ever been. The smell of certain foods that I normally loved could now make me physically nauseated. I had relied on my body for so much, as an athlete, a fighter pilot, and a generally active person. Now my body was going off script.

The more pleasant aspect of my pregnancy was how my fellow Marines reacted to it. Getting pregnant in uniform was uncharted territory; there were no mentors I could turn to for direction or support. I wasn't sure how other Marines would react, so I was overjoyed when all the guys I had served with in different squadrons were incredibly upbeat and supportive. Most of the officers I worked with in the Pentagon were just as encouraging, including the one-star general who was in charge. That widespread backing made me want to work even harder and deliver a solid new strategy for the Marine Corps.

I felt the weight of that responsibility. Although I had made life-and-death decisions in the cockpit, I was now researching and writing an overarching strategy that—if I did it right and it was fully accepted and implemented—could influence how the American military conducted future conflicts and wars. A well-thought-out plan for interagency cooperation could feasibly save scores of lives, help end or prevent some of these conflicts our country found itself involved in, and make the world safer. There was little margin for error; I wanted to get it right.

The pressure made the work exciting and rewarding. I pored over existing policies of engagement and planning, identifying where the corps had missed opportunities to exploit what the Department of State, USAID, the Justice Department, DHS, and even the CIA were doing overseas. The heart of the challenge was that Marines didn't train to conduct operations with other agencies. We were the tip of the spear. We kicked down doors and killed bad guys. Even in 2011, traditional warfare was still the baseline for most Marine Corps training. In that way, our policies of engagement weren't much different than they had been in 1945. Unfortunately, that method of conducting a military campaign was long outdated and could actually be destructive in the framework of the modern, more complex global environment. We had taken our antiquated philosophy into Iraq and Afghanistan, and it was a big part of why we were still mired in a decade-long engagement in those countries. Even though the traditional warfare mentality had been incredibly effective for the Marine Corps at one time—and still has its place in some modern conflicts—relying completely on a blunt-force, military-only approach could easily lay waste to years of hard, careful work done by agencies like USAID and the State Department. Instead of "winning" a war and getting our troops home, we set ourselves back and did untold damage to local populations and cultures. Many times, we wound up stuck and hated, creating as many problems as we solved.

Each day I went to work and dove into decoding how international aid, diplomacy, and intelligence agencies functioned. Slowly but surely, I began to see clearly how the Marine Corps could realistically coordinate a military mission with various other agencies. I loved the work. It was challenging, and it injected life into everything I was learning in books and lectures at Johns Hopkins.

Ultimately, it took me almost two years to research and write an exhaustive new strategy. Along the way, I gave birth to Theodore Joseph Henderson after twelve hours of labor. I've been fortunate to enjoy many happy moments in my life, but I had never experienced such pure joy as holding Teddy in my arms for the first time. Looking into that small face, I was struck that I was now responsible for two lives. I might have the opportunity to deploy into combat again, and to sit in the cockpit of an F/A-18, but now this little being would play a major role in that decision. I just wanted to protect and love him. I wasn't alone. Erik was more moved than I had ever seen him be. He is not a man who cries easily, and he was close to tears looking at our newborn. We took pictures with Teddy and sent them to everyone we knew. Like most new, first-time parents, we wanted to shout the news out to the world.

As much as I was overwhelmed with love for Teddy, my maternity leave was as big a challenge as the pregnancy had been. My body remained out of whack, and I was frustrated that it didn't seem quite mine anymore. With feedings every two to three hours, I started to feel as if I were nothing more than a drive-through Dairy Queen. I had relied so long on my mental prowess, on my ability to study hard, learn, and figure out the best way to do things. As fit as I had been, it was my mind that had propelled me in my military career and in life. Now my mind was largely irrelevant. I was nothing more to Teddy than a food source. I loved him to pieces, but I was happy when my maternity leave came to an end and I got back to work.

There was a lot to be done. Drafting the new strategy had been a monumental effort. I had all kinds of help from professionals in the Pentagon and other agencies, but putting the strategy together was only half of what I had to do. The second part was an exercise in diplomacy and patience. The strategy had to be approved up the chain of command, ultimately signed by the commandant of the Marine Corps, and then instituted throughout the Marine Corps as official policy.

It involved persuading old-school Marine officers to think outside the box about how the next generation of officers would be trained. There was a lot of resistance to the idea that the corps needed to integrate better with other government agencies. Change is always difficult in large, formal institutions like the Marine Corps. Many older, more senior officers felt the strategy meant giving up warfare planning autonomy. It looked like a pure negative to them. I had to win over skeptical minds, one at a time. As frustrating as it could be, the bureaucracy was actually useful in honing the strategy. Amid the grumbling were legitimate concerns that needed to be addressed. I was able to refine and improve the strategy as it went through the approval process.

Between my work at the Pentagon and writing my master's thesis, Teddy's first year flew by in a blur. Watching him grow and change so quickly made me think carefully about our family's future, including what was next in my Marine Corps career. As I worked to get sign-off on the new strategy from the various stakeholders up the chain of command, it had come time to make a choice between military and family.

Any military career involves a series of life-changing decisions. Perhaps the most significant one is this: What are you going to sacrifice? The military is a life and a calling, not a job. I had given up a lot to fly an F/A-18. Now I had to decide how much of my family life I was still willing to sacrifice. Erik had already chosen to retire from the navy at his twenty-year mark. He wanted to go back to school and get his MBA. I, too, was approaching twenty years in service. If I was going to continue with a career on the command track, the path was clear. The best, most obvious move for me would be to go back to flying and deploy again. Following Marine Corps orthodoxy, the next step would be selection for command of a squadron. The goal would be to become, in time, a full-bird colonel. That was a monumental achievement by any measure, but it would come at a high price. The reality was that I would spend months away from both Teddy and Erik. I'd see them only on a scratchy video feed, if that. Having any more kids would be out of the question. That led to a lot of soul-searching.

Eventually, I realized that I wanted to focus on family. I had to accept that my military career would essentially be stalled from that point on. A new and different future would blossom. In the short term, I had to figure out what my next move would be. That pondering came to a head in a conversation with one of the few Marine aviator generals in the Pentagon.

He called me into his office and got right to the point: "You've got your kid. Now you need to get back in the cockpit."

"Sir, I'm pretty sure I want another kid."

"The corps really wants you to get back into the fleet." He meant a flying squadron.

"I understand that. But my heart's not there."

He frowned and said, "Okay, so long as you're aware of what that means to your opportunity to command and future chances for promotion."

"I know the deal, sir. I know."

I was effectively stalling future promotions and limiting where I would go next. I knew that I could probably continue working at the Pentagon. As interesting as that option was, military staff in the Pentagon work crazy hours. It's a terrible place to be if you're raising a young family. I also considered requesting an assignment to a European command, which would have certainly been exciting. Erik wanted to go back to school for his MBA, though, so Europe was out of the question.

The more I thought about it, the more I came back to Annapolis. It was a beautiful place to live, and half the teaching staff were military officers. I felt as though I had a lot to offer as an instructor. I was well on my way to finishing my master's degree, and I had significant real-world experience on the Hill. I thought I could bring value to a classroom and give midshipmen a unique perspective on how politics and international policy would affect what they did as officers. As if on cue, I found out that I was pregnant again.

I contacted Headquarters Marine Corps, Personnel Division, and asked how I'd go about getting orders to the naval academy. I found out that the senior Marine officer at the academy has the freedom to select officers for teaching positions. I emailed him my résumé and outlined what I had done. He got back to me the same day. He wrote that he would gladly put in a special request to get me orders to the academy. As things began to fall in place, the idea of teaching a new generation of Marine officers became even more alluring.

My work at the Pentagon wasn't done. After the strategy had been approved up the chain of command, and even with the commandant's signature on it—making it a formal order throughout the Marine Corps—someone had to oversee the implementation. That someone was me, and so the work continued. It meant fostering a process that had never existed before and a lot of nuts-and-bolts work. I was the one, for instance, who had to arrange a meeting between the appropriate State Department contacts and the Marine colonels who would lead various expeditionary forces around the world. It was my role to touch base with State to make sure they knew what Marine Corps assets were at their disposal should they need them. There was still plenty of work to be done.

One day, I checked the Marine Corps messaging system to find that my orders to Annapolis had come through. I stared at the message. It seemed a perfectly fitting place to finish my twenty-year career, back where I started. I could give future military leaders the benefit of my experience and education and raise my young family in a place I loved. The assignment would offer me the opportunity to have more kids. It was a different path than I might have taken, but I was profoundly happy. You can't plan for every eventuality. The best you can do is seek your own true north. An academic life, with a growing family, was the right direction for me.

I contacted Captain Coward, my mentor at Annapolis. I told him about my new orders. He and his wife, Croom, were Navy football season ticket holders, and they invited Erik, Teddy, and me to the next game. A long, fun weekend would be the perfect chance for us to scout out where we might want to settle in Annapolis.

It was wonderful to see the Cowards and experience the exhilarating nostalgia of sitting in Navy–Marine Corps Memorial Stadium with a roaring crowd on a sunny November Saturday. The team was winning, and Erik and I were having fun. I felt the camaraderie of the school, and it made me happy. As the Drum and Bugle Corps took the field at halftime, Croom leaned over to me.

"We're so excited that you're coming back, Amy."

I smiled at her. "Me too. I can't wait."

"Do you have a place to live?"

"Not yet. We're going to look around tomorrow."

"Do you want to buy our house?"

I was shocked. For a moment, I thought she might be kidding. Then, as she continued to smile at me, I realized she wasn't.

"What? That would be incredible."

The Cowards lived in a beautiful, well-appointed gray three-dormer Cape Cod, with a two-acre, wooded backyard. It had lots of room, tons of sunlight, and a comfortable family feel. I had always loved their house. Erik and I gave ourselves a week to think it over and discuss it. In the end, though, it was just too good an offer to pass up. It turned out to be the easiest real estate deal I had ever done.

Returning to Annapolis was a pure pleasure. The school represented both the rich traditions of the military and the changes that were transforming it. It was rewarding to bring twenty years of experience back to that hallowed place, to give students the benefit of real-life knowledge and offer them the type of insight I wanted when I was a midshipman. The staff was an interesting and equal mix of civilian professors and military officers. It was a great blend for students who would be in Iraq, Afghanistan, or the South China Sea in a couple of years.

Shortly after we moved, I was promoted to lieutenant colonel. That rank is no small accomplishment in the Marine Corps, and I valued it as recognition of what I had done in my deployment in Afghanistan and at the Pentagon. I had done a third tour, fulfilled all the requirements of special military education, and spearheaded a game-changing strategy for interagency coordination. I felt I had justly earned my new silver oak leaves. Even though we had moved to Annapolis, I decided to have my promotion ceremony in the Pentagon's Marine Corps hallway. All the people I had worked so closely with over the prior three years were there, and it seemed like a fitting place. It was an unusual ceremony because I was eight and a half months pregnant with my second child. The presiding officer had to literally lean in over my belly to pin one of the oak leaves onto my collar. Erik pinned on the other, and I was officially a lieutenant colonel. We took pictures, spent a little time with all my Pentagon friends and well-wishers, and headed home before I ran out of energy for the day.

That same week, I walked the stage at Johns Hopkins, graduating with my master's degree in global security. Less than two weeks later, I gave birth to my second child, George. Life got much busier with two young children, as Erik began a two-year MBA program at the University of Maryland.

Time flew by with our busy schedules, especially when I returned to the classroom after my maternity leave. As hectic as my days were, it was comforting to be working somewhere so steeped in tradition. The rituals of life at the U.S. Naval Academy gave it a pleasing rhythm unlike any of my other assignments. As fixed in convention as the school is, I was happy to see that there were also heartening, progressive changes on campus. The student body was now almost a third women, whereas it had been about 13 percent when I was a midshipman. The Marine Corps and the military were changing. That change could seem painfully slow at times, but it happened. I was ecstatic to see a vast number of women getting the opportunities that I was one of the first to enjoy. I took pride in teaching and felt it was as important as anything else I had done in my career. I was giving future military officers direction in how a changing world could impact their role and duties in the military at home and abroad. I was providing them with a framework to understand their leadership responsibilities, and giving them a better grasp of how American politics influenced military operations and day-to-day life in the country—as well as in an international setting.

The school semesters unfolded at a fast clip, faster than when I was a midshipman. Somewhere in the back of my mind, I understood that this was the sunset of my military career and that Annapolis was not where I would be in ten years. I didn't ponder that. I savored the experience—campus life, our beautiful home, our growing family. It was an exceptional moment in time, and I enjoyed it as much as I possibly could. As Erik worked through his MBA program, I became pregnant for the third time.

Erik and I closely watched the emerging front-runners for the Democratic and Republican presidential nominations, with the new perspective of parents concerned about our family's future. It looked as if it would be a historic presidential race. The cast of Republican candidates seemed thrown together from the far edges of the party. Donald Trump lent a circus atmosphere to the primary season, and both Erik and I thought his candidacy was a pure public-relations stunt. His appeal was as an anti-establishment outsider, but he made completely unrealistic promises and seemed to not have a clue as to how to lead a government. His candidacy seemed anything but viable. Then he won the primary. It was a sign to me of just how desperate the Republican Party had become. I felt that the party was increasingly straying from traditional core conservative values and had truly lost its way, dating from the moment John McCain picked Sarah Palin as his running mate. Donald Trump was the end point of the party's deteriorating ideology.

I gave birth to our daughter, Eleanor, in May 2016. Two months later, the Democrats nominated Hillary Clinton. Erik and I thought America would soon have its first woman president. It seemed so obvious. We did not anticipate the rise of Donald Trump or Trump-ism at the time. As the presidential campaign moved closer and closer to November, the Marine Corps offered to extend my billet at the naval academy for another year. We were so comfortable and happy in Annapolis that it was a tempting proposition. Then came the election.

November 8, 2016, fundamentally changed me. Like many Americans, I was shocked that we could elect someone with no political or governmental experience. The idea that we would vote in someone who acted so differently from what I had come to expect of an American leader stunned me. Far from revering the sacrifice members of the military made, President-elect Trump insulted the American military hero John McCain. He insulted women and minorities and mocked people with disabilities. I had always prided myself on being nonpartisan. I was an independent for many years and considered myself a political moderate. I embraced certain mainstay Republican values, such as fiscal conservatism, free trade, and a strong defense. Throughout the campaign, I was shocked at the ease with which the Republican Party fell in line, adopting and supporting lies and a platform that wasn't truly conservative at all. I was stunned and then saddened by our country's embrace of divisiveness and the gross labels being given to anyone with different opinions or positions. It shook me to my core. Like all military leaders, I had learned what leadership was from the officers who had gone before me. I taught my students that model of leadership, based on integrity, honor, character, and sacrifice for the greater good.

I wasn't surprised that my students were visibly shocked at what had happened. I could see that they had little faith in the honor and trustworthiness of America's political leadership of all stripes and in the commander in chief they would serve. That alarmed me. More than anything, though, it saddened me to see our country deeply divided, with leaders in Congress and the White House lacking in vision, decency, thoughtfulness, or even basic competency.

It has always been in my nature to attack problems. They are challenges to be overcome. Just as I had fought to be a combat fighter pilot long before there was a path for a woman to become one, I now wanted to do something to help my country. I saw in the danger of that moment, in the threat that this poor leadership posed to America and American democracy, a personal obligation.

I have always been keenly aware that I am blessed. I was blessed with a wonderful, loving family and parents who nurtured my passions even when those passions took me in unusual directions. I was blessed with above-average athletic ability and a nimble mind that allowed me to study, absorb, test well, and earn good grades. Ultimately, I was blessed with opportunities that many women before me simply didn't have. Doors opened at just the right time. Knowing all that, in the wake of the 2016 presidential election I kept thinking about a biblical passage that has resonated with me from a young age—Luke 12:48: "To whom much is given, much is expected."

I realized that it would not be right or moral for me to sit idly by in the face of what was happening to my beloved country. I was obligated to act, to do whatever I could.

Two years before, as part of a guest lecturer program called Congress to Campus, the former Kentucky congressman Ben Chandler came and spoke to my class. He had given me his card afterward, and I had tossed it into my desk drawer. He was the only politician from Kentucky that I had ever met. He seemed as good a starting point as any. I fished the card out of the drawer and emailed him. Ben had represented Kentucky's Sixth Congressional District as a Democrat, until he was defeated by a Republican in 2012. I reminded him of how we had met and asked if he thought a Democrat could win the seat again. Ben was honest about how hard the battle would be for a Democrat, even a centrist like me. It was a long shot, but one he urged me to explore. He told me he would help in any way he could. To start with, he introduced me to Mark Nickolas, a longtime political pro who would ultimately become my campaign manager.

The more I thought about running for office, the more sense it made. I was coming to the end of my time in the Marine Corps. I wouldn't just retire and do nothing; that wasn't my nature. Entering national politics, having an impact, and trying to display the leadership I believed we needed seemed a profoundly good use of my time and effort. Moving back to Kentucky appealed to me for personal reasons as well. My father had done battle with cancer for fourteen years and had gone through many ups and downs. He was stable at that point, but no one could predict what lay ahead. I didn't know how many more battles he had in him. I liked the idea of being close by if my mom or dad needed my help or support.

Erik and I had an ongoing conversation about the possibility of my running for the Sixth District seat. We also did our homework. We attended a candidate training workshop put on by the Veterans Campaign, a group founded to help military veterans run for office. Then we met with our financial adviser. Erik and I would soon be living off our retirement checks, and we had to make sure that a long congressional campaign was even going to be financially feasible. Our adviser's first reaction was one of disbelief. "You're going to do what? You're not going to make any money doing that."

I nodded. "We understand that. We're career military; we know how to live frugally. We'll sell the house in Maryland and downsize to something more modest. We'll tighten our belts."

He reluctantly ran the numbers and let us know that we could do it but it would hurt. Erik and I just about talked it to death. Finally, he said, "You need to do this. We need to do this. Here's the thing, Amy. You know what you want to do right now. I can figure out what I'll do later. We'll get retirement checks, and that will hold us through this. We can move back to Kentucky and do this. Make a difference and see what happens."

I was so grateful for those words. For the millionth time, I thanked God that I had found the right partner in life. We were a military family, so the idea of moving wasn't a big deal to us. We could sell a house and move somewhere else; we had done it before. The bigger relief for me was that Erik was like me in that he was okay with taking a well-thought-out risk. Neither of us was a gambler, but we were both comfortable making sacrifices to take a long shot at something we believed in. It was important, a sacrifice for the country. Sure, we would take a hit financially, a big hit, but there wasn't a more important cause to a veteran. We wanted to be able to tell our children that we stood up and did the right thing, even if it was difficult. We did what we needed to do for them to have the country we loved. So, just like that, "Amy McGrath for Congress" launched.

17

Politics is a money sport. Most candidates start out rich or have rich friends. It's a matter of necessity and the reality of modern campaigning. Counting primaries, the run for a state or federal office can stretch almost two years. It's a full-time job and then some, which means two years in which you can't earn a living doing anything else. The campaigns themselves are expensive. That's why candidates spend an inordinate amount of time and effort chasing down donors. My problem was that military officers aren't used to asking for help or money; they do things themselves and earn every promotion they get. Fund-raising was a hard pill to swallow. It was the biggest challenge and worst aspect of campaigning for me.

Getting the campaign started was hectic and difficult. I put in for retirement just as Erik finished his MBA. We listed our beautiful house in Annapolis for sale. It had been the perfect home and we would cherish the memories, but any accomplishment worth achieving requires real sacrifice. My political campaign meant sacrificing that warm, wonderful home on Meadow Gate Drive.

We found a smaller house in Georgetown, Kentucky, north of Lexington. It was the perfect location, not too far from my parents and near a Montessori school for Teddy, George, and Ellie. Georgetown is a beautiful tree-lined suburb in the heart of horse country. It is quiet, with a warm, small-town vibe. Erik found a business opportunity there. A colleague from the navy introduced him to a friend who was in the construction business in Georgetown. He was interested in expanding, and Erik decided to help him build his business. Things came together. At least beyond the campaign.

I started with a handicap; I didn't know many wealthy people. That meant I had no obvious sources to tap for a campaign launch budget. Mark Nickolas and I realized that without rich friends fundraising was going to be an issue. He introduced me to a political media strategist named Mark Putnam. Putnam had the idea to make a short video that would capture who I was as a candidate. We'd use the video to launch the campaign. The goal was to raise my profile quickly and make it possible for me to legitimately approach large donors. The hitch was that the video cost thirty thousand dollars to produce, which seemed like an insurmountable sum.

I started trying to raise that money on our drive to Kentucky from Annapolis. As soon as we watched the moving truck head off with our stuff, we bundled the kids into our SUV and began the trek to Kentucky. I sat in the passenger seat, making calls as we drove. I reached out to every one of my aunts and uncles. I gave them all the same pitch. "Aunt Dee, you've known me my whole life. I think it's my duty to run for Congress. I believe it's the right thing for the country. I've never asked anybody for money in my life, and I wouldn't ask now if it wasn't so important. Could you contribute to my campaign so that I can get started?" Every single one of my aunts and uncles contributed, some close to the federal maximum of twenty-seven hundred dollars. Between my large extended family and close friends, I raised just enough money to make the video.

Even with that bankroll, the campaign was in the red on the day we launched. The video took every last cent I'd raised. We distributed it to the media and put it online to announce the campaign. Then we held our breath. I knew—everyone knew—that it was a risky strategy, essentially a Hail Mary. If the video fell flat, if nobody responded to it, my campaign was over before it began. We were flying in the face of conventional wisdom. They had taught me in the Veterans Campaign seminar that you never bet it all. You start slowly, build momentum, and raise funds more actively the more coverage you get. We didn't have that option. We didn't have a war chest, and I didn't have wealthy connections. So, we swung for the fences . . . and hit a home run. The video went viral.

By the end of the first day, it had been played on the blog *Politico* and on NBC. It got shared on social media sites like crazy. I had friends from around the country calling me to say, "I'm watching your video! People who don't even know you are sharing it with me."

We got lucky; the gamble paid off. The campaign raised more than $400,000 in contributions off that video in the first week. The money poured in, not just from Kentucky, but from all over the country. We got checks from Georgia, Alaska, New York, and beyond. Suddenly I had a budget. I hired a modest staff, foot soldiers to complement my tiny team of a manager, finance director, and part-time compliance accountant. We started running ads and traveling to get my message out. I was a legitimate candidate running a legitimate campaign.

The primary turned out to be almost as tough as the general election. My main opponent was the mayor of Lexington, a political veteran named Jim Gray who jumped into the race five months after I launched my campaign. He had the backing of the Democratic Party, including the support of most of the major donors I might have tapped. The first poll we got into the field showed that I was trailing him by forty points.

Never underestimate the power of a determined Marine. I traveled around the district nonstop, making my case to voters. We picked up steam and slowly ate into Gray's lead. Much as I hated the money part of campaigning, I loved getting out and talking to all these great everyday people. As an active-duty Marine officer, it's not considered proper to publicly voice political opinions. There is a clear separation between the military and the political world. As a fellow in Congress, I don't think many people I worked with knew exactly where I stood on the political spectrum. I don't think anybody there would have been able to say whether I was a Republican, Democrat, or independent. At the naval academy, I took pride in the fact that my students could not figure out my political orientation. On the campaign trail, though, I could say exactly what I believed. I wasn't a polished speaker, and it gave me an authenticity many candidates don't have. I loved connecting with people and learning their stories. I wanted to discover what they most needed from their leaders and government, and then figure out how to deliver it. I also wanted to be as honest as possible in that communication, something that created a few surprising moments on the campaign trail.

One of them was during a town hall I held in Richmond, Kentucky. Typically, I introduced myself, gave a short speech about why I was running and what issues I saw as most important. Then I would open the forum up to a long question-and-answer period. I made clear that I wanted the gathering to be a dialogue. In Richmond, the second-largest town in my district, we packed into the auditorium of the local library. Almost fifty people crowded in. We were halfway through the town hall when one man in the back of the auditorium raised his hand. I called on him.

"What is your stance on marijuana? Medical and recreational."

The issue of marijuana decriminalization or legalization hadn't come up in any questions I'd received prior to that moment. I looked at him and, after a pause, said, "You know, sir, I don't know."

The auditorium fell silent. You could have heard a pin drop. I continued, "I don't want to bullshit you. I don't know anything about marijuana. I just got out of the Marine Corps, and I never dealt with marijuana in the service. What's your stance?"

Like so many people who asked loaded questions, he had an agenda. He was an advocate for complete legalization and took the opportunity to make his case in front of an audience. When he was done, I said, "I appreciate your stance. Here's what I'll promise you. I'll develop a position. I don't know what it's going to be. I'll talk to experts, and I'll take what you've said here seriously. Within the next month, I'll post a stance on marijuana." Then I moved on to the next question.

At the end of the event, a middle-aged woman came up to me and said, "I've met so many politicians in my lifetime. I've come to a lot of these events, and I have never once heard anyone say they don't know." She leaned in and said, "It's just so refreshing to listen to you, because you don't make things up. You don't dance around. When you don't know, you don't know. And you don't have an answer for everything. I really like that about you."

I took her comments as a compliment. It was a lesson to never give up my honesty and candor. As far as I was concerned, I didn't have an option. I had to be who I was and not bend to whatever political winds were blowing at the moment. That was how I was going to connect to voters and stay true to myself. That strategy served me well. I continued to put on town halls, and the race got tighter and tighter. With less than a month to go in the primary, I attended a dinner in Richmond, Kentucky, hosted by the Madison County Democratic Party. Although I wasn't speaking, I needed to be there. It was a high-profile party event, and Jim Gray would be there. I was seated at a table right in the middle of the room, the best spot in the house as far as a politician is concerned. As I listened to the keynote speech, I got a text from my sister. It said, "Call Mom right now."

My sister is a levelheaded person who doesn't get flustered by much, so I immediately thought that there might be a problem with my dad. I got up and walked out to the parking lot and called my mom. She was calm and clear but sad. She said, "Your dad . . . Papa . . . is gone." She told me that the two of them had been in the kitchen when he had suddenly slumped over. She had tried to get him up but could not. She called 911. By the time EMS arrived, he was dead.

I fell to my knees on the parking lot gravel. Something inside me crumbled. My father had always been a pillar, someone I could lean on. It was a shock because he had been doing so well and seemed to have regained much of his health and a little bit more stamina. One of my staff came out to check on me. As soon as he saw me, he realized that something was wrong.

"Amy, are you okay?"

"No. My father just died. I have to get home."

"Right now?" He looked back toward the banquet hall doors.

"Yes."

"Do you want me to drive you?"

"No, I'll drive myself. Just go back inside and let the county party chairs know what's happening."

It was a dark drive to my house. I called Erik and told him what had happened. He was dealing with the kids, so we kept our conversation short. Then I called my brother. "Matt, can you just talk to me? Talk about Dad?"

He understood. He talked me through the drive. He told me funny stories about Dad, talking until I was safely home.

Time slowed down, and everything seemed strange and out of sync. Erik took care of the kids, and I headed to my mom's the next morning. On the hour drive north, I ached to see my dad one last time and tell him how much I loved him. I was having trouble believing that I would never get that chance. Matt and Jane were already at the house when I got there. We spent the next few days supporting our mom, preparing for the funeral, sharing memories, and grieving in our own ways. Each night, I sat on the back porch steps staring at the sky, thinking that my dad now knew the truth about all those religious mysteries he and I had pondered.

I was supposed to take part in a debate with the other Democratic challengers the next night. Mark Nickolas agreed that it made no sense for me to participate in my frame of mind. There were more important places for me to be, like sitting next to my mom. He put out a statement, and the debate went on as scheduled without me. The media barely covered it.

My family and I took some time to celebrate my father's life. His love of people, his strong religious faith, and his lifelong devotion to both learning and teaching. He had been an honorable and loving man and had instilled in me a soul-deep love of Kentucky and America. My father had fostered my Catholicism but also taught me to be curious about the world around me and question everything. He had enjoyed a good practical joke and adored meeting new people and learning about them. He absolutely loved to laugh, eat, and enjoy a cold beer on a hot day. As fathers go, I had the best. I would miss him every day from that point on, but perhaps that's one of the measures of a life well lived.

Erik was incredibly understanding and made the grieving process easier than it might have been by being a rock I could lean on. He took care of the kids and gave me all the time I needed with my siblings and my mom. After four days, though, I had to get back to the campaign. Much as I would have loved to stay with my mom, I was in the middle of a fight. My dad would have been the first one to demand I get back into it, that I keep moving forward. The primary was right around the corner—about a month away—and it was no time to let up.

I went back on the road, hitting town after town, giving speeches, asking questions, and answering more. On May 22, I won the primary and became the Democratic candidate for Kentucky's Sixth Congressional District. The real battle began. The general election was a roller coaster. My opponent, the Republican incumbent, Andy Barr, had won his last race by twenty-five points. Nobody expected us to win. Barr came swinging almost immediately. We started seeing what would be a series of ads attacking me and my positions with nasty, outright lies. Barr ran a campaign of divisiveness and fear, everything we would expect from a Republican in the age of Trump. I wouldn't go negative. I wanted to run with an optimistic message of "country over party," building on a bright, forward-looking vision for the future. Negative ads were the opposite of that. They also ran counter to who I was and what I considered honorable and decent.

We opened campaign offices in every county in the district, and the sheer number of volunteers and supporters inspired me. So did the everyday Kentuckians I met on the campaign trail. Rarely a day went by that I didn't run into someone who said, "I registered to vote so I could vote for you!" Or, "I'm a Republican, but I'm voting for you!" It was humbling and energizing. We gained momentum and support, and the polls got tighter and tighter. People across the district and throughout Kentucky began to believe we could win.

I was full of hope on election night. My family, my staff, and I crowded into a hotel suite to watch CNN report on the house races across the country, including mine. As the numbers came in from across the district, it became clear that we were lagging. We were losing the rural counties even while winning big in Lexington. Finally, the election was called for Andy Barr in an incredibly close finish: 51 percent to 49 percent.

I stepped out into the stairwell to gather myself, and Erik followed me. We sat down on the top step, side by side. He put his arm around me, and I realized I was exhausted. I leaned into him and thought about all the people in the hotel suite—and the bigger crowd gathered in a ballroom half a mile away—who had worked so hard on my behalf. I felt bad for all of them. Eventually, we got up and returned to the suite. I composed myself and then thanked everyone in the suite. Teddy was playing *Minecraft* on his iPad, oblivious to everything around him. Sensing the quiet in the room, he paused the game and looked up at me. He asked, "Did you win, Mom?"

"No, honey, I lost."

He frowned. "I'm sorry, Mom." Then he went back to playing his game. That moment was when I knew everything would be okay. It put everything into context. You can take a defeat as the end, as the worst thing in the world, but that's not what Marines do. They can get knocked down, but they never stay down. If they go down ten times, they get up eleven, and they keep on fighting. I didn't wear a uniform anymore, but I was still a Marine, and I wasn't done fighting for my country. Far from it. We all piled into black SUVs and headed to the ballroom. Backstage, I stood up tall, took a breath, and went out to give a short concession speech.

I didn't see the campaign as a failure. We had, in fact, helped many others around the country. By late that evening, it was clear that the Democrats had regained the House of Representatives. We now had hope of checking the president and working toward a functioning government again. Two years earlier I said that I wanted to do *something* to help our country . . . and I had. Of course, there was much more to do. Most people see defeat as loss. A wound that you move on from as quickly as possible. Not my campaign manager. The day after my concession speech, Mark Nickolas called me excited. He didn't sound the way I felt. In fact, he sounded energized.

"Okay, don't be mad at me."

"Why?"

"We need to change the narrative."

"The narrative, Mark, is that I lost. Not sure how you're going to change that."

"Well, think about it this way. We didn't win the election, sure. But you know what we did? We moved a conservative Kentucky red state district twenty-three points over the course of a campaign. That's an incredible accomplishment. And, by the way, no other politician—not even the ones that won their House races—moved their district anywhere close to that. Joe Cunningham won in South Carolina in a Trump plus-thirteen district, but that was an open seat. He didn't have to fight an incumbent. You almost beat an established incumbent in a Trump plus-sixteen district."

"So what?" I was still stung from the loss and didn't see all that as terribly heartening.

"You should consider running for governor."

I laughed. "Seriously? Come on."

"Yes, seriously."

"I'm not running for governor."

"But you could. The election is next year, you have donors and a fund-raising network. You've got the campaign structure in place. You have me. You've just been through it, so you know how to do it. Matt Bevin is universally hated. A strong challenger will beat him."

"I'm not sure I want to run again."

"Just let me put it out in the press. You don't have to make a decision now. You have time, and you should think about it."

The next day, a news article told the story of a unique political accomplishment, and it said that I was exploring a run for governor. It made the front page of the local paper.

I spent November and December trying not to be devastated about the loss and pondering whether I could put my family—not to mention myself—through another campaign. I asked myself again and again if I even wanted to be governor. I turned to my mom as a sounding board. She was worried about me because a campaign moves a mile a minute right up to election night. Then it stops like a car running into a brick wall. Losing is a huge psychological blow, and my mother was concerned that I might spiral down into depression. As a doctor, she was looking for any sign that I was struggling. She would call and ask, "All right, are you working out today? Are you going to take a walk? Are you drinking water?"

I think she suspected that running for office again was my way of recapturing the campaign "high." It can be exciting and addictive. It's true that I missed the full-on schedule day to day, missed the edginess of running. When it came down to it, though, I just didn't think I wanted to be governor. So, at the end of December, I put out a statement that I wouldn't be running.

Looking over the research we had done on how likely I would be to win a governor's race, Mark noticed something unusual. It was so tough to run as a Democrat for statewide office in Kentucky that the chance of winning a governor's race was about the same as my chance of winning a race against Kentucky's senior senator, Mitch McConnell. Looking at those numbers, I thought, "Now, that's a guy I'd like to beat, and that's a job I'd love to have." A governor was mired in the politics of a state; a senator could change the trajectory of the country. Running against McConnell was a brutal proposition. It would be a hard uphill battle. He was not only a thirty-three-year incumbent; he was also the Senate majority leader with the full weight of the Republican National Committee behind him. Even in Vegas, I don't think anyone would have taken a bet on my chances. It didn't look like something I wanted to take on. Then we got a call from Senator Chuck Schumer, the Democrat from New York. He said, "I'd like to fly you out to D.C. I want to talk to you about running against McConnell."

"I'm not sure I'm ready to do that, Senator."

"It's just a discussion. Let's meet and talk."

Both Erik and Mark urged me to go and sit down with Senator Schumer. It was, as he said, just a discussion. Erik said, "Look, just go out there and meet with him. See what he has to say." It seemed harmless enough. I wasn't committing to anything. Mark and I booked a flight.

In D.C., as we waited to meet with Senator Schumer, I imagined what a day as a senator would be like. I could imagine myself reviewing judicial appointments, reading pending legislation, and writing my own. There would be the opportunity to do a tremendous amount of good. As far as I was concerned, I would help the country simply by sending Mitch McConnell into retirement and stopping the damage he was single-handedly inflicting on American values, our democracy, and the Constitution.

Senator Schumer was, like most senators, convincing. He was earnest and made me feel as if the race against McConnell were winnable.

"Amy, McConnell is as vulnerable as he's ever going to be. I'd like to do some polling, and the party will pay for it. We'll go out and see how you match up against McConnell. Frankly, though, of everybody in Kentucky, you're the strongest candidate to go against him. If you do it, I'll be behind you. The party will be behind you." I agreed to carefully consider it.

The research took a couple of months. The results weren't surprising. Was it possible that I could win? Sure. Was it a 10 percent chance? The research told us I had a better chance than that, but certainly less than a 50 percent shot. I knew, though, what Mark and any political pro knows: it was a turbulent, disruptive time. All any challenger would need was for the political winds to blow a certain way, and even an entrenched politician like McConnell could be toppled. The more I thought about it, the more I realized I would love the job. I also agreed with Mark and Senator Schumer that of the three top candidates in Kentucky who had a chance against McConnell, I was the best equipped to take him on.

Much as I might have wanted it, though, the most difficult question was, could I put my family through this again? As we had the first time, Erik and I talked and talked about it. Could we weather another campaign? What would a senatorial campaign involve? How would we manage? What would we do differently, and could we make it work financially? It would be another two years of no income for me.

Erik was, as always, supportive. He reassured me that we could manage financially if I were to run again. I had all the tools to run, but I was definitely torn on the issue. Then Senator Schumer invited me to D.C. again, to talk more. I flew out again, this time with Erik. We listened to Senator Schumer talk about the leadership of our country, the Senate, and what it would mean for our democracy if we could get rid of Mitch McConnell. That evening Erik sat down across from me. He looked at me and said, "What are you doing? You have a chance to change the world here, and you're still wavering? You need to do this."

I thought, "All right, if Erik's saying this, I really should take this on." Even more, it dawned on me that our country was still in peril. The president needed to go, and Mitch McConnell needed to go, too. Our democracy, the rule of the law, the Constitution—they couldn't take much more of the Republicans' corruption. I was the best chance Kentucky and the country had of getting rid of someone who was damaging our institutions, corrupting our system of government, and really hurting Kentucky. How could I look myself in the mirror if I let that chance slip away? How would I look my kids in the eye in ten years? How would I tell them that I could have done the hard thing and fought for the country, fought for democracy, but it was just too inconvenient? I knew it was going to be a really rough campaign. Mitch McConnell is a cunning and vicious political operator with a seasoned team of the best political pros in the country behind him. At the end of the day, though, I wanted to tell my kids that I had done everything I could possibly do to ensure their America was as incredible as mine had been. I had to try to make a difference. I made the decision. I was going into battle one last time. Now I'd be fighting the second most powerful man in the United States.

18

Iᴛ'ꜱ ᴀ ᴄᴀʟᴍᴇʀ ᴛɪᴍᴇ for my family now. I'm happy to be off the campaign trail and spending more time with Erik and the kids. I think we're all ready for in-person classes to start again and looking forward to life becoming somewhat normal. Georgetown is a nice, family-oriented small town. Kentucky will always be home to me. That word carries tremendous power for anyone who has bounced around the globe in a twenty-four-year military career. Erik, too, has enjoyed his time living here in Kentucky. He was incredibly supportive of my Senate run, picking up the domestic slack when I was out speaking, making appearances, and raising funds. I do more "mom" things now that I'm off the campaign trail. I have to admit, I love the routine of a busy house—small, simple domestic joys that are the opposite of what I've endured for the last three years.

My Senate campaign was just as nasty, if not worse, than my run for the House of Representatives. Even before I got to the general election and Mitch McConnell's win-at-all-cost tactics, he spent millions of dollars to smear my name and spread lies about me and what I believed. That was a tactic that unfortunately worked.

I'm far from naive; I understand that political fights are typically rough-and-tumble. I've never shied from a tough fight. But sending a wave of trolls to jam up my campaign's social media pages is one thing. Blatant dishonesty is something altogether different. I remember watching a McConnell campaign ad in which a western Kentucky sheriff stood there in his fresh-pressed uniform, with his badge of authority gleaming. He looked right at the camera and said that Amy McGrath encouraged looting and rioting, and that if I was elected I would defund the police and sheriff's department. There was no basis whatsoever for that attack. I never once said anything like that and don't support defunding law enforcement. I thought, "There is no bottom for these people. They're just fine with flat-out lying."

That type of outright dishonesty shouldn't be a part of public discourse or politics. It's one of the many things I don't miss about campaigning. It might have been unpleasant asking complete strangers for large sums of money, but the underhanded, unethical tactics were worse. As a candidate, you feel as though perhaps you should reevaluate the sanctity of honesty. Is lying what it takes to win?

On election night, as I made my way back to my campaign headquarters from my final event, the exit polls didn't look good for us. The reality—both in Kentucky and across the country—was far worse than the polls made out. I had barely settled into my office and was sitting there with Erik when my campaign manager came in and closed the door behind him.

"They called the race."

I nodded. "Okay."

"What do you want to do?"

"Make the call and then I'll shoot a video."

"Right now?"

"There's no reason to wait."

I called McConnell for a twenty-second conversation. Then my video team set up while I tweaked the speech my communications team had written. They entered it into my iPad teleprompter and I read it to the camera, thanking my supporters and conceding the race. Erik and I tried to eat dinner, but I had no appetite. We drove home, and I went into each of my kids' bedrooms in turn and kissed each child. I struggled to keep perspective. After all, even though I had lost a hard-fought race, the most important people in the world to me were still safe and asleep in our house.

I tried to sleep but eventually gave up, went into our family room, and turned on the TV. No winner had yet been called in the race for president. I was very worried as to what another four years of Trump in the White House would do to our democratic institutions. The results of other congressional races were disheartening. The blue wave that was supposed to sweep out venal Republican legislators had not materialized.

As the dust settles, I'm disappointed and saddened by the disinformation and the results of the election. Partly, I'm working through the grief of losing a contest that was so important to me and the country. More than that, I have grave concerns about the future of American democracy. I ran for the Senate because the country was at a historic crossroads. Mitch McConnell, Donald Trump, the Republican Party, disinformation, and polarization were ripping this country apart. My race was about embracing the values I served in uniform to protect. In becoming a candidate, I wanted to be part of a movement restoring competence, thoughtfulness, and humanity to our federal government. My entire adult life has been dedicated to protecting this country, its ideals, and the Constitution. I never thought I'd see the day when America's ideals were attacked from within. I don't think I lost to a conservative or a Republican. I didn't come up short in a battle over ideologies. I lost to a man who has spent the last four years enabling a deeply flawed leader. Mitch McConnell supported a pathological liar who violated the Constitution, empowered this nation's enemies, eroded trust in core institutions, and showed absolute contempt for the rule of law. I don't believe Senator McConnell cares about traditional Republican or conservative values. He doesn't seem to have an ideology, ethics, or an inner North Star. His only inspiration seems to be power and money. Unfortunately, the voters did not hold him accountable in the voting booth.

People vote their emotions more often than they choose a candidate based on a careful analysis of the issues, or even their own self-interest. Voters can be swayed with a sound bite, even a dishonest one. That's how Donald Trump built a successful presidential run on a slew of lies. Those fabrications resonated with a vast number of people, making them feel strong, heard, and supported. I had hoped to counteract the lies by promoting the values at the heart and soul of America. On the campaign trail, I used words like "justice," "democracy," "integrity," "decency," "compassion," and "humanity." After a career as a Marine, those are more than words to me. They represent who we are as Americans, and everything Donald Trump and Mitch McConnell are not.

Unfortunately, in Kentucky and other states, many voters are afraid of change and find it easier to embrace anything that reinforces their own world view than to research facts. It wasn't uncommon to come across people who actually thought I was a communist, thanks to McConnell's propaganda machine. Many Americans don't have the time and energy to learn more about their government. Civics isn't a part of the core public education curriculum, as it once was. I was surprised to find, among many people I met on the campaign, deep misunderstandings about how government worked and what a senator's job was.

Democracy is hard. It requires an electorate that is engaged and informed. Democracy only works if most voters take the responsibility to research the facts, learn the truth, and hold candidates accountable. Without most Americans' active engagement in the process, democracy cannot survive.

I had hoped for a full-scale, no-doubt rejection of Trumpism. The country needed that. I learned at the naval academy that the traits that define true leadership are honor, character, integrity, responsibility, and ethical behavior. That's why you can make mistakes, fail tests and even classes at the academy, and still remediate and graduate. But lie, cheat, or steal at a certain rank and you'll be kicked out without a second chance. Honor and trust are difficult to rebuild. Those values don't matter much in politics anymore, especially among Republicans.

As I watched the election results pour in that night, I started to believe that maybe I had been wrong in what I taught my students at the academy. I always emphasized that federal officials, individuals who made it to that level, should strive to be honorable, and that the American people respected that. The rise of Donald Trump and the reelection of Mitch McConnell called all that into question for me. Trump held the highest office in our country and clearly sold out America to line his own pockets, stroke his own ego, and enrich his family and friends. Mitch McConnell was right there with him. They have both, along with multiple Republican elected leaders, made a mockery of the ideals and values I was taught were essential for true American leadership.

As I watched invaders breach the Capitol on January 6, 2021, for the first time since 1814, I was stunned. Eventually other emotions started to sink in—outrage at seeing broken glass in the marble halls, shame of seeing a Confederate flag fluttering in the rotunda, and despair at the senseless violence and deaths. What happened was not politics. It was not protesting. It was not about tax policy, or the size of government, or even an election. It was treason, plain and simple. It was an attack by a violent cult, aided and abetted by a deeply flawed president and a complicit Republican Party. An act fueled by lies and conspiracies.

It should not, however, have been unexpected. The GOP has spent the last four years failing to uphold American values, working for their own narrow interests rather than for Americans or America.

People say to me, "I don't care for politics." They know I ran for office and they are trying to be polite. The January 6 insurrection at the Capitol changed how I think about that comment. A Capitol Hill police officer died in the insurrection. Republican members of Congress and in statehouses must be held accountable. It is not acceptable at this painful historic moment to abdicate our responsibility as Americans to be involved in government, in politics. If our democracy is to survive, Americans must step up. They must participate and commit to rebuilding and serving our neighbors and our country. The best way we can defend our democracy from this attack is to stay engaged. That takes courage and work. That work starts in the halls of Congress and in the chambers of our statehouses. If we are patriots, we must care about politics. Because, right now, "politics" is a life-and-death struggle for American democracy.

This country faces so many tough challenges. We have let special interest groups and money dominate our democracy. We haven't done the hard work citizens need to do. As terrible as the events that rang out on January 6, 2021, were, we need to remember there was a time in the not-so-distant past when everyday Americans were invested in American ideals and American politics. Voters rightfully expected politicians to be patriots serving country over party or self. Our representatives worked for We the People. They dedicated themselves, as Marines dedicate themselves, to serve the nation and the Constitution. We need to return to those ideals.

I'll never stop being a Marine. I want to help, and I'll always want to serve. Ultimately, I'll get up, dust myself off, and get back to it.

I'll figure out the next steps that will allow me to have the greatest impact. What direction those steps will take is unclear to me now. Whether it's in the public or the private sector, I am honor bound to continue to be a voice, to fight for my family, my home, and to defend my country.

ACKNOWLEDGMENTS

The story of my life could not have happened without so many people who have influenced, mentored, befriended, and loved me. There is no way to specifically thank everyone, so this is just a snapshot.

In no particular order, I'll begin by thanking Vicky Wilson, my editor, who strove to keep me on track and put forward the best literary work that could reach as many people as possible. For someone who has never written and published a book before, you really have been a tremendous help during this process. Thank you, too, to everyone at Knopf.

Thanks to Jane Dystel, my agent, who believed my story could inspire others, and who walked me step by step through the long development of this project. She has been a wonderful advocate for me personally, a tremendous supporter of the campaigns I ran to defend our democracy, and just a genuinely good person.

Thanks to Chris Peterson, an incredibly gifted writer (and listener), without whom I would never have been able to write my story. The product of his work are the words you read, but the labor included many late-night phone interviews, listening to my recollections, which sometimes brought laughter and other times tears. He was masterful at deciphering the many rather haphazard writings I had already put down in prose and at weaving together my story.

This book, my campaigns, and the most important parts of my life (my children) would not have been possible without my husband, Erik. He has been behind me since I first met him so many years ago. He has read and edited much of this book, as well as numerous speeches, op-eds, my master's thesis . . . the list goes on. He hasn't fallen asleep while reading yet. Well, maybe once or twice.

My children, Teddy, George, and Ellie, while very young, inspired me in the most important way. They were the ones for whom this work was meant, an incomplete record of their mother, what she stood for, and what shaped her. My hope is that, at a certain age, this work will help them to understand their parents, and themselves, just a little bit more.

Thanks again to my parents—my father, Donald, who is no longer with us but always encouraged me to write. He was an English teacher, of course. I have kept the handwritten letters he would send me while I was deployed and throughout my time in the Marines. I also received valuable input from my mother, Marianne. Not only did she help me edit this work, but she helped me remember the events of my childhood, as well as my feelings during and after my combat deployments. My mother had kept all the emails I sent home during that time, and those were a tremendous source for me in writing.

I could have written a whole chapter on how amazing my sister, Janie, has been to me growing up and remains to this day. Her belief in me has always been a source of strength, whether I tackled flight school or a U.S. Senate campaign. Her family, including her husband, Greg, and their wonderful young adult children, Jackson, Charlie, and Maddie Sora, have been stalwart supporters of my endeavors. Janie is also the best writer in our family and helped me edit this work.

My brother, Matt, was always my challenger growing up. He inspired me to excel in sports in early life, and then academically later in life. Matt's love of American history and his wife Jamie's and their daughter Hadley's belief that we can build a better America based on values of inclusion also inspired me to run for office.

Members of my extended family have had a special influence on me. My godparents, Betsy and Ernie Disantis, have always believed in me; their encouragement in all of my endeavors has been above and beyond. I'd also like to thank other aunts and uncles: Pat and Mike Sumida, Marian and Jim McGrath, Diana and Fritz Smith, Margie and Bill Klesse, Sally and Reed Borie, Judy and Jim Smith, Joan and Tim McCarthy, and Joanne and Dave Vogel. Your love, acceptance, and support over the years has been tremendous. Your letters to me overseas kept me sane, and I will never forget your real investment in me and my crazy idea to get my first congressional campaign off the ground.

There are so many people from my past who shaped me that I can't possibly thank them all, but a few stand out. The late Eleanor Eckerle was the most loving and kind nanny a little girl could ever have. She, along with my parents, influenced me the most in my early childhood. Beth and Ken Bronsil were and are close family friends. Together with their sons, Tim and Matt, they were a formative fixture in my childhood. Thanks to Carlotta and Lloyd Owens and to Carlotta's daughter Kristin for showing me the great outdoors, and for opening up their home to me as a young adult. Carlotta's son, Bobby, whether he knew it or not, was a great influence on my desire to join the military. Thanks to Jacquie Newberry for being such a wonderful friend for so long and encouraging me to write along the way.

Aimee Molique has remained one of my best friends since the seventh grade. I thank her for her grace, love, and support. Many other high school friends, such Sharon Gronotte and Natalie MacDonald, I've grown to love and respect.

Thanks to the late Joe and Bette DiNunno, part of the Greatest Generation, who opened their home to me as a midshipman. Their patriotism, faith, counsel, and kindness will be etched in me forever.

A very special thanks to Captain Sandy and Croom Coward. They have been like a second set of parents to me. Sandy provided invaluable mentorship throughout my career. His love of country and his life dedicated to defending our country continued to inspire me long after my USNA days. I'm so grateful also to Croom for her years of love and support.

I would like to express my admiration for my teachers during and after high school, who challenged me, opened my eyes, and took me seriously when I told them what I wanted to do. This list is long, but includes Connie Roenker, Nisia Thornton, and the sisters of Notre Dame, especially Sisters Ethel, Rita, Dolores, Judith, and Sister Maria Francine.

I was also fortunate to have some amazing professors and instructors at the USNA, who challenged me and instilled in me the values of academic and professional excellence. They include Major Locke and Colonel Glynn. Some special professors taught me as a midshipman and then taught alongside me when I came full circle back to the USNA as an instructor. They include Eloise Malone, Gale Mattox, and Stephen Wrage. Those who were my colleagues instructing the next generation of our military's officers, who influenced my decision to run for political office—Brendan Doherty, Howard Ernst, Deb Wheeler, and many others.

To the many coaches in my life who taught me hard work, dedication, teamwork, and composure under pressure: Bill Westerman, Dick Maile, and Nancy Armbruster in basketball; Tim Prieshoff, Mike Wolf, Carin Gabarra, and Rob Blanck in soccer—thank you.

Each of my former teammates had her own dedication, challenge, friendship, laughter, support . . . it all mattered. In high school, I had amazing soccer, basketball, and softball teammates. At the USNA, my soccer teammates shaped me more than they will ever know.

My 2nd Company roommates, Rachel McNary, Nicole Peoples, Ty Westinghouse, Alison Johnson, and Maureen Moroney, endured our years at USNA together with grace and laughter. Other amazing Americans from the USNA have remained my friends, even though we have all gone off to do other things after our service days. These include Sarah Rhodes, Jeannette Haynie, Sara Stires, Bridget Ruiz, and Laura Maasdam, among others. Thanks to my longtime friend and inspiration who has done it all in the navy, CDR Natalia Henriquez. Guy and Mihae Ravey have been friends since we were in the same platoon at TBS. Being a former F/A-18 pilot and LSO, Guy helped remind me of the aircraft carrier landing terminology. Thanks to them both.

I thank the late Bob and Nelly Jones from San Diego. Bob, another part of the Greatest Generation, was a blast from the past in my mother's life, and he welcomed me as a grandchild or niece.

To the Marines of my first tour with VMFA(AW)-121 Green Knights, I thank you for some of the most amazing three years one could ever have serving in the Corps. Some aircrew whom I'd like to thank personally for either their mentorship and leadership or their friendship and comradery include Dudley, Blow, Doogie, Bean, Mullet, ChimChim, Happy, Legs, Gunner V, Peepers, and WB. Thanks to Tegan Owen for her friendship and patience in serving our Green Knight years together in the boys' club and beyond.

Thanks to all the Green Knights of my second tour under the leadership of Rosie and Paste. Your professionalism and service made the squadron even better than it was during my first tour, and I'll forever be proud to have served with you.

Major General Charles F. Bolden has modeled servant-leadership to me for over twenty-five years. He has been someone I've reached out to for advice during my big career decisions, and he has always taken the call. Additional former operational commanding officers Gumby, Stress, Jams, and Pappy each taught me a great deal about leadership and dedication. I thank them all.

With much admiration, I thank all the senior enlisted whom I've learned invaluable leadership lessons from over the years, especially Top Tonne, Sergeant Major Siaw, Gunnery Sergeant McKeown, and Gunny Abbott.

To my friends who gave the ultimate sacrifice in service to our country, I hope that I have stood in my remaining life in defense not only of our democracy, but for the ideals and values that are the best of America. I live each day knowing that it easily could have been me in that cockpit that day, or that night, who did not return. You will never be forgotten— JB Blackmon, Zilby, Laura M, "Sugar Bear," and too many others.

Thanks to Congresswoman Susan Davis, who allowed me to be a member of her Hill team for a year. She made me believe that there are some wonderfully good people in elected office. To Team Davis, including Lisa Sherman, Rekha Chandrasekaran, Quinn Dang, Aaron Hunter, and others, thank you not only for teaching me, but also for your service to America.

To my colleagues in the Pentagon, you made my time in the five-sided puzzle palace way more bearable, and actually productively pleasant: Kelly Comstock, Colonel Rice, and Col Outz. Special thanks to Rebecca DeGuzman, who wrote and published the USMC Interagency Integration Strategy with me, for your friendship and your support of me.

Thanks to my colleagues at the U.S. Naval Institute Editorial Board, especially Fred Rainbow, who sparked in me the idea that to "dare" at this point in my life meant not flying high-performance jets, but speaking out, writing, and being a courageous voice on the things that matter, even when it's uncomfortable.

My political campaigns were made possible by many individuals who deserve recognition. Before I even knew that I wanted to get into politics, former congressman Ben Chandler connected me to the right people; I'm so thankful he believed in my message and my background enough to have done so. None of this would have been possible without Mark Nickolas, my campaign manager, one of my closest advisers, and candidate coach. It was his political savvy together with his communication and management skills that powered my campaigns. Mark Putnam, my brilliant media consultant, took my story and condensed it into a form that would catch attention and inspire people to get involved in our democracy. My consultant team of Fred Yang, Joe Hansen, Lori LaFave, Mitch Stewart, Anita Dunn, Bill Knapp, and Toby Falsgraff helped make our campaign possible. Sannie Overly, the most influential person during my Senate campaign, provided honest counsel and guidance. She was unwavering in her commitment and work for the campaign, and in her encouragement of me to finish this book. I'm enormously grateful for our friendship.

Thanks to Senator Kirsten Gillibrand, who was the first elected official to endorse me, and to others who have believed in my message, including former governors Martha Layne Collins and Paul Patton and congressman Seth Moulton. President Joe Biden came down to Kentucky to support my congressional run. For his time and encouragement, I'm enormously grateful.

To my amazing campaign staff, the thousands of volunteers who made phone calls, knocked on doors, wrote postcards, and to the million-plus donors to my campaigns—you were inspired, as I was, to make a difference for our country at a critical moment. It mattered, and I thank you.

INDEX